The Political Economy of Customs and Culture: Informal Solutions to the Commons Problem

The Political Economy Forum

Terry L. Anderson and Randy T. Simmons, Editors

Rowman & Littlefield Publishers, Inc.

ROWMAN & LITTLEFIELD PUBLISHERS, INC.

Published in the United States of America
by Rowman & Littlefield Publishers, Inc.
4720 Boston Way, Lanham, Maryland 20706

British Cataloging in Publication Information Available

Library of Congress Cataloging-in-Publication Data

The political economy of customs and culture : informal solutions to
the commons problem / edited by Terry L. Anderson and Randy T.
Simmons.
p.   cm. — (The Political economy forum)
Includes bibliographical references.
1. Commons.   2. Property.   I. Anderson, Terry Lee, 1946–   .
II. Simmons, Randy T.
HD1286.P64   1993   333.2—dc20   92–32790 CIP

ISBN 0–8476–7786–9 (cloth : alk. paper)

Printed in the United States of America

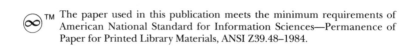
™ The paper used in this publication meets the minimum requirements of
American National Standard for Information Sciences—Permanence of
Paper for Printed Library Materials, ANSI Z39.48–1984.

Contents

Tables and Figures

Acknowledgments

The Political Economy Research Center is well known for its research on the use of private property rights as a solution to resource allocation problems. Indeed, the first volume in the Political Economy Forum series examined *Property Rights and Indian Economies*. In considering how formal property rights structures affect resource allocation, however, we have come to realize the important role that less formal institutions play in conditioning human action.

The fact that customs and culture constrain human relations has long been apparent to anthropologists, but political economists are only now beginning to comprehend their importance. More economics journals are publishing articles focusing on non-market social controls, books such as Robert Ellickson's *Order Without Law: How Neighbors Settle Disputes*, Douglass North's *Institutions, Institutional Change, and Economic Performance*, and Elinor Ostrom's *Governing the Commons: The Evolution of Institutions for Collective Action*, are focusing on informal institutions, and even the International Association for the Study of Common Property has been formed.

Though political economists may be late realizing the importance of customs and culture, this second volume in the Political Economy Forum series suggests that the tools of economics can bear fruit in this area of inquiry. Why are informal institutions chosen rather than more formal property rights? How effective are they in preventing the tragedy of the commons? What historical role have informal institutions played? What predictions can be made regarding the likelihood of free riding under informal constraints? These are some of the questions addressed by the authors in this volume, and we hope that this collection will raise even more questions and stimulate further research.

The pages included between these covers cannot possibly indicate the effort that lies behind them. In particular, it is the staff at the Political Economy Research Center which takes care of all the details that makes the process work with typical efficiency. Monica Lane Guenther coordinated the conference where the papers were first presented, and Pamela Malyurek helped with word processing. But then the real work started as Dianna Rienhart put the manuscript into "camera-ready copy," checking every detail from punctuation to bibliographic citations. Without her continually pushing the editors and authors to make sure that every detail was addressed, the Political Economy Forum series would not exist.

Finally we wish to thank the M. J. Murdock Charitable Trust for providing funds for the Political Economy Forum. Since the Political Economy Research Center depends solely on private funding for its operation, the generosity of foundations like the Murdock Trust are crucial to our research, conference, and publishing efforts.

Terry L. Anderson
Randy T. Simmons

1

Method, Metaphor, and Understanding: When Is the Commons Not a Tragedy?

Randy T. Simmons and Peregrine Schwartz-Shea

> The inherent logic of the commons remorselessly generates tragedy . . . Ruin is the destination toward which all men rush, each pursuing his own best interest in a society that believes in the freedom of the commons. Freedom in a commons brings ruin to all. (Hardin 1968, 1244)

Among social scientific topics, the commons problem is notable for the interdisciplinary attention it has received due in large part, to the power of the "tragedy" metaphor with which Garrett Hardin (1968) described it. Social, natural, and physical scientists use the commons problem and Hardin's tragedy metaphor to study a broad range of environmental and social problems and possible solutions. This volume reflects this interdisciplinary attention, with contributions by political scientists, anthropologists, and economists.

The interdisciplinary attention received by the commons problem is matched by diversity in method: some scholars focus primarily on elaborating the game-theoretic bases for possible solutions to the commons problem (Roberts, chapter 4, this volume); others use field work to describe the carrying capacity, customs, and legal-regulatory aspects of particular real-world commons (Acheson, chapter 5; Ensminger and Rutten, chapter 6 this volume); more recently, scholars have begun to use the experimental method to explore both game-theoretic arguments and inferences based on real-world commons (Ostrom, Walker and Gardner, chapter 8, this volume; for a review see, Messick and Brewer 1983).

By combining theory and data across disciplines and method, it is possible to gain a more complete picture of commons problems and their solutions. One clear result, from more that two decades of research, is the finding that the commons is not necessarily the problem suggested by theory: people do not always follow the inexorable logic of the tragedy metaphor.

The contributors to this volume explain this discrepancy between theory and reality in diverse ways, but one theme that emerges is the importance of culture and norms whether expressed through evolved or consciously designed cultural institutions (rules, procedures, prohibitions, rewards) or through psychological effects such as "group identity." Note, however, that notions of culture and norms are missing from the game-theoretic formulations of the commons and certainly from Hardin's metaphor. This omission may explain a large part of the difference between the predictions of tragedy and the real-world outcomes of many commons.

Limits of the Tragedy Metaphor

As Gigerenzer and Murray (1987) document, metaphors may crucially influence scientific thinking and the development of knowledge in both positive and negative ways. In the case of research on the commons, Hardin's metaphor of the tragedy has been particularly valuable because it has provided an interdisciplinary research community with the common language, questions, and concerns that facilitate cross-disciplinary communication. At the same time, however, this disciplinary diversity has often meant that the biases of the tragedy metaphor go unexamined.

As Schlager and Ostrom (chapter 2) note, the very parsimony of the commons model that proves so attractive can mask many facets and distinctions that could be critical at both theoretical and field levels. They begin by pointing out that when researchers use the term "the commons," it is often not clear whether they are talking about "property owned by government, property owned by no one, or property owned and defended by a community of users" (p. 13). Part of this ambiguity can be traced back to Hardin who uses examples of each of these categories (national parks, air pollution, the English commons) in his original article as if the incentives in each situation were identical.

It is necessary, therefore, for theorists and field researchers to be more precise and to improve their models of the various types of commons. But notice that such theoretical development confronts a "realism-manageability" tradeoff: As the commons model is made more realistic with the addition of new variables, its heuristic power may be lessened. Conversely, a powerful theoretical model (i.e., one including only the most important variables) is often "unrealistic" precisely because it leaves out many factors. Thus, one issue confronted by researchers using the commons metaphor is the marginal value in improved predictions from each additional variable.

A qualitatively different explanation of the divergence between predictions and empirical evidence focuses on the assumptions of the model. Whether used by game theorists, economists, or biologists, the commons model is based on a highly stylized portrait of human behavior—humans are assumed to be rational, narrowly self-interested, myopic maximizers. Thus, the tragedy predicted by commons logic is, in part, a function of these assumptions. Even though Hardin argues at the end of his article that the only hope of avoiding tragedy is if farsighted people use "mutual coercion, mutually agreed upon" to change institutions, his tragedy *metaphor* assumes myopic human beings.

This portrait of human nature has colored not only the predictions of the commons model but approaches to solutions as well.[1] Many believe the logic implies state control of some kind. As C. Ford Runge (1984, 6) explains in a critique of Hardin:

> Since the premise of the "Tragedy of the Commons" is that free-rider behavior is dominant, it follows that any agreement—however mutually agreed upon— will be unstable without a heavy dose of state control. This is because no one has an incentive other than fear of authority to keep it.

The argument that the state is the best and, in fact, only solution to tragedy is perhaps best developed by William Ophuls (1973, 229), who wrote in "Leviathan or Oblivion," that "we will be required to submit ourselves to a higher power as a means of solution," and that "even if we avoid the tragedy of the commons, it will only be by recourse to the tragic necessity of Leviathan."[2]

Another solution to the commons problem, that also relies on the assumption of narrowly self-interested humans is private property. Steve Hanke, a former staff member of President Reagan's Council of Economic Advisers expressed this view as follows: "Either you want property rights, or you want public, collectivized arrangements. There is no middle of the road" (Shute 1983, 42).

The broad range of alternatives that lie between Olphus's "higher power" and Hanke's property rights has become evident from the work of those using an historical or evolutionary methodology. Based, in part, on field research this approach embraces the notion that humans can anticipate tragedy and organize to prevent it. In other words, the assumption of myopia is relaxed, so that the self's interest has a longer time horizon. Demsetz's (1967) and Anderson and Hill's (1975) work has been influential in documenting the reasons why self-interested (but not myopic) individuals modify open-access commons arrangements. Vernon Smith's chapter (chapter 9) is in this tradition. He emphasizes the pervasive fact of resource scarcity and human beings' ability to adapt to this fact or face extinction.

"Group Identity" and the Commons

The assumption of self-interest can be enlarged (some would say fundamentally changed) in another way as well. In contrast to the game-theoretic portrait of human nature, many social scientists (for a review, see Brewer 1979) begin with a social human being for whom "group identity" is critical. Group identity is defined as "those aspects of an individual's self-image that derive from the social categories to which [the individual] perceives himself as belonging" (Tajfel and Turner 1979, 37). Once an individual has identified self with group, then group outcomes are means of improving self-image or esteem. As Brewer (1979, 322) argues, a consequence of group identity is that "outcomes to other group members, or to the group as a whole, come to be perceived as one's own."

Group identity is linked to the efficiency problem of the commons in a fundamental way. To understand this point, consider another classic metaphor often used to explain commons logic—the prisoners' dilemma. Solving the efficiency problem for the collectivity of the prisoners (lowest total of the two prison terms) creates an inefficiency from the perspective of the wider society (letting guilty prisoners go too soon). Similarly, when cartel members solve their "public goods" problem, they create a "public bad" for consumers in the form of restricted output and higher prices. As economist Hirshleifer expresses this point:

> efficiency is always relative to the boundaries of the society or group envisioned. . . . outcomes efficient for our nation as a whole may be adverse to the well-being of other nations; even gains for the whole human species may be achieved at the expense of other species. My point is that no one, probably, favors efficiency is a totally universalistic sense. We all draw the line somewhere, at the boundary of "us" versus "them." *Efficiency thus is ultimately a concept relating group advantage over other competing groups.* (1982, 8, original emphasis)

The notion of group identity, then, is not just some "add on" that threatens the parsimony of the game-theoretic model. Instead, definitions of group boundaries and the concept of group identity are fundamental to thinking about commons problems and their solutions.

In the contributions to this volume, the salience of group boundaries and group identity varies. In the purely theoretical pieces, group identity or the definition of groups is only implicit. Schlager and Ostrom analyze the commons problem in terms of three levels of action (operational, collective choice, and constitutional). At each level the issue of who may or may not participate/harvest is implicitly recognized. This schema could be enriched (and more fruitfully utilized in historical studies of commons) by recognizing the ways in which these formal decisions are related to psychological attachments, e.g., group identity. Similarly, Roberts recognizes the social significance of "groups" when he points out that fishermen are likely to organize to "oppose any improvement and potentially oppose it with much intensity" while those who would benefit from establishing the fee are "likely to be dispersed relative to the concentrated opposition of the fishermen" (p. 64). His argument depends critically on how the polity (as well as subgroupings within the polity) is defined.

The remaining contributions deal with empirical evidence of varying precision. Smith surveys a broad literature for consistency with his argument that prehistoric cultural practices and changes can be understood as adaptations to changing resource scarcities. Implicit in his argument is a cultural/evolutionary model of ingroup practices shaped by between-group competition for survival as a function of scarcity.

In contrast, Ostrom, Walker, and Gardner generate precise predictions (based on game-theoretic analysis) and data to address those predictions (using the experimental method). Their data suggest that, given the power of face-to-face communication, group identity plays a key role in monitoring and sanctioning behavior in real-world commons.

The field studies by Acheson, Lueck, and Ensminger and Rutten—because they are field studies—cannot escape the ubiquitous fact of group identity in social reality. Acheson's informal institutions for protection of the lobster commons depend critically on this variable. To be a legitimate harvester one must be a member of a gang. Membership is a function of familial ties, whether or not one is native to the area, willingness to abide by group norms and, in the case of island gangs, small numbers, kinship ties and ideology, and dependence on harvesting.

Similarly, Eggertsson's review of the history of the Icelandic aféttir shows that membership in the hreppur (the local governance institution) was determined by being adjacent with other farmers—they were small *communities* of farmers who managed common property by excluding non-members, enforcing rules, and suppling collective goods. Lueck's analysis emphasizes group identity. Hutterites, Cree Indians, lobster gangs, and Swiss villages all define their group clearly and have strict rules and customs that enforce membership.

The importance of changes in group identity is evident in the history of the Kenyan commons detailed by Ensminger and Rutten. When all group members are herders, group identity does not appear to be particularly important for managing access to the commons. But an increase in resource scarcity produces conflicting subgroups as some herders become sedentary. And encroachment by outsiders (herders from Somalia) makes ingroup/outgroup distinctions salient. Appeals to the state for help in enforcing internally-developed access rules are most insistent (and most successful) in the case of encroachment by outsiders.

The ubiquity of group identity in interdisciplinary field studies calls for greater attention to this variable at the theoretical level. Researchers should investigate the emergence, maintenance, and strength of group identity as a function of identifiable mechanisms: group boundaries, culture, supporting norms and institutions, and political entrepreneurship.[3] The relative efficacy of these mechanisms is unclear as is the broader question of the relative importance of group identity vis-a-vis other factors. Exogenous changes in costs (e.g., a drought, new technology) may be the driving force to which group identities adapt or group identities may facilitate collective action useful for promoting societal-level change.

Why hasn't group identity received more theoretical attention? Part of the answer lies in the limits of the metaphor discussed earlier. That is, the concept of group identity may seem quite foreign to researchers immersed in the tragedy tradition with its emphasis on the bifurcation between self-interest and collective interest. Another part of the answer is "method." For those who investigate the commons problem primarily in game-theoretic terms, incorporating psychological variables (i.e., modifying the strict assumptions of self-interest) could make the use of mathematical tools extremely difficult if not, in some cases, impossible.

Understandably, then, game theorists have been reluctant to modify their very useful assumptions short of convincing evidence that there is considerable predictive ability to be gained from such a project. But that evidence now exists. Results from twenty years of experimental research challenge the portrait of humans as rational, narrowly self-interested, myopic maximizers who always defect. The experimental data show that approximately 30 percent of subjects still cooperate even under conditions most favorable to game theory (i.e., no discussion, anonymity of choices, etc.). And when discussion is allowed, cooperation rises to levels between 60 percent and 100 percent—despite a dominant material incentive to defect.[4] Still game-theorists have been slow to react to this evidence as well as to the evidence from the field that game-theoretic predictions of tragedy are not always borne out in real-world commons. But some progress is occurring. Kinder and Palfrey (1991, 5), for example, report that mathematical utility theory is now being revised in response to robust experimental results.

We believe that experimentalism can lead to similar progress in research on the commons. The Ostrom, Walker, and Gardner chapter is an example of how to link the concerns of researchers from different disciplines and methodological traditions. Their experiments show how ideas from theory and the field can be melded and tested in rigorous ways[5] while providing specific evidence useful to game theorists who confront the manageability-realism tradeoff referred to earlier.

In Ostrom, Walker, and Gardner commons experiments, group members monitor and sanction each other's behavior. The experiments show that, given appropriate information and "an arena where they can discuss joint strategies and perhaps implement monitoring and sanctioning," group members can develop effective management strategies by themselves (p. 149). In the real world, the rules and institutions for monitoring, sanctioning, and rewarding behavior would evolve based on how the group is defined and the strength of group identity. In fact, group identity is likely to motivate the development of institutions for defining the group's membership and use rights.

Rethinking Rights and Institutions

When political economists evaluate common property institutions, the (now) conventional question they ask is whether the institutions are "incentive compatible," i.e., whether the institutions are designed so that self-interested individuals have an incentive to preserve rather than destroy the commons. This approach has been enormously fruitful, particularly in the ways that it has been used to understand and justify systems like private property rights which economize on the need for collective management and administration (Hardin 1977). But when incentive-compatibility is based on narrow definitions of self-interest, it often implies there must be an exogenous force (i.e., government) that conceives of and enforces rules and regulations (including the rules of private property) to benefit the group.

In contrast, modifying assumption of self-interest and recognizing group identity creates a broader understanding of incentive-compatibility that encompasses endogenous solutions to commons problems. As Coleman (1990, 49, 50) points out, "the concept of a right intrinsically involves more than one person" and "rights imply intersubjective consensus." Thus, while it is certainly correct that rights and institutions can be enforced by a higher power, they can also evolve within the group, reflecting that group's culture, norms, and history.

It is clear from the contributions to this volume that collective institutions for managing common property do arise endogenously. Moreover, the examples cited by Acheson (chapter 5), Eggertsson (chapter 7), Ensminger and Rutten (chapter 6), Lueck (chapter 3), and Schlager and Ostrom (chapter 2) show that a variety of institutional types may evolve—as a function of the particularities of resource characteristics, group identity, and historical-political experience. Perhaps, in part, because of their evolved particularity, these institutions can be, as Eggertsson claims, "fragile structures, vulnerable to pressures from population growth, technological change, and shifts in political power and processes."

Viewing rights and institutions as (potentially) evolved encourages a research mind set and agenda different from that of the conventional incentive-compatibility approach. It is a Hayekian (c.f., 1973) approach eschewing design by an omniscient scholar in favor of respect for the human capacity to adapt to circumstances, thereby producing unintended (i.e., not consciously designed) institutional arrangements peculiarly adapted to time and place.

In evaluating these institutions, we suggest that the group processes they put in place and support are critical. That is, if a user of the commons acts in his or her immediate self-interest at the expense of the group interest what will be the consequences for that person? Can the action be monitored? Will there be sanctions? Is the sanction an effective deterrent? Does the act violate group norms? Are these norms substantial or inconsequential? More specifically, this approach means emphasizing the subtle interaction between formal and informal definitions of rights and formal and informal enforcement mechanisms. The evolution of rights is a function of changing resource costs, but also of shared (i.e., group-defined) views of what constitutes a "legitimate" right. If formal rights are not viewed as legitimate, that can be a impetus to change—to the organization of groups of individuals who feel slighted by the current distribution of rights.

Conclusion

A core reading in our graduate training in political economy was "The Tragedy of the Commons." We were taught to look for commons problems in all kinds of social situations and, not surprisingly, we found the commons problem to be ubiquitous. Specifically, as political scientists, some of our professors used commons problems to justify the state. Another part of our training, however, lead us to examine property rights solutions to commons problems. But cultural and normative, or informal, solutions to commons problems were not emphasized, implying, however, that culture and norms are seldom powerful explanatory variables.

In our own research we found that culture and norms are critical to understanding behavior in a commons. We found, for example, that parochial behavior is rather easily triggered and that appeals to more universal norms of behavior can be effective under a narrow set of circumstances (Schwartz-Shea and Simmons 1990, 1991, N.d.). The contributions to this volume reinforce the findings of our own research and lead us to the following conclusions that at least modify the understandings from our graduate training:

1. Common property is sometimes more efficient than other forms of ownership and management.
2. The effectiveness of common property management depends on the rights and responsibilities protected and enforced by social institutions.
3. Social institutions can be informal (i.e., culture and group identity) as opposed to the formal institutions that rely on the power of the state.

We want to emphasize that these conclusions do not negate the very real problems of managing a commons, even in homogeneous communities. When a resource is managed collectively there is an incentive for irresponsibility that is not present with private property. Because costs of decisions are shared collectively, wants can be elevated to the rank of needs, the variety of management options can be reduced, and information about the effects of political choices can be suppressed. Depending on the kinds of institutions relied upon, rules can be changed on whims or they can be so rigidly in place that they do not respond to changing resource costs.

We also suggest caution about using these conclusions in inappropriate settings; they are unlikely to hold for large societies the way they do for small groups. Incentives would change for the Maine lobster fishers if the harbor and island gangs were done away with and all fishers were joined in one large group. Buchanan (1977, 162) summarized this caution against extrapolating to large groups from small group interactions:

> Volunteer fire departments arise in villages, not in metropolitan centers. Crime rates increase consistently with city size. Africans behave differently in tribal culture than in industrialized urban settings. There is honor among thieves. The Mafia has its own standards. Time-tested honor systems in universities and colleges collapse when enrollments exceed critical size limits. Litter is more likely to be found on heavily traveled routes than on residential streets. Even the old adage, Never trust a stranger, reflects the recognition of this elemental truth, along with, of course, additional ethical predictions. Successful politicians organize grassroots support at the precinct level.

Buchanan's point is that group identities and ties may be dramatically reduced by the anonymity created by increasing group size. The quality of the cultural connection may also change as well as a function of mobility and rapid dissemination of information and images. Many scholars have commented on the apparent movement toward a mass international culture, but whether these trends would necessarily undermine the cultural underpinnings necessary to efficient commons management is unclear. On the one hand, group identities and ties seem to be lessening; they certainly have lessened in the movement from feudal to market societies. On the other hand, as the Balkanization of the former Soviet empire demonstrates, group identities can be amazingly robust.

As commons scholars we must, therefore, pay attention not only to the peculiarities of a particular setting but to the wider historical trends as well. And as the contributors to this volume so clearly show, we must recognize there are instances in which common property is not a tragedy, that we do not have to accept Ophuls's leviathan or oblivion, and that we should not automatically advocate private property solutions for what we perceive to be commons problems.

Notes

1. Hardin (1968, 1247), for example, said his call for "mutual coercion, mutually agreed upon" did not necessarily imply "arbitrary decisions of distant and irresponsible bureaucrats"; but Hardin did not further clarify the meaning of the phrase.
2. Leviathan refers to Thomas Hobbes's formulation of a government powerful enough to "overawe" self-interest, without which, Hobbes said, life would be "solitary, poor, nasty, brutish, and short."
3. Political and social entrepreneurs use group identity often: politicians invoke patriotism, business and labor groups seek protection from foreigners and ask

consumers to "buy American," cheerleaders stress school spirit, Native American tribal leaders seek to keep their tribes pure from the contamination of "white ways," environmental group leaders call themselves "greens" in contrast to the polluters whom they call "browns," church leaders call the members of their churches "brothers and sisters" to remind them of their group affiliation and, therefore, commitments.

4. These results occur without side payments (Olson 1965), iteration (Axelrod 1984), designated contributing sets (van de Kragt, Orbell, and Dawes 1983), or other formal mechanisms that provide self-interested reasons for cooperation (i.e., "incentive compatibility"). Moreover, Goetze and Orbell (1988) showed that the effects are not due to misunderstanding on the part of subjects.

5. Issues of general concern (i.e., the commons problem) can be studied in the laboratory and findings can be derived which have real-world relevance. The key is to use laboratory "analogues"—laboratory situations which model aspects of the social world in a simplified manner. It is critical to note that analogue experiments are not simulations. Simulations use role-playing where subjects are asked to respond as if they occupied the role in the hypothetical situation. In laboratory experiments, in contrast, there are no "imagined responses but actual responses to the situation at hand" (Brewer 1965, 161). Participants are not asked to play a role and are generally completely unaware of the real-world problem being modeled. Moreover, there are monetary consequences from their decisions, for themselves, and for others. The monetary incentives are large enough that subjects regard the situation as a real one in which they are emotionally involved occasionally quite involved, as indicated by their reactions after experiments.

References

Anderson, Terry, and P. J. Hill. 1975. The evolution of property rights: A study of the American West. *Journal of Law and Economics* 12:163–79.

Axelrod, Robert. 1984. *The evolution of cooperation.* New York: Basic Books.

Brewer, Marilyn B. 1979. Ingroup bias in the minimal intergroup situation: A cognitive-motivational analysis. *Psychological Bulletin* 86:307–24.

———. 1985. Experimental research and social policy: Must it be rigor versus relevance? *Journal of Social Issues* 41:159–76.

Buchanan, James M. 1977. *Freedom in constitutional contract.* College Station: Texas A & M University.

Coleman, James S. 1990. *Foundations of social theory.* Cambridge, MA: Belknap Press of Harvard University Press.

Demsetz, Harold. 1967. Toward a theory of property rights. *American Economic Review* 57:347–59.

Gigerenzer, G., and D. J. Murray. 1987. *Cognition as intuitive statistics.* Hillsdale,

NJ: Erlbaum Associates.

Goetze, David M., and John M. Orbell. 1988. Understanding cooperation in social dilemmas. *Public Choice* 57:275–80.

Hardin, Garrett. 1968. The tragedy of the commons. *Science* 162:1243–48.

———. 1977. An operational analysis of responsibility. In *Managing the commons,* edited by Garrett Hardin and John Baden. San Francisco: W. H. Freeman and Company.

Hayek, F. A. 1973. *Law, legislation, and liberty.* University of Chicago Press.

Hirshleifer, Jack. 1982. Evolutionary models in economics and law: Cooperation versus conflict strategies. In *Research in law and economics: Evolutionary models in economics and law,* edited by Paul H. Rubin. Greenwich, CT: JAI Press.

Kinder, Donald, and Thomas R. Palfrey. 1991. An experimental political science? Yes, an experimental political science. *The Political Methodologist* 4 (1): 2–8.

Messick, David M., and Marilyn B. Brewer. 1983. Solving social dilemmas: A review. In *Review of personality and social psychology,* edited by L. Wheeler and P. Shaver, vol. 4. Beverly Hills: Sage.

Olson, Mancur. 1965. *The logic of collective action.* Cambridge, MA: Harvard University Press.

Ophuls, William. 1973. Leviathan or oblivion? In *Toward a steady-state economy,* edited by Herman Daly. San Francisco: W. H. Freeman.

Schwartz-Shea, Peregrine, and Randy T. Simmons. 1990. The layered prisoners' dilemma: Ingroup or macro-efficiency? *Public Choice* 65:61–83.

———. 1991. Egoism, parochialism, and universalism: Experimental evidence from the layered prisoners dilemma. *Rationality and Society* 3:106–32.

———. N.d. Social dilemmas and perceptions: Experiments on framing and inconsequentiality. In *Social dilemmas,* edited by David A. Schroeder. New York: Praeger.

Tajfel, Henri, and John C. Turner. 1979. An integrative theory of intergroup conflict. In *The social psychology of intergroup relations,* edited W. G. Austin and S. Wrochel. Monterey, CA: Brooks/Cole.

Runge, C. Ford. 1984. The fallacy of privatization. *Journal of Contemporary Studies* 7 (1): 3–17.

Shute, Nancy. 1983. The movement to sell America. *Outside* (September).

van de Kragt, Alphons J. C., John M. Orbell, and Robyn M. Dawes. 1983. The minimal contributing set as a solution to public goods problems. *American Political Science Review* 77:112–22.

2

Property-Rights Regimes and Coastal Fisheries: An Empirical Analysis

Edella Schlager and Elinor Ostrom*

Political economists' understanding of property rights and the rules used to create and enforce property rights shape perceptions of resource degradation problems and the prescriptions recommended to solve such problems. Ambiguous terms blur analytical and prescriptive clarity. The term "common-property resource" is a glaring example of a term that is repeatedly used by political economists to refer to varying empirical situations including: (1) property owned by a government, (2) property owned by no one, and (3) property owned and defended by a community of resource users.[1] The term is also used to refer to any common-pool resource used by multiple individuals regardless of the type of property rights involved. The purpose of this paper is to develop a conceptual schema for arraying property-rights regimes that distinguishes among diverse bundles of rights that

* Portions of this chapter are reprinted with permission from "Property Rights Regimes and Natural Resources: A Conceptual Analysis," *Land Economics*, vol. 68, no. 3 (1992) 249–62. This paper has benefited from the critical and helpful comments from many colleagues at Indiana University and elsewhere. In particular, we would like to thank William Blomquist, Ed Connerley, Louis DeAlessi, David Feeny, Howard Frant, Roy Gardner, Larry Kiser, Ron Oakerson, Vincent Ostrom, Tai-Shuenn Yang, and two anonymous reviewers. Financial support provided by the National Science Foundation (Grant # SES-8921884) is gratefully acknowledged.

may be held by the users of a resource system. We define a property rights schema ranging from authorized user, to claimant, to proprietor, and to owner. We do *not* find that "owners" are the only resource users who make long-term investments in the improvement of resource systems. Proprietors face incentives that are frequently substantial enough to encourage similar long-term investments. Even claimants may manage use patterns to an extent not predicted by a simpler property rights dichotomy. We apply this conceptual schema to analyze findings from a variety of coastal fisheries.

Rules, Rights, and Property Regimes

As individuals conduct day-to-day activities and as they organize these activities, they engage in both operational and collective-choice levels of action (Kiser and Ostrom 1982).[2] Operational activities are constrained and made predictable by operational-level rules regardless of the source of these rules. By "rules" we refer to generally agreed-upon and enforced prescriptions that require, forbid, or permit specific actions for more than a single individual (Ostrom 1986).[3] Examples of operational rules are those used by fishers to specify the types of fishing equipment authorized or forbidden at particular locations within a fishing ground.

Operational rules are changed by collective-choice actions. Such actions are undertaken within a set of collective-choice rules that specify who may participate in changing operational rules and the level of agreement required for their change. Changing the types of fishing equipment authorized or forbidden at different locations within a resource is an example of a collective-choice action. The particular set of operational rules that are actually in use and enforced may have been devised in multiple arenas. Operational rules related to inshore fisheries are as apt to be devised in a local meeting place, even a tavern, as they are in a court, a legislature, or a governmental bureau.[4]

The terms "rights" and "rules" are frequently used interchangeably in referring to uses made of natural resources. Clarity in analysis is enhanced by recognizing that "rights" are the product of "rules" and thus not equivalent to rules. "Rights" refer to particular actions that are authorized (Ostrom 1976). "Rules" refer to the prescriptions that create authorizations. A property right is the authority to undertake particular actions related to a specific domain (Commons 1968). For every right an individual holds, rules exist that authorize or require particular actions in exercising that property right. In addition, all rights have complementary duties. To possess a right implies that someone else has a commensurate duty to observe this right (Commons 1968). Thus rules specify both rights and duties.

In regard to common-pool resources, the most relevant operational-level property rights are "access" and "withdrawal" rights. These are defined as:

Access: The right to enter a defined physical property.

Withdrawal: The right to obtain the "products" of a resource (e.g., catch fish, appropriate water, etc.).[5]

If a group of fishers hold rights of access, they have the authority to enter a resource. Rules specify the requirements the fishers must meet in order to exercise this right. For instance, fishers may be required to reside in a specified jurisdiction and to purchase a license before entering a fishing ground. In addition, fishers, through a lottery, may be assigned particular fishing spots (Faris 1972; Martin 1973). The assignment of fishing spots is an operational-level withdrawal right authorizing harvesting from a particular area.[6]

Individuals who have access and withdrawal rights may or may not have more extensive rights authorizing participation in collective-choice actions. The distinction between rights at an operational-level and rights at a collective-choice level is crucial. It is the difference between exercising a right and participating in the definition of future rights to be exercised. The authority to devise future operational-level rights is what makes collective-choice rights so powerful. In regard to common-pool resources, collective-choice property rights include management, exclusion, and alienation. They are defined as follows:

Management: The right to regulate internal use patterns and transform the resource by making improvements.
Exclusion: The right to determine who will have an access right, and how that right may be transferred.
Alienation: The right to sell or lease either or both of the above collective-choice rights.

The right of management is a collective-choice right authorizing its holders to devise operational-level withdrawal rights governing the use of a resource. Individuals who hold rights of management have the authority to determine how, when, and where harvesting from a resource may occur, and whether and how the structure of a resource may be changed. For instance, a group of fishers who devise a zoning plan that limits various types of harvesting activities to distinct areas of a fishing ground are exercising rights of management for their resource[7].

The right of exclusion is a collective-choice right authorizing its holders to devise operational-level rights of access. Individuals who hold rights of exclusion have the authority to define the qualifications that individuals must meet in order to access a resource. For instance, fishers who limit access to their fishing grounds to males above a certain age who live in a particular community and who utilize particular types of gear are exercising a right of exclusion.[8]

The right of alienation is a collective-choice right permitting its holder to transfer part or all of the collective-choice rights to another individual or group. Exercising a right of alienation means that an individual sells or leases the rights of management, exclusion, or both.[9] Having alienated those rights, the former rights-holder can no longer exercise these authorities in relation to a resource or a part thereof.

Arraying these rights, as shown in Figure 2.1, enables us to make meaningful distinctions among four classes of property-rights holders related to fisheries. The five property rights are independent of one another but, in relation to fisheries, are frequently held in the cumulative manner arrayed in Figure 2.1. It is possible to have entry rights without withdrawal rights, to have withdrawal rights without management rights, to have management rights without exclusion rights, and to have exclusion rights without the rights of alienation.[10] In other words, individuals or collectivities may, and frequently do, hold well-defined property rights that do not include the full set of rights defined above. On the other hand, to hold some of these rights implies the possession of others. The exercise of withdrawal rights is not meaningful without the right of access; alienation rights depend upon having rights to be transferred.

Figure 2.1
Bundles of Rights
Associated With Positions

	Owner	Proprietor	Claimant	Authorized User
Access and Withdrawal	✓	✓	✓	✓
Management	✓	✓	✓	
Exclusion	✓	✓		
Alienation	✓			

We call individuals holding operational-level rights of access and withdrawal "authorized users."[11] If specified in operational rules, access and withdrawal rights can be transferred to others either temporarily, as in a lease arrangement, or permanently when these rights are assigned or sold to others. Transfer of these rights, however, is not equivalent to alienation of management and exclusion rights as we discuss below.

The rights of authorized users are defined by others who hold collective-choice rights of management and exclusion. Authorized users lack the authority to devise their own harvesting rules or to exclude others from gaining access to fishing grounds. Even though authorized users may be able to sell their harvesting rights, nevertheless, they lack the authority to participate in collective action to change operational rules.

An example of authorized users are the salmon and herring fishers of Alaska. In 1972, the Governor's Study Group on Limited Entry was created to research and develop limited entry legislation, which the Alaskan legislature adopted in 1973 (Adasiak 1979, 771). The Alaskan limited entry system divides Alaskan salmon and herring fisheries into a number of different fisheries. An Entry Commission determines the number of permits available for each fishery. The Commission can make adjustments in the numbers as circumstances change, either by issuing additional permits or by buying back existing permits. Fishers cannot hold more than one permit per fishery. The permits are freely transferable, but cannot be used as collateral. The Alaskan fishers who hold permits are authorized users. The Alaskan legislature in conjunction with a study group devised the fishers' rights of access and withdrawal, which fishers can transfer. The fishers do not directly participate in making collective choices, and thus cannot devise their own operational-level rules concerning the use of their fisheries.

We define as "claimants" individuals who possess the same rights as authorized users plus the collective-choice right of management.[12] With the right of management, claimants have the collective-choice authority to devise operational-level rights of withdrawal. They cannot, however, specify who may or may not have access to resources, nor can they alienate their right of management.

For instance, the net fishers of Jambudwip, India, are claimants (Raychaudhuri 1980). Jambudwip is an island in the Bay of Bengal which is only occupied during fishing seasons when fishers establish camps and fish off its southwestern shore. The Jambudwip fishers, exercising management rights, have devised a set of withdrawal rules that permit them to coordinate their use of the fishing grounds. At the beginning of a fishing season each crew chooses a spot on which to set their net. A large bag net is suspended between two posts which are then driven into the ocean floor. Rules, as well as environmental conditions, govern the placing of nets. As Raychaudhuri explains:

According to the convention of the fisherfolk, one is not allowed to set his net in a line, either in front or behind another's net. But there is no bar to set on any side of it. . . . If one net is set in front of another, both lose the catch, either of the tide or of the ebb. (1980, 174)

In addition, a spot once claimed by a fishing crew belongs to that crew for the remainder of the fishing season. Even if the crew removes its net from the spot and moves to another spot, no other crew can fish the abandoned spot unless first gaining permission from the original crew (Raychaudhuri 1980, 167–68). While the Jambudwip fishers have exercised management rights by devising rules that define withdrawal rights, they do not exercise the authority to decide who can and who cannot enter the fishing grounds that they utilize. Consequently, the Jambudwip fishers are claimants and not "proprietors."

"Proprietors" are defined as individuals who possess collective-choice rights to participate in management and exclusion. Proprietors authorize who may access resources and how resources may be utilized, however, they do not have the right to alienate either of these collective-choice rights. Scholars who have recently undertaken theoretical and empirical research on "common-property regimes" focus primarily on those regimes organized by proprietors (National Research Council 1986; Berkes 1989; McCay and Acheson 1987; Ostrom 1990). To use the same term for regimes composed of proprietors, who possess four bundles of property rights, and regimes composed of individuals who possess no property rights, clearly confounds the capacity to communicate about important scientific and policy issues.

The fishers who participate in the cod trap fisheries of Newfoundland are proprietors. Cod trap berths are allocated by lottery. To gain access to a berth, a fisher must participate in a lottery. "Only fishermen from the local community are allowed to participate in the lottery" and to sit on the local cod trap berth committee that operates the lottery (Martin 1979, 282). The lottery system is significant in that "the organization of cod trap committees since 1919 has legally codified the boundaries of the fishing space over which a community has political jurisdiction" (Martin 1973, 15).

Turkish fishers who harvest from coastal lagoons are also proprietors. The Turkish government leases lagoons to fishers' cooperatives. For instance, it leases the Ayvalik-Haylazli lagoon to a fishers' co-op of the same name. To access and harvest fish from the lagoon, a fisher must belong to the co-op. In order to belong to the co-op a fisher must reside in one of the three adjacent villages for at least six months and not have wage employment income (Berkes 1986, 72). The fishers of Ayvalik-Haylazli lagoon

> have exclusive and legal rights to the fish of the lagoon and the lagoon's adjacent waters. All fishermen are cooperative members, and all cooperative members are active fishermen. They protect their rights by patrolling the boundary of their fishing area and chasing off or apprehending intruders. (Three outside fishing boats were apprehended in 1983.) (Berkes 1986, 72)

Neither the fishers of Ayvalik-Haylazli lagoon nor the cod fishers of New-foundland, however, can sell or lease their rights of management and exclusion.

If in addition to collective-choice rights of management and exclusion, individuals also hold the right of alienation, that is, they can sell or lease their collective-choice rights, then they are defined as "owners."[13] For instance, fishers of Ascension Bay, located in Quintana Roo State, Mexico, are members of the Vigia Chico cooperative. Co-op members have divided Ascension Bay into "individually held capture areas ('parcelas' or 'campos') ranging from 0.5 to more than 3 km[2]" from which they harvest lobster (Miller 1989, 190). Each co-op member holds complete sets of rights over specific areas. The fishers may transfer their rights of management and exclusion over their particular spot to other fishers of Ascension Bay. "Several campos are sold or bartered each season and such transactions are common knowledge. On occasion, sales are registered with the co-op" (Miller 1989, 192). Once having sold their campos, however, fishers no longer can exercise rights of exclusion or management in relation to Ascension Bay lobstergrounds.

De Facto and *De Jure* Property Rights

The sources of the rights of access, withdrawal, management, exclusion, and transfer are varied. They may be enforced by a government whose officials explicitly grant such rights to resource users. If so, such rights are *de jure* rights in that they are given lawful recognition by formal, legal instrumentalities. Rights-holders who have *de jure* rights can presume that if their rights were challenged in an administrative or judicial setting, their rights would most likely be sustained.

Property rights may also originate among resource users. In some situations resource users cooperate to define and enforce rights among themselves. Such rights are *de facto* as long as they are not recognized by government authorities. Users of a resource who have developed *de facto* rights act as if they have *de jure* rights by enforcing these rights among themselves. In some settings *de facto* rights may eventually be given recognition in courts of law if challenged, but until so recognized they are less secure than *de jure* rights.[14]

Within a single common-pool resource situation a conglomeration of *de jure* and *de facto* property rights may exist which overlap, complement, or even conflict with one another. A government may grant fishers *de jure* rights of access and withdrawal, retaining the formal rights of management, exclusion, and alienation for itself. Fishers, in turn, may cooperate and exercise rights of management and exclusion, defining among themselves how harvesting must take place, and who may engage in harvesting from their fishing grounds. In many situations where local fishers possess *de jure* authorized user or claimant rights, field researchers have found *de facto* proprietor arrangements that are commonly understood, followed, and perceived as legitimate within the local community (Cordell and McKean 1987; Berkes 1986, 1989; Davis 1984; Acheson 1975).

In many instances government officials simply pay little attention to inshore fisheries, leaving fishers with sufficient autonomy to design workable arrangements. For many years this was the case for fishers of Valenca, Brazil, who fished from the adjacent estuary (Cordell 1972). These fishers held *de jure* rights of access and withdrawal when they first developed the fishery at the beginning of this century. Initially, they experienced a number of problems due to the diverse technologies in use. Gear became entangled and was destroyed, leading to violence among the fishers. In addition, fishers fought over the choicest fishing spots (Cordell 1972, 105). Over a period of time fishers designed harvesting arrangements that addressed many of the problems they had experienced. The fishers divided the estuary among different technologies so that diverse gears were not utilized within the same area (Cordell 1972, 42). In addition, fishers allocated fishing spots by drawing lots to determine the order of use of a particular spot. The Valenca fishers did not initially experience exclusion problems. No other fishers exhibited interest in fishing the estuary. While the Valenca fishers were *de jure* authorized users, they were *de facto* claimants.

The Brazilian government, in an attempt to "modernize" fisheries, made nylon nets available to anyone who qualified for a bank loan arranged by the government through the *Banco do Brasil*. The Valenca fishers did not qualify for bank loans and could not purchase nets. A number of wealthy individuals around Valenca did qualify, and purchased nets. These individuals hired men to fish with the nets, men who had no prior fishing experience. The men invaded the Valenca estuary. Conflict erupted between the established fishers and the new entrants. Fishers were shot and equipment destroyed. The *de facto* property rights crumbled as fishers fought for whatever fishing spots they could gain. The fishery was overharvested and eventually was abandoned (Cordell 1978).[15]

De facto property systems are important for several reasons. First, the resource economics literature examining property rights and fishery regulation is generally pessimistic about the likelihood of fishers undertaking self-regulation so as to avoid inefficient economic outcomes, such as rent dissipation and the extinction of valuable species. And yet, an extensive empirical literature exists that documents a diversity of indigenous institutions devised by fishers without reference to governmental authorities (Alexander 1977; Berkes 1986, 1989; Cordell 1972; Davis 1984; Faris 1972; Forman 1970; Martin 1979; McCay and Acheson 1987; Pinkerton 1989). Many of these *de facto* arrangements substantially reduce the incentives to overinvest in harvesting effort and to dissipate rent that fishers face in an open access fishery. Understanding the *de facto* arrangements that have enabled some fishers to reduce inefficient use of resources permits the development of better explanations of the conditions that inhibit or enhance effective self-organized collective solutions.

Second, self-organized collective-choice arrangements can produce operational rules closely matched to the physical and economic conditions of a particular site. Within the context of *de facto* proprietor regimes fishers have devised maps of their fishing territories that could not be generated by central authorities. The maps reflect local knowledge of where fish spawn, their habits in particular waters, and where technologies can be used without the efforts of one boat adversely affecting the success of another boat (see, for example, Cordell 1972 or

Berkes 1986). The knowledge needed to establish agreement concerning a set of productive fishing spots is achieved by a community of fishers who learn from their accumulated daily experience on a particular fishing ground. The cost of assigning a government official to devise a similar arrangement would be prohibitive. Nor is such an arrangement enforceable without the commitment of the fishers to the legitimacy of their self-imposed constraints.[16]

Third, since the professional literature is so pessimistic about fishers adopting effective self-regulation, this literature is used by policy analysts to recommend sweeping reforms. These reforms, however, may "sweep away" successful human efforts to solve extremely difficult problems.[17]

Fourth, since the regulation of these *de facto* proprietor regimes is undertaken by local fishers who benefit from these regimes, the costs of regulation are largely borne by these same beneficiaries. Institutional arrangements that internalize the costs of monitoring and exclusion among beneficiaries reduce inefficiencies.

Property Rights, Incentives, and Outcomes

Different bundles of property rights, whether they are *de facto* or *de jure,* affect the incentives individuals face, the types of actions they take, and the outcomes they achieve. An important difference often discussed in economics is that between owners, who hold a complete set of rights, and all other users who do not hold complete rights. In particular, the right of alienation is believed crucial for the efficient use of resources.[18] Alienation rights, combined with rights of exclusion, produce incentives for owners to undertake long-term investments in a resource. Through sale or lease of all or part of the property rights owners hold, they can capture the benefits produced by long-term investments. In addition, alienation permits a resource to be shifted from a less productive to a more productive use (Posner 1975). Ownership, however, does not guarantee the survival of a resource. If owners use a relatively high discount rate, they may still destroy a resource (Clark 1973, 1974) or engage in activities leading to substantial "overexploitation, resource abuse, and overcapitalization" (van Ginkel 1989, 102).[19]

Owners of natural resources often invest in the physical structure of resources that maintain or increase the productivity of the resource. For instance, the fishers of Ascension Bay, discussed earlier, place artificial habitats, called casitas, on the sea floor in each of their campos, which attract lobsters (Miller 1989). Lobsters are attracted because they "are gregarious; because they remain in dens during the day; and because they do not modify existing habitat or build new habitat" (Miller 1989, 190). In addition, casitas may enhance the productivity of the campos because they provide "refuge sites from predators," and those located near feeding grounds of lobsters "have the potential to reduce predation risk" (Miller 1989). Fishers of Ascension Bay regularly make long-term investments in their fishing grounds.

Rights of alienation, however, are not the only important distinction among rights-holders. Another important difference is that between claimants and authorized users on the one hand, and proprietors and owners on the other hand, based on the right of exclusion. The right of exclusion produces strong incentives for owners and proprietors to make current investments in resources. Because proprietors and owners can decide who can and cannot enter a resource, they can capture for themselves and for their offspring the benefits from investments they undertake in a resource.[20] Owners and proprietors are reasonably assured of being rewarded for incurring the costs of investment (Posner 1975). Such investments are likely to take the form of devising withdrawal rights that coordinate the harvesting activities of groups of owners or proprietors so as to avoid or resolve common-pool resource dilemmas. In addition, owners and proprietors devise access rights that allow them to capture the benefits produced by the withdrawal rights (Dahlman 1980).

Claimants, because of their rights of management, face stronger incentives than do authorized users to invest in governance structures for their resources even though their incentives are weaker than proprietors or owners. Claimants can devise operational-level rights of withdrawal for their situation. Without collective-choice rights of exclusion, however, they can no longer be assured of being rewarded for investing in withdrawal rights. Consequently, whether claimants exercise their rights of management depends upon whether they act within a set of circumstances that allows them to capture the benefits of coordinating their activities even without rights of exclusion.

For instance, claimants may utilize resources that no other groups are interested in using, or claimants may be physically isolated from other populations so that exclusion is not problematic. In such situations, claimants are likely to be able to capture the benefits from exercising their rights of management. The fishers of Valenca, Brazil, discussed earlier, even though claimants, utilized fishing grounds of no interest to other potential users. Over a period of time the fishers devised a number of withdrawal rights that resolved the common-pool resource dilemmas that they faced. For several decades the Valenca fishers enjoyed the benefits produced from coordinating their use of the Valenca estuary. Of course, such arrangements are vulnerable to external invasion as the Valenca fishery attests.

Finally, authorized users possess no authority to devise their own rules of access and withdrawal. Their outcomes are dependent primarily upon the operational-level rights that others define for them. Whether the incentives they face induce them to act so as to achieve efficient outcomes depends upon the institutional design skills of those who hold the collective-choice rights. Since authorized users do not design the rules they are expected to follow, they are less likely to agree to the necessity and legitimacy of the rules. Authorized users may engage in a game with rule enforcers, seeking to gain as much as possible. This leads to an overinvestment in the fishery and inefficient outcomes.

Common Pool Resource Dilemmas

The institutional arrangements fishers may invest in to govern the use of their fishing grounds are often designed to address and resolve common pool resource (CPR) dilemmas (Schlager 1990). CPR dilemmas that fishers typically experience are appropriation externalities, technological externalities, and assignment problems (Schlager N.d.) Assuming a homogeneous distribution of fish over space and time, and identical fishers harvesting from the stock of fish, the dilemma that arises is one of appropriation externalities. The dilemma arises because fishers are withdrawing fish from a common stock without taking into account the effects of their harvesting upon each other. When a fisher harvests fish, he subtracts from the amount of fish available to be harvested increasing the marginal costs of appropriating additional fish and lowering the marginal product of additional fishing effort. Thus, the increased costs of harvesting due to reducing the stock not only affect the fisher who harvested the fish—the fisher who generated the costs—but all fishers who fish that stock. As Wilson explains:

> each individual fisherman cannot perceive the marginal external costs of his fishing activity on the rest of the fleet. Consequently, fishermen as a whole tend to commit too much capital and labor to the fishery, i.e., too much fishing effort. (1982, 423–24)[21]

Another dilemma fishers potentially face are technological externalities. Technological externalities are produced when fishers physically interfere with each other in harvesting fish. Wilson defines technological externalities as:

> gear conflicts or other forms of physical interference which arise because fishermen often find it advantageous to fish very close to one another. (1982, 423)

Technological externalities may also be produced by indirect physical interference. Gear does not become entangled or destroyed, but it is set so close together that the flow of fish among gear is obstructed. As Smith explains:

> externalities may also enter via crowding phenomena: If the fish population is highly concentrated the efficiency of each boat may be lowered by congestion over the fishing grounds. (1968, 413)

A third dilemma that coastal fishers potentially face are assignment problems. Fish are unevenly distributed across fishing grounds, congregating in areas that provide food and shelter. Consequently, particular areas or spots of fishing grounds are more productive than others, with fishers desiring to fish the most productive spots. Assignment problems occur when fishers, in their uncoordinated choice of a fishing spot, do not allocate themselves efficiently across spots. Problems arise over who should have access to the productive spots and how access should be determined. Failing to solve assignment problems can lead to violence among fishers and increased production costs.

Combining the above arguments concerning property rights and CPR dilemmas a general research question emerges that will be carefully examined in the following sections.

> *The more complete the bundle of property rights fishers hold in relation to a fishing ground the more likely fishers are to invest in institutional arrangements that govern their access and harvesting activities of that ground; the institutional arrangements fishers adopt are designed to address and resolve typical CPR dilemmas fishers face; consequently, fishers who adopt institutional arrangements to govern the use of their fishing ground are much less likely to face CPR dilemmas.*

Data From the Field

The above research question will be examined using data collected from case studies of the coastal fishing grounds located around the world (see Table 2.1). The data were extracted from these case studies using a set of detailed coding forms containing mostly close-ended questions that captured the physical, institutional, and community attributes of coastal fishing grounds and the fishers who utilize them.[22]

In choosing case studies two criteria were used. First, the study had to describe a coastal fishery dilemma. Second, the study had to contain information on the rules that fishers used to organize their harvesting activities. After searching through hundreds of documents, *thirty* in-depth coastal fishery case studies were identified and coded.

These case studies are not a random sample from the population of coastal fishing grounds located throughout the world. Consequently, one must be cautious in generalizing these findings. On the other hand, a consistent set of variables were collected across the cases permitting controlled comparisons.

The unit of analysis used is the subgroup. A subgroup is a group of fishers who harvest from the same fishing ground and who are relatively similar in relation to the following five characteristics:

1. Their legal rights to appropriate fish.
2. Their withdrawal rate of fish.
3. Their exposure to variation in the supply of fish.
4. Their level of dependency on fish withdrawn from the resource.
5. Their use of the fish they harvest.

Table 2.1
Coastal Fishing Grounds Case Studies

Country	Location	Fish Harvested	Sub-groups	Positions	Documentation
Belize	Caye Caulker	Lobster	1	Claimants	Sutherland (1986)
	San Pedro	Lobster	2	Proprietors	Gordon (1981
Brazil	Arembepe	Mixed	1	Authorized Users	Kottak (1966)
	Coqueiral	Mixed	1	Proprietors	Forman (1966, 1970)
	Valenca	Mixed	5	Claimants	Cordell (1972, 1974,
				Authorized Users	1978, 1983, 1984)
Canada	Baccalaos Cove	Cod	2	Proprietors	Powers (1984)
	Cat Harbour	Cod	2	Proprietors	Faris (1972)
	Fermeuse	Cod	2	Proprietors	Martin (1973, 1979)
	James Bay	Whitefish	1	Proprietors	Berkes (1977, 1987)
	Petty Harbour	Cod	2	Proprietors	Shortall (1973)
	Port Lameroon, Pagesville	Lobster	1	Proprietors	Davis (1975, 1984)
	Port Lameroon, Pagesville	Mixed	1	Proprietors	Davis (1975, 1984)
Greece	Messolonghi Etolico	Mullet, Seabream	2	Claimant, Authorized User	Kotsonias (1984)
India	Jambudwip	Mixed	2	Claimants	Raychaudhuri (1980)
Jamaica	Fraquhar Beach	Mixed	1	Proprietors	Davenport (1956)
Japan	Ebibara	Shrimp	1	Claimants	Brameld (1968)
Korea	Kagoda	Anchovy	1	Proprietors	Han (1972)
Malaysia	Kampong Mee	Mixed	1	Authorized Users	Anderson and Anderson (1977)
	Perupok	Mixed	1	Proprietors	Firth (1966)
Mexico	Andres Quintana Roo	Mixed	1	Authorized Users	Miller (1982)
	Andres Quintana Roo	Lobster	1	Proprietors	Miller (1982)
	Ascension Bay	Lobster	1	Owners	Miller (1982, 1989)
Nicaragua	Tasbapauni	Turtle	2	Proprietors	Nietschmann (1972, 1973)
Sri Lanka	Gahavalla	Mixed	3	Proprietors, Claimants	Alexander (1982)
Thailand	Rusembilan	Mackerel	1	Claimants	Fraser (1960, 1966)
Turkey	Alanya	Mixed	1	Proprietors	Berkes (1986)
	Ayvalik-Haylazi	Mixed	1	Proprietors	Berkes (1986)
	Tasucu	Mixed	1	Proprietors	Berkes (1986)
Venezuela	Chigauan	Lisa	1	Authorized Users	Breton (1973)
U.S.A.	Mount Desert Island	Lobster	1	Proprietors	Grossinger (1975)

Table 2.2
Guttman Scale of Property Rights

Access	Withdrawal	Manage	Exclusion	Transfer	Number of Subgroups
Yes	Yes	Yes	Yes	Yes	1
Yes	Yes	Yes	Yes	No	26[a]
Yes	Yes	Yes	No	No	10[b]
Yes	Yes	No	No	No	7

CR (coefficient of reproductivity) = 1

[a] 18 subgroups hold *de facto* rights of exclusion

[b] 5 subgroups hold *de facto* right of management

This definition of a subgroup depends on the sharing of similar characteristics and not on the presence or absence of an organization of fishers. More than one subgroup of fishers may utilize the same fishing grounds simultaneously. Forty-four subgroups utilize the thirty fishing grounds listed in Table 2.1.

Property Rights and Rules

Among the forty-four subgroups of fishers, the sets of property rights each possesses varies (see Table 2.2). One subgroup possesses all five rights, those of access, withdrawal, management, exclusion, and alienation. The fishers of this subgroup reside at Punta Allen in Quintana Roo State in Mexico and harvest lobster from Ascension Bay, and are owners of their grounds (Miller 1982, 1989). Twenty-six of the subgroups are proprietors, possessing the four rights of access, withdrawal, management, and exclusion. Another ten subgroups are claimants. These subgroups do not possess the rights of exclusion or alienation. Finally, the remaining seven subgroups are authorized users, possessing only rights of access and withdrawal.

Authority and Scope Rules

How these collectively held rights are exercised is important. Rules define how fishers within a group can exercise their rights in relation to each other and in relation to nongroup members. Without rule definition, even given a more complete set of property rights, a group of fishers can utilize the resource inefficiently, and even possibly destroy it, if they do not organize their harvesting activities. Rule definition, however, is more likely to take place as fishers possess more complete sets of rights in their fishing grounds. More complete sets of rights grant fishers greater authority to make decisions concerning the use of the grounds. They are more likely to capture the benefits of investments they make in rules that order their harvesting activities.

Among the forty-four subgroups of fishers this expectation holds (see Table 2.3). Subgroups that possess at least the right of management are much more likely to devise authority and scope rules—rules that define how harvesting is to take place.[23] Among proprietors and owners, 88 percent devised authority and scope rules. Ninety percent of the claimants devised authority and scope rules, whereas only one group of authorized users use authority and scope rules.

As shown in Table 2.4, five different types of authority and scope rules are used in these groups: location rules, size rules, season rules, order rules, and time-slot rules. Subgroups frequently rely on more than one authority or scope rule. The most often used rule is a scope rule that limits harvesting activities to specific locations or spots. Every subgroup in the sample used a location rule to determine how choice fishing spots are distributed. Access to fishing spots is dependent on meeting any of a variety of requirements. The gear that a fisher uses may determine where the fisher can locate it (Davis 1975). Or a fisher may gain access to a choice fishing spot through a lottery (Faris 1972).

Table 2.3
Required Authority Rules
By Property Rights Holders

	Authorized Users	Claimants	Owners, Proprietors	(Total)
No Required Rules	86% (6)	10% (1)	11% (3)	(10)
Required Rules	14% (1)	90% (9)	89% (24)	(34)
(Total)	100% (7)	100% (10)	100% (27)	(44)

Gamma = .75

Table 2.4
Required Authority and Scope Rules

Type of Rule	Number of Subgroups Using Rule (N = 34)	% of Subgroups Using Rule
Withdraw at Specific Locations/Spots	34	100
Withdraw Fish of at Least a Specific Size	9	26
Withdraw in a Fixed Order	7	21
Withdraw Only During Specific Seasons	7	21
Withdraw at a Fixed Time Slot	4	12

The second most frequently used rule is a size rule requiring that fishers harvest fish greater than a minimum size. The rule is typically used to ensure that fish achieve maturity and have a chance to spawn before being harvested. Nine of the thirty-three subgroups utilize this rule. In all but one instance an external authority has imposed the size rule on the fishers.[24]

The third most frequently used rules are seasonal restrictions and harvesting in a fixed order. Seasonal restrictions forbid the harvesting of fish during specific times of the year, typically when fish spawn. In the case of seasonal restrictions, all but one of the rules was devised by a government authority. Harvesting in a fixed order defines how choice spots on the grounds can be accessed and harvested from. Often times the rule requires that fishers take turns in accessing particular spots. All of the order rules were devised by fishers.

The fourth most frequently used rule is a fixed time slot rule. This rule is often combined with a fixed order rule or a location rule. It limits the amount of time that a boat can remain on a choice fishing spot. Typical limits involve one casting of a net, or one day (Alexander 1982, Cordell 1972).

The authority and scope rules reveal a clear attempt on the part of fishers to resolve CPR dilemmas. Assignment problems are addressed by location rules that allocate choice spots, minimizing destructive competition among fishers.

Relegating particular technologies to different areas of a fishing ground addresses technological externalities by separating incompatible types of gear.

Boundary Rules

In addition to authority and scope rules that define how rights of withdrawal may be exercised, boundary rules are also used among the fishers. Boundary rules define how rights of access may be exercised. The required boundary rules reveals attempts on the part of fishers to limit the number of fishers who can access fishing grounds and the types of technology that can be utilized (see Table 2.5).

Twelve different types of boundary rules are utilized among the forty-four subgroups. The rules used by most subgroups (34 out of 44) are residency rules that require fishers to reside in a particular village to gain access to particular grounds. After residency requirements, twenty-seven subgroups (61 percent) limit access to their fishing grounds on the basis of the type of technology used. Boundary rules based on gear assist in alleviating technological externalities. By limiting the types of gear that can be brought into the grounds, interference among gears is minimized.

Note, however, that boundary rules can have an indirect effect upon appropriation externalities. Limiting both the number of individuals who can access a ground and the type of technologies they can utilize limits the amount of fishing effort applied in harvesting, and thereby possibly affecting the magnitude of appropriation externalities.

Performance of Institutional Arrangements

While fishers have adopted institutional arrangements that appear to address CPR dilemmas, have fishers successfully resolved such problems?[25] In Table 2.6, property rights holders are arrayed by the level of assignment problems.[26] Altogether, nineteen subgroups, at some point in time faced assignment problems. But, as Table 2.6 illustrates, fishers have been very successful in addressing and resolving them. Of the nineteen subgroups of fishers who faced assignment problems, 74%, or 14, of the groups have resolved them. The successful resolution of assignment problems is particularly high among proprietors and owners. Of those eleven subgroups, ten, or 91%, have minimized such problems. Among the claimants, 67% no longer face problems of assignment. Authorized users, however, continue to experience assignment problems.

The finding that institutional arrangements make a difference in resolving assignment problems also holds for the resolution of technological externalities.[27] Table 2.7 arrays property rights holders by the level of technological externalities. Of the forty-four subgroups, twenty-one have experienced technological externalities. Of the twelve subgroups that are proprietors or owners, 67% no longer experience problems with technological externalities. The outcomes for claimants is quite different. Of the six subgroups, 17%, or one, has resolved its technological externality problems, while five, or 83%, have not. Not one of the three subgroups of authorized users have resolved their problems of technological externalities. Clearly, the types of institutional arrangements fishers have devised affect whether they are able to solve technological externalities.

Table 2.5
Required Boundary Rules Among Fishers

Type of Rule	Number of Subgroups Using Rule (N = 44)	% of Subgroups Using Rule
Residency—Local	34	77
Use of Particular Technology	27	61
Membership in an Organization	15	34
License	8	18
Ownership of Property Related to Harvesting (i.e., fishing berths)	7	16
Lottery	5	11
Race	6	14
Registration on Lottery Eligibility List	5	11
Continuing Usage of Access Rights	3	7
Ethnicity	7	16
Ownership or Leasing of Land in Area	7	16
Caste	2	5

Table 2.6
Property Rights Holders
By Level of Assignment Problems

	Owners, Proprietors	Claimants	Authorized Users	(Total)
Minimal Assignment Problems	91% (10)	67% (4)	0% (0)	(14)
Moderate Assignment Problems	9% (1)	33% (2)	100% (2)	(5)
(Total)	100% (11)	100% (6)	100% (2)	(19)

Gamma = .85

Table 2.7
Property Rights Holders
By Level of Technological Externalities

	Owners, Proprietors	Claimants	Authorized Users	(Total)
No Technological Externalities	67% (8)	17% (1)	0% (0)	(9)
Technological Externalities	33% (4)	83% (5)	100% (3)	(12)
(Total)	100% (12)	100% (6)	100% (3)	(21)

Gamma = .68

Conclusion

DeAlessi (1980, 42) argues that "differences in the structures of rights to use resources affect behavior systematically and predictably." Clearly, this assertion holds true for the forty-four subgroups of fishers examined here. Fishers who hold more complete sets of property rights are more likely to invest in authority and scope rules that define how they exercise their right of withdrawal. Defining how fishing grounds may be used substantially affects whether fishers resolved common pool resource dilemmas. Owners, proprietors, and claimants fare much better than do authorized users. Another important difference emerges between owners and proprietors who possess the right of exclusion and claimants who have no such right. Owners and proprietors are more successful in resolving assignment problems and technological externalities. Being able to exclude is an important right.

Since different bundles of rights affect the behavior of resource users it is crucial that in analyzing common pool resources the types of property rights held by users be made explicit. The term "common property" cannot begin to capture the diversity of rights held in common by resource users. Instead, a more precise language must be developed that captures meaningful differences among different property rights regimes. We have begun such a process through the schema presented here.

Notes

1. The confusion in the use of the term "common property" has been addressed frequently in the past (Ciriacy-Wantrup and Bishop 1975; Bromley 1982, 1986, 1989; Runge 1981) without much impact on its careless usage. Even scholars, who are meticulous theorists and observers of behavior related to natural resource systems, use the terms "open access" and "common property systems" inter-changeably (see Johnson and Libecap 1982, 1005; for other examples, see Agnello and Donnelly 1975; Bell 1972; Christy 1975; Gordon 1954; Scott 1955; Scott and Christy 1965; Smith, Weber, and Wiesmeth 1991; Sinn 1988).
2. A third level of action is also available and that is the constitutional level. Constitutional-choice actions entail devising collective-choice rules. In establishing an organization or changing the process by which operational rules are to be devised within an existing organization, individuals engage in constitutional-choice actions. Fishers creating a marketing cooperative is an example of a constitutional-choice action.
3. A plan adopted by an individual for how that individual wishes to undertake future actions is better thought of as a "strategy" rather than as a "rule." The concept of "rule" relates to shared understandings about prescriptions that apply to more than a single individual. A marriage contract can be viewed as a set of

rules authorizing and forbidding future actions for the two individuals involved. A court decision outlawing some types of agreements among fishers using inshore fisheries is a set of rules affecting future actions for all individuals using the coastal fisheries under that court's jurisdiction. Rules, be they operational, collective choice, or constitutional choice, instruct individuals to take actions that are required or permitted, or to avoid taking action that is forbidden (Gardner and Ostrom 1991; Ostrom 1986). See Buck (1989) for an analysis of the rules creating property rights in the American Southwest.

4. Not all actions taken in collective-choice arenas affect rules-in-use. Passing a new law or writing a new regulation is not the equivalent of establishing a new rule. Laws and regulations must be enforced to become rules (see Ostrom 1991). To be effective they must be accepted as legitimate by resource users.

5. Rules defining the rights of access and withdrawal may or may not permit those rights to be transferred.

6. See Copes (1986) for an analysis of quota systems in relation to fisheries. See Wilson (1982) for an effective critique of standard economic theory's limited view of institutional alternatives in relation to fisheries.

7. See, for example, Davis (1984) and Cordell (1972).

8. If these same fishers revise the conditions that constitute the right of access by expanding the number of fishers who can enter their fishery, they have not exercised a right of alienation. They have not transferred rights to additional individuals. Rather, they have exercised their right of exclusion to redefine who may or may not enter. The right of alienation refers only to the authority to alienate collective-choice rights, that is, to sell or lease such rights.

9. By alienation we specifically mean the authority to sell or lease collective-choice rights. We do not include the ability to bequeath. In most common-property regimes, users have the ability to bequeath their rights in a resource. Rights rarely die with an individual. In many situations, however, resource users do not have the right to sell or lease their rights to others. Limiting alienation to sale or lease also brings it closer to its economic usage. The importance of a right of alienation for many economists is that it provides the possibility that resources will be transferred to their highest valued use. While being able to sell or lease collective-choice rights provides that potential, the right to bequeath these rights is usually presumed by economists to be an insufficient property right to achieve full efficiency. Larson and Bromley (1990) effectively challenge this commonly held view and argue that much more needs to be known about the specific values of a large number of parameters in a particular setting before analysts can make careful judgements whether the right of alienation leads to higher levels of efficiency than the right to bequeath. See also Anderson and Hill (1990) for an analysis of three different alienation rules that the U.S. government used in transferring public lands to individuals.

10. While theoretically it is possible to hold entry rights without withdrawal rights, in practice this rarely occur. The distinction between access and withdrawal

becomes crucial at a collective-choice level. Often times individuals who hold rights of management and thereby define withdrawal rights are not the same individuals who hold rights of exclusion and thereby define access rights. We provide a number of examples throughout the remainder of the paper.

11. One could also define a position called "squatter" to consist of individuals who possess no rights at any level in relation to a common-pool resource. Squatters use natural resources, such as fisheries, but they do so at their own risk. If challenged by a person who holds collective-choice or operational rights, squatters lack authority to enforce their claims. Squatters stand entirely exposed to the actions of others as concerns the use of a resource.

12. Alchian and Demsetz refer to the possession of the right of management, but not exclusion or alienation as "communal rights" (1973, 19).

13. The rights of alienation can be exercised in total or to a limited set of rights for a limited duration. Given the latter capability, "hybrid" legal arrangements related to the same resource are possible and occur frequently. Alchian and Demsetz (1973, 18) point out that some of the "ambiguity in the notion of state or private ownership of a resource" occurs "because the bundle of property rights associated with a resource is divisible." In fact, all coastal fisheries in the U.S. are apt to be hybrid legal arrangements of one or another variety since the ownership rights to the coastal waters are vested in states. Each state decides whether to assign claimant status to all residents, to all residents who obtain licenses, or to allow various forms of proprietorship to come about through self-organization or through formal lease-hold arrangements.

14. Note that unchallenged *de facto* rights are as much a factor affecting action as are *de jure* rights. Only if *de facto* rights are challenged do the differences between the two classes of rights become apparent.

15. See Matthews (1988) and Matthews and Phyne (1988) for discussions of the impact Canadian fishing policies are having on the institutional arrangements devised by fishers in Newfoundland.

16. See, for example, McGuire and Langworth (1991).

17. See, for example, Berkes (1989) and Davis (1984).

18. By efficiency, we focus in this article on the level of resource rents that are obtained by fishers and not dissipated through overinvestment or other inefficient practices. Copes (1972) points out that in relation to fisheries, however, not only can resource rent be dissipated but producer and consumer surplus can be lost, depending upon the institutional arrangements that govern the use of a fishery. We have not attempted to expand our analysis of efficiency to that of total social surplus, as we are not examining property rights to resource units in commodity markets.

19. Also, see Larson and Bromley (1990).

20. See Larson and Bromley (1990) for an important analysis of the "bequest motives" that exist under common property versus the "market incentives that exist under private property." They conclude: "There is no scientific knowledge

that can rank the relative magnitudes of the terminal value under private property . . . and common property . . . even assuming a perfect land market" (1990, 254).

21. Anderson (1986, 47) defines stock externalities as follows: "The individual fishermen do not consider the effect that their production will have on the production of all others in the current period. . . . At the same time, however, the stock is being nonoptimally depleted because individual operators do not consider the user cost they are imposing on harvesters in future periods." Smith (1968, 413) states that stock externalities occur because: "No individual competitive fisherman has control over population size as a private decision variable yet it enters as a parameter in each fisherman's cost function". Gordon (1954, 451) argues that stock externalities arise because: "It is not the relative *marginal* productivities of the two grounds but their *average* productivities. The fisherman does not ask what allocation of effort will maximize the aggregate production of the fishing fleet but what action will give him, individually, the greater yield".

22. See Tang (1992) and Schlager (1990).

23. See Ostrom (1986) for a complete discussion of rule types.

24. That exception is the Cree Indians in northern Canada as reported by Berkes (1977, 1987).

25. Appropriation externalities are not examined because of measurement problems and a lack of data. Obtaining a measure of production externalities is highly problematic. Not only do fishers have little information concerning stock dynamics and the effects of their actions upon each other's harvest, but neither do most researchers. Thus, direct measures of production externalities are not reported in the case studies. The only information reported in the case studies that may relate to production externalities is whether the stock of fish appeared to be abundant. Stock abundance is not, however, a good measure of production externalities since declining stocks of fish may be due to environmental factors and not necessarily the harvesting activities of fishers. Since no reliable measure of production externalities is available, whether fishers organize when confronted with production externalities will not be explored.

The following discussion of assignment problems and technological externalities involves thirty-one distinct subgroups. Ten subgroups have experienced assignment problems only, twelve have faced technological externalities only, and nine have experienced both. For thirteen subgroups, not enough information was presented to determine the type of problem the fishers experienced.

26. This discussion involves nineteen subgroups—ten of which have experienced assignment problems only and nine which have experienced both.

27. The question concerning technological externalities appears on the operational level form and is worded as follows: *As of the beginning and end of this period, what is the extent of technical externalities resulting from the appropriation activities of participants from this resource? 1) the level of technical externalities is quite low, 2) the level of technical externalities is relatively low, 3) modest*

levels of technical externalities exist, 4) relatively high levels of technical exter-
nalities exist, 5) very high levels of technical externalities exist. For Table 2.7, I
collapsed answers 1), 2) no technological externalities, and answers 3), 4), and 5)
as technological externalities.

References

Acheson, James M. 1975. The lobster fiefs: Economic and ecological effects of
territoriality in the Maine lobster industry. *Human Ecology* 3 (3): 183–207.

Adasiak, A. 1979. Alaska's experience with limited entry. *Journal of the Fisheries
Research Board of Canada* 36 (7): 770–82.

Agnello, Richard, and Lawrence Donnelly. 1975. Property rights and efficiency
in the oyster industry. *Journal of Law and Economics* 18:521–33.

Alchian, Armen, and Harold Demsetz. 1973. The property rights paradigm.
Journal of Economic History 33 (1): 16–27.

Alexander, Paul. 1977. South Sri Lanka sea tenure. *Ethnology* 16:231–55.

———. 1982. *Sri Lankan fishermen: Rural capitalism and peasant society.*
Canberra: Australian National University.

Andersen, Raoul. 1979. Public and private access management in Newfoundland
fishing. In *North Atlantic maritime cultures.* New York: Mouton, 299–336.

Anderson, Eugene N., Jr., and Marja L. Anderson. 1977. *Fishing in troubled
waters: Research on the Chinese fishing industry in West Malaysia.* Taipei:
Chinese Association for Folklore.

Anderson, Lee. 1986. *The economics of fisheries management,* 2nd edition.
Baltimore, MD: Johns Hopkins University.

Anderson, Terry, and Peter Hill. 1990. The race for property rights. *Journal of
Law and Economics* 33:117–97.

Bell, Frederick W. 1972. Technological externalities and common property
resources: An empirical study of the U.S. lobster industry. *Journal of Political
Economy* 80:148–58.

Berkes, Fikret. 1977. Fishery resource use in a subarctic Indian community.
Human Ecology 5 (4): 289–307.

———. 1986. Marine inshore fishery management in Turkey. In *Proceedings of
the conference on common property resource management,* National Research
Council. Washington, DC: National Academy Press, 63–83.

———. 1987. Common property resource management and Cree Indian fishermen
in subarctic Canada. In *The question of the commons: The culture and ecology
of communal resources,* edited by Bonnie J. McCay and James M. Acheson.
Tucson: University of Arizona Press, 66–91.

———, ed. 1989. *Common property resources: Ecology and community-based
sustainable development.* London: Belhaven Press.

Brameld, Theodore. 1968. *Japan: Culture, education, and change in two communities.* New York: Holt, Rinehart, and Winston.

Breton, Yvan D. 1973. A comparative study of rural fishing communities in Eastern Venezuela: An anthropological explanation of economic specialization. Ph.D. dissertation, Michigan State University.

Bromley, Daniel. 1982. Land and water problems: An institutional perspective. *American Journal of Agricultural Economics* 64 (December): 834–44.

———. 1986. Closing comments at the conference on common property resource management. In *Proceedings of the conference on common property resource management*, National Research Council. Washington, DC: National Academy Press, 591–97.

———. 1989. *Economic interests and institutions: The conceptual foundations of public policy.* Oxford: Basil Blackwell.

Buck, Susan J. 1989. Cultural theory and management of common property resources. *Human Ecology* 17:101–16.

Christy, Francis T. 1975. Property rights in the world ocean. *Natural Resources Journal* 15 (4): 695–712.

Ciriacy-Wantrup, S. V., and Richard C. Bishop. 1975. Common property as a concept in natural resource policy. *Natural Resources Journal* 15 (4): 713–27.

Clark, Colin W. 1973. Profit maximization and the extinction of animal species. *Journal of Political Economy* 81 (4): 950–61.

———. 1974. The economics of overexploitation. *Science* 181:630–34.

Commons, John R. 1968. *Legal foundations of capitalism.* Madison: University of Wisconsin Press.

Copes, Parzival. 1972. Factor rents, sole ownership, and the optimum level of fisheries exploitation. *Manchester School of Economics and Social Studies* 41: 145–63.

———. 1986. A critical review of the individual quota as a device in fisheries management. *Land Economics* 62 (August): 278–89.

Cordell, John C. 1972. The developmental ecology of an estuarine canoe fishing system in Northeast Brazil. Ph.D. dissertation, Stanford University.

———. 1974. The lunal-tide fishing cycle in northeastern Brazil. *Ethnology* 13:379–92.

———. 1978. Carrying capacity analysis of fixed territorial fishing. *Ethnology* 17 (January): 1–24.

———. 1983. Social marginality and sea tenure in Brazilian fishing. Occasional Papers in Latin American Studies Association, no. 7. Stanford, CA: Joint Center for Latin American Studies, 1–21.

———. 1984. Traditional sea tenure and resource management in Brazilian coastal fishing. In *Management of coastal lagoon fisheries,* edited by James M. Kapetsky and G. Lasserre, GFCM Studies and Reviews, no. 61. Rome: Food and Agriculture Organization, 429–38.

Cordell, John C., and Margaret A. McKean. 1987. Sea tenure in Bahia, Brazil. In *Proceedings of the conference on common property resource management*, National Research Council. Washington, DC: National Academy Press, 85–114.

Dahlman, Carl J. 1980. *The open field system and beyond: A property rights analysis of an economic institution.* Cambridge: Cambridge University Press.

Davenport, William H. 1956. A comparative study of two Jamaican fishing communities. Ph.D. dissertation, Yale University.

Davis, Adam F. 1975. The organization of production and market relations in Nova Scotian inshore fishing community. Ph.D. dissertation, University of Manitoba.

Davis, Anthony. 1984. Property rights and access management in the small boat fishery: A case study from Southwest Nova Scotia. In *Atlantic fisheries and coastal communities: Fisheries decision-making case studies,* edited by Cynthia Lamson and Arthur J. Hanson. Halifax: Dalhousie Ocean Studies Programme, 133–64.

DeAlessi, Louis. 1980. The economics of property rights: A review of the evidence. *Research in Law and Economics* 2:1–47.

Dewar, Margaret E. 1990. Federal intervention in troubled waters: Lessons from the New England fishers. *Policy Studies Review* 9 (Spring): 485–504.

Faris, James. 1972. *Cat harbour: A Newfoundland fishing settlement*, Newfoundland Social and Economic Studies, no. 3. Toronto: University of Toronto Press.

Firth, Raymond. 1966. *Malay fishermen: Their peasant economy,* 2nd ed. London: Routledge and Kegan Paul.

Forman, Shepard L. 1966. Jangadeiros: Raft fishermen of Northeastern Brazil. Ph.D. dissertation, Columbia University.

————. 1970. *The raft fishermen: Tradition and change in the Brazilian peasant economy.* Bloomington: Indiana University Press.

Fraser, Thomas M., Jr. 1960. *Rusembilan: A Malay fishing village in Southern Thailand.* Ithaca, NY: Cornell University Press.

————. 1966. *Fishermen of South Thailand: The Malay villagers.* New York: Holt, Rinehart and Winston.

Gardner, Roy, and Elinor Ostrom. 1991. Rules and games. *Public Choice* 70 (2): 121–49.

Gardner, Roy, Elinor Ostrom, and James Walker. 1990. The nature of common-pool resource problems. *Rationality and Society* 2 (3): 335–58.

Gordon, Edmund T. 1981. Phases of development and underdevelopment in a Caribbean fishing village: San Pedro, Belize. Ph.D. dissertation, Stanford University.

Gordon, H. Scott. 1954. The economic theory of a common property resource: The fishery. *Journal of Political Economy* 62 (April): 124–42.

Grossinger, Richard. 1975. The strategy and ideology of lobsterfishing on the back side of Mount Desert Island, Hancock County, Maine. Ph.D. dissertation, University of Michigan.

Han, Sang-Bok. 1972. Socio-economic organization and change in Korean fishing villages: A comparative study of three fishing communities. Ph.D. dissertation, Michigan State University.

Johnson, Ronald N., and Gary D. Libecap. 1982. Contracting problems and regulation: The case of the fishery. *American Economic Review* 72 (5): 1005–022.

Kiser, Larry L., and Elinor Ostrom. 1982. The three worlds of action: A metatheoretical synthesis of institutional approaches. In *Strategies of political inquiry,* edited by Elinor Ostrom. Beverly Hills: Sage, 179–222.

Kotsonias, G. 1984. The Messolonghi-Etolico Lagoon of Greece: Socioeconomic and ecological interactions of cooperatives and independent fishermen. In *Management of coastal lagoon fisheries,* edited by James M. Kapetsky and Georges Lasserre, GFCM Studies and Reviews, no. 61. Rome: Food and Agriculture Organization, 521–28.

Kottak, Conrad. 1966. The structure of equality in a Brazilian fishing community. Ph.D. dissertation, Columbia University.

Larson, Bruce A., and Daniel W. Bromley. 1990. Property rights, externalities, and resource degradation: Locating the tragedy. *Journal of Development Economics* 33:235–62.

Martin, Kent O. 1973. 'The law in St. John's says . . .': Space division and resource allocation in the Newfoundland fishing community of Fermeuse. Master's thesis, Department of Anthropology, Memorial University of Newfoundland.

_____. 1979. Play by the rules or don't play at all: Space division and resource allocation in a rural Newfoundland fishing community. In *North Atlantic maritime cultures: Anthropological essays on changing adaptations,* edited by R. Anderson. The Hague: Mouton, 276–98.

Matthews, R. 1988. Federal licensing policies for the Atlantic inshore fishery and their implementation in Newfoundland, 1973–1981. *Acadiensis: Journal of the History of the Atlantic Region* 17:83–108.

Matthews, R., and J. Phyne. 1988. Regulating the Newfoundland inshore fishery: Traditional values versus state control in the regulation of a common property resource. *Journal of Canadian Studies* 23:158–76.

McCay, Bonnie J., and James M. Acheson. 1987. *The question of the commons: The culture and ecology of communal resources.* Tucson: University of Arizona Press.

McGuire, Thomas R., and Mark Langworth. 1991. Behavioral and organizational modification of enforcement/avoidance theories: The fisheries case. Department of Anthropology, University of Arizona.

Miller, David. 1982. Mexico's Caribbean fishery: Recent change and current issues. Ph.D. dissertation, University of Wisconsin-Milwaukee.

————. 1989. The evolution of Mexico's spiny lobster fishery. In *Common property resources ecology and community-based sustainable development,* edited by Fikret Berkes. London: Belhaven Press, 185–98.

National Research Council. 1986. *Proceedings of the conference on common property resource management.* Washington, DC: National Academy Press.

Nietschmann, Bernard. 1972. Hunting and fishing focus among the Miskito Indians, Eastern Nicaragua. *Human Ecology* 1 (1): 41–67.

————. 1973. *Between land and water: The subsistence ecology of the Miskito Indians, Eastern Nicaragua.* New York: Seminar Press.

Ostrom, Elinor. 1986. An agenda for the study of institutions. *Public Choice* 48:3–25.

————. 1987. Institutional arrangements for resolving the commons dilemma: Some contending approaches. In *The question of the commons: The culture and ecology of communal resources,* edited by Bonnie J. McCay and James Acheson. Tucson: University of Arizona Press, 250–65.

————. 1990. *Governing the commons: The evolution of institutions for collective action.* New York: Cambridge University Press.

Ostrom, Elinor, Roy Gardner, and James Walker. N.d. *Rules, games, and common-pool resources.* Ann Arbor: University of Michigan Press. Forthcoming.

Ostrom, Vincent. 1976. John R. Common's foundations for policy analysis. *Journal of Economic Issues* 10 (4): 839–57.

————. 1991. *The meaning of American federalism: Constituting a self-governing society.* San Francisco: Institute for Contemporary Studies Press.

Pinkerton, E., ed. 1989. *Co-operative management of local fisheries: New directions for improved management and community development.* Vancouver: University of British Columbia Press.

Posner, Richard. 1975. Economic analysis of law. In *Economic foundations of property law,* edited by Bruce Ackerman. Boston: Little Brown & Co.

Powers, Ann M. 1984. Social organization in a Newfoundland fishing settlement on the Burin Peninsula. Ph.D. dissertation, State University of New York, Stony Brook.

Raychaudhuri, Bikash. 1980. *The moon and the net: Study of a transient community of fishermen at Jambudwip.* Anthropological Survey of India. Calcutta: Government of India Press.

Runge, C. Ford. 1981. Common property externalities: Isolation, assurance and resource depletion in a traditional grazing context. *American Journal of Agricultural Economics* 63:595–606.

Schlager, Edella. 1990. Model specification and policy analysis: The governance of coastal fisheries. Ph.D. dissertation, Indiana University.

————. N.d. Fishers' institutional responses to common-pool resource dilemmas. In *Rules, games, and common-pool resources,* by Elinor Ostrom, Roy Gardner, and James Walker. Ann Arbor: University of Michigan Press. Forthcoming.

Scott, Anthony D. 1955. The fishery: The objectives of sole ownership. *Journal of Political Economy* 63 (April): 116–24.

Scott, Anthony D., and Francis T. Christy, Jr. 1965. *The common wealth in ocean fisheries*. Baltimore: Johns Hopkins University Press.

Shortall, D. 1973. Environmental Perception in two local fisheries: A case study from Eastern Newfoundland. Master's thesis, Memorial University of Newfoundland.

Sinn, Hans-Werner. 1988. The Sahel problem. *Kyklos* 41:187–213.

Smith, J. Barry, Shlomo Weber, and Hans Wiesmeth. 1991. Heterogeneity, interdependence and equilibrium industry structure in fisheries. Department of Economics, York University, Toronto.

Smith, Vernon. 1968. Economics of production from natural resources. *American Economic Review* 58 (3): 409–31.

Sutherland, Anne. 1986. *Caye Caulker: Economic success in a Belizean fishing village*. Boulder, CO: Westview Press.

Tang, Shui Yan. 1992. *Institutions and collective action: Self-governance in irrigation*. San Francisco: Institute for Contemporary Studies Press.

van Ginkel, Rob. 1989. Plunders into planters: Zeeland oystermen and the enclosure of the marine commons. In *Dutch dilemmas anthropologists look at The Netherlands*, edited by Jeremy Borssevain and Jojada Verrips. Assen/Maastricht, The Netherlands: Van Gorcum, 89–105.

Wilson, James. 1977. A test of the tragedy of the commons. In *Managing the commons,* edited by Garrett Hardin and John Baden. San Francisco: Freeman, 96–111.

———. 1982. The economical management of multispecies fisheries. *Land Economics* 58 (November): 417–34.

3

Contracting Into the Commons

Dean Lueck

Introduction

Though economists argue that the lack of property rights leads to dissipation of the wealth associated with valuable natural resources, many anthropologists have noted that common ownership is a pervasive form of property for many natural resources.[1] Economists contend that the dissipation takes many forms—over-harvest of fish, over-pumping of an oil field, or excessive grazing of grasslands. Non-economists counter, noting that in many cases common property institutions have not resulted in a "tragedy of the commons."

While this debate has generated many case studies to refute the idea that common ownership always leads to dissipation, there has been little theoretical effort to explain successful common ownership. This chapter offers a contractual rationale for common ownership. Rather than taking the ownership regimes as exogenous, this contractual approach not only makes institutions endogenous but also brings attention to the incentives inherent in the choice of different systems of ownership.

The analysis ignores the open access (unrestricted) cases and focuses on limited-access (restricted) common property.[2] The key question is who limits access and how? The contractual approach considers common property as a joint wealth maximizing share contract among members of a group who have exclusive ownership of a resource. Although there are potentially many ways to allocate use among group members, I examine only egalitarian (equal) sharing rules because they are common. I distinguish between cases in which the group members share the output from the resource and cases in which members share access to the resource and compare both with individual private ownership in order to derive conditions for which each system maximizes wealth. The explanatory power of the model is illustrated with applications to four examples of common property.

Contracting for Common Property

Consider the production of a good (Y) that is sold in a competitive market, where $Y = f(\sum x_i)$ and x_i is the effort of the ith person.[3] Production requires the application of individual effort to a fixed natural resource that can be owned under alternative property rights regimes.[4] Several assumptions help simplify the analysis. First assume that marginal products are positive and declining and that the cost of x is $c(x) = c(x_1, x_2, \ldots x_n)$ where marginal costs are positive and increasing. The increasing marginal costs of effort not only take into account the opportunity cost of individuals' effort but also consider the congestion costs of using the resource which in turn implies that the fixed resource is *not* a pure public good. In order to focus on enforcing property rights rather than on risk avoidance, assume that all input suppliers are risk neutral. Finally, assume input owners have costs and productivity that are not directly affected by each other.[5] Under these conditions, individuals will shirk in their provision of effort because it is impossible for other claimants of the output to implicitly calculate the level of inputs simply by observing the final output.[6]

As Coase (1960) showed, if contracts could be enforced without cost, there would be no shirking and net expected value would be maximized. Under these conditions, expected net wealth is $V^* = f(X^*) - c(X^*)$, regardless of the organization of the input owners. The optimal aggregate level of effort is X^* which satisfies the usual condition that marginal product of effort equals marginal cost of effort.

Now consider three alternative ownership schemes with positive contracting costs.

1. Private Ownership with Input Monitoring

Where contracting costs are positive, all contractual forms, including private ownership, result in $V < V^*$.[7] Consider a simple form of private ownership in which one person owns the fixed resource and the resulting output. Using a fixed payment contract, the resource owner hires and polices effort on a per unit basis. This requires the owner to monitor the effort of hired inputs in order to mitigate shirking. If such monitoring costs are $m = m(x)$, where marginal monitoring costs are positive and increasing with number of inputs hired, the problem is to maximize $V^P = f(\sum x_i) - c(x) - m(x)$. The result is that the optimal amount of employed inputs and the expected net wealth is less than in the zero contracting cost example; in other words, $X^P < X^*$ and $V^P < V^*$.

2. Sharing Output with Common Ownership

Suppose that members of a group jointly own the fixed asset, individually supply their own inputs, and equally share the final output. Examples include tribal cattle herds grazing on reservation land or fishermen splitting their catch from a jointly-owned fishery. Group members must exclude nonmembers from the resource in order to prevent open access dissipation. Assume the costs of excluding nonmembers, $e = e(n)$ are inversely related to the size of the group (n); if the group excluded no one, exclusion costs would be zero. For a "group" with only one member (private property), exclusion costs would be at their maximum. Because each member of the group is a partial output owner, the incentive to shirk is reduced compared to a fixed payment contract, but shirking is not eliminated because each member receives only a portion of the output. By excluding outsiders the group implicitly chooses its membership size, n, and the resulting overall level of effort, X^S, which is less than the zero transaction cost level, X^*. When choosing group size (n^S) the tradeoff is between the increased shirking associated with a larger group and the increased exclusion costs associated with a smaller group. Obviously, as the costs of exclusion rise, the optimal group size will increase, *ceteris paribus*. Also as the marginal net value of effort increases, the shirking losses can be reduced by reducing group size (increasing share size) so that each member has less incentive to shirk when supplying effort.

3. Sharing Resource Access with Common Ownership

Rather than sharing the output, suppose a group jointly owns a resource and chooses to allow members equal access. For instance, instead of a tribal cattle herd, the rules could allow individual members equal access to the tribal pasture for grazing private herds. Here the exploitation of the commons does not result from shirking, but rather from excessive effort. Contrary to the output sharing model, common ownership with access sharing results in excessive effort, or $X^C > X^*$. This result is similar to the classic tragedy of the commons except that the dissipation results from contracting costs rather than open access. Here, however, a contract among group members mitigates the tragedy by restricting membership to an optimal size (n^c) in light of the tradeoff between exclusion costs and rent dissipation.[8]

The Choice of Ownership Regime

What determines the type of property institution that will prevail? If common ownership is chosen, what will determine whether the common owners of a resource choose to share final output or resource access? Answers can be found by recognizing the incentives in each contract. Fixed payment contracts precisely ration input use by explicit unit pricing. Common property contracts ration by making each group member a partial residual owner, thus avoiding the costs of monitoring and pricing input units. In particular, output sharing contracts take advantage of cooperative production but require shared output measurement, while access sharing ignores cooperative production and avoids output measurement.

Determinants of Ownership Rules

Contract choice can be examined by comparing net value functions for the three contract choices with the zero transaction cost world. For the fixed payment contract with private ownership, $V^P = f(X^P) - c(X^P) - m(X^P)$, where f is the total output of the good (Y), c is the total cost of the effort, m is the total cost of effort, and $X^P < X^*$. For input sharing with common ownership, $V^C = f(X^C) - c(X^C) - e(n^C)$, where e is the cost of excluding nonmembers and $X^C > X^*$. For the output sharing with common ownership, there are costs of dividing the output, d,[9] as well as costs of excluding nonmembers, so that $V^S = f(X^S) - c(X^S) - e(n^S) - d$, where $X^S < X^*$.

The problem is to choose the contract that yields the greatest net value of the resource; that is, maximize $\{V^P, V^C, V^S\}$. This choice will depend on five parameters—output division costs, marginal exclusion costs, marginal policing costs, marginal input costs, and marginal input productivity—which in turn determine the actual value realized under each contract. By considering changes in these parameters, it is possible to predict changes in the relative values of the contracts and to predict jointly maximizing outcome. In many cases the contract comparisons are straightforward. For example, an increase in the cost of dividing output renders the output sharing contract less valuable relative to either private property ("fixed payment contract") or access sharing with common ownership. However, an increase in the cost of dividing output has no impact on the choice between fixed payment and access sharing contracts.

Figure 3.1 illustrates the effect of a change in output division costs on the choice between access sharing and output sharing contracts. For both contracts the net values (V^C and V^S) are plotted against output division costs (d). As the figure shows an increase in d does not affect V^C but it unambiguously decreases V^S. At some point these costs will become high enough to make the access sharing contract superior to output sharing. This cutoff point is noted as d′; for division costs less than d′ output sharing is the value maximizing contract, but for values greater than d′ the access sharing contract generates greater wealth. The hatched line indicates the maximum wealth for various values of d. As the costs of dividing output increase it is more likely that access sharing will be chosen over output sharing.

The results of pair-wise comparisons for all parameters and all contract choices are shown in Table 3.1.[10] Each entry in the table, (+), (−), and (0), indicates an increase, decrease, or no change, respectively, in the relative value of one contract to another as the parameter changes. Consider the choice between access sharing and output sharing examined in Figure 3.1. The third column shows how changes in parameter values affect the value of access sharing relative to output sharing (V^C/V^S). The entry (+) at the intersection of V^C/V^S and Output Division Costs indicates that an increase (decrease) in these costs will increase (decrease) V^C/V^S. Alternatively, an increase in the marginal policing costs reduces the value of access sharing relative to output sharing.[11]

Figure 3.1
The Effect of Changes in Output Division Costs
On the Choice Between Common Property
With Output Sharing and Common Property With Access Sharing

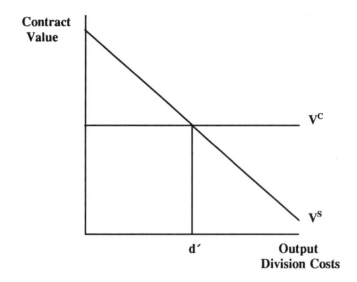

As a final example, consider how shifts in the marginal cost of hired inputs affect the choice between a fixed payment contract and common property with output sharing. When input costs are low, common property is inferior to private property. For high input costs this relationship is reversed because the shirking inherent in common property acts to economize on input costs. The entry (−) in Table 3.1 indicates the inverse relationship between changes in marginal input costs and the value of a fixed payment contract relative to an output sharing commons.

To this point the assumption has been that production technologies are the same across the contractual choices, but the choice between the two common property contracts could also hinge on differential production technologies. It may be more productive to organize use of a commonly owned resource by having group members working together and sharing output, rather than have members use the resource individually and retain their own output. For instance, grazing cattle together on the commons may be less costly than grazing them in individual herds because of economies in herding or dispatching predators. This productive advantage, however, could be overwhelmed by the output division costs inherent in an output sharing commons.

Table 3.1
Pairwise Comparison of Contract Values
For Changes in Various Parameters

Parameters	Contract Comparison		
	$\dfrac{V^P}{V^C}$	$\dfrac{V^P}{V^S}$	$\dfrac{V^C}{V^S}$
Output Division Costs	0	+	+
Marginal Exclusion Costs	+	+	0
Marginal Policing Costs	−	−	−
Marginal Cost of Effort	+, −, 0	−	−
Marginal Product of Effort	−	+, −, 0	+

Homogeneity as an Enforcement Device

In both common property models, the assumption was that sharing rules were egalitarian. The following argument explains why equal sharing rules are, in fact, optimal with homogeneous members of the group. Furthermore, once an equal sharing rule is chosen, there is an incentive for the group to maintain homogeneity. In an egalitarian system individuality is costly to the group and its members. With output sharing, group members shirk when providing effort. With access sharing, members overuse the asset. Under shared ownership, dissipation of the potential resource value results from deviations between marginal costs and marginal products of individual effort. For common property to maximize resource value, or minimize dissipation, these deviations must be made as small as possible.

One way to minimize these deviations is to use equal sharing rules *and* maintain group homogeneity, so that each member has identical costs and productivity. Homogeneity does not eliminate dissipation, but minimizes it by equating the deviations (between marginal costs and marginal products) across all group members. Indeed, with equal sharing, optimality is achieved with a homogeneous membership.[12] Egalitarian sharing and group homogeneity are expected to go together because they promote efficient use of common property resources. In contrast to the impact of homogeneity in the open access case where Cheung (1970) has shown that homogeneity leads to complete rent dissipation, homogeneity in the common property sharing cases described here actually minimizes dissipation. If the sharing group were heterogeneous, less productive members would have to bribe the more productive members to reduce their shirking or to limit their access. Such side payments would raise the costs of shirking and overuse by essentially eliminating the equal sharing provision. Because such side payments are costly to negotiate and enforce, however, maintaining group homogeneity provides an alternative way of minimizing costs.

The impact of homogeneity among members of the commons manifests itself in several ways. Not only must the members of the commons restrict entry, they must screen potential members for traits that reflect homogeneity and indoctrinate members in the group's ways. In this latter capacity, culture or ideology play an important role. Further, prohibiting or restricting membership transfers can also maintain homogeneity.[13] In the case studies examined below some or all of these practices are observed.

Four Case Studies of Common Ownership

Below I examine four cases in which natural resources are held in common by well-defined groups. These cases illustrate the importance for contractual choice of the key parameters identified in the model. While there is private ownership of many inputs in these cases, common property results from private contracting to first exclude outsiders and then share output from or access to a specific resource. As predicted by the model equal sharing dominates the allocation among homogeneous members. Furthermore, cultural norms, education, and restrictions on membership transfers strengthen this homogeneity. Table 3.2 summarizes these characteristics for each of the four cases examined.

The Lobster Gangs of Maine

The lobster fishery described by Acheson (1988 and 1993) show how private groups known as harbor gangs have effectively owned the lobster fishery for more than one hundred years. Harbor gangs are composed of individuals who harvest lobsters and exclude outsiders from a specific harbor. Although gang members act in concert when dealing with trespassers, each lobsterman owns his own boat, traps, and ultimately the catch in his traps. Gang members invariably come from the local harbor town and have familial and ethnic ties. New members are admitted into the gangs only after group acceptance, which can require years of subordinate work. For example, an adult nephew of a gang member may join the group after successfully working for the uncle as an adolescent. Gang members agree to limit the number of traps each person uses and may agree on other limits on take. The lobster territories are marked by the harbor's shoreline and defended from outsiders by the group.[14] Interlopers are swiftly punished by gang members who destroy the interloper's traps and other gear.

The model present above explains several features of harbor gangs. The formation of gangs is a contractual choice in favor of common property. Exclusion costs dictate an optimal group size. Acheson (1987, 61) notes that "Successful defense . . . often demands the coordinated efforts of a group of fishermen, and even then the costs can be quite high." Because of economies of scale in enforcement, private (one lobsterman-one boat) territories are apparently a more costly alternative to common property. Also gangs composed of family members from tiny, ethnic coastal towns are unusually homogeneous. They stay homogeneous because outsiders cannot buy their way into the group. Given this homogeneity, the limits on traps is a way to institute equal sharing.

Communal Farming Among the Hutterites[15]

On the prairies straddling the American-Canadian border, Hutterites (members of an Anabaptist Christian sect) operate communal farms. Three original colonies established in South Dakota in 1872 have grown into over 300. An average colony owns from 5,000 to 10,000 acres of land and the attendant equipment, sharing the spoils among 100 people. Once a colony reaches a population of 130–150, plans are made to find land for a new colony. Except for personal belongings such as clothes and tools, there is no individually owned property.

The day-to-day life of the Hutterite society is notable for its lack of specialization, except between men and women, and reliance on egalitarian rules. Most work is done in groups with tasks, like baking and field work, rotating on a weekly basis. Hutterites also share the production of the colony, from meals to material for clothes. Even food at the table is shared: "One duck is for four persons—always the same four, since persons are always seated in the same position. Informal courtesy requires that two persons eat the breast and better pieces one Sunday, giving the other two the preferred portions the following Sunday" (Hostetler and Huntington 1967, 54). The society is highly structured and rules of social behavior are extremely strict. Daily religious training begins almost from birth and continues throughout each person's life. Entertainment such as dances, movies, and television are prohibited. Dress codes are strict. Men wear black trousers held up by suspenders, long-sleeved shirts, and beards; women wear long patterned dresses, no makeup, long braided hair, and head scarfs.

Several aspects of the Hutterite communes are explained by the model. Egalitarian sharing and private contracting are both apparent. The Hutterite's common property is different from the harbor gangs because the Hutterites also share output. The contractual nature of common property is especially clear during the formation of a new colony. Plans for a new colony begin with the purchase of *private* farmland. This splitting-off also confirms the idea of an optimal group size that is the result of a tradeoff between exclusion costs and member shirking. As colonies grow to exceed 100 people, scholars have observed problems of "efficiency" and "supervision" in managing the farms. As the model implies, behavioral restrictions serve to maintain a homogeneous population and thus reduce the shirking problems. One close observer noted: "The chief objective of training is to assure voluntary conformity to communal interests" (Hostetler 1983, 26).

Common Pastures in Swiss Alpine Villages[16]

In Switzerland the existing pattern of land ownership developed centuries ago in the alpine villages. Individual village members typically own private hayfields and pastures surrounding the village. High alpine meadows, however, called "alps," are nearly always owned in common by the citizens of the village community.[17] The alps are used during a rather short summer grazing season to supplement the forage gotten from the private valley pastures and fields that surround the village. The fertile lower elevation fields and pastures are most often privately owned, while the high elevation alps tend to be common property. The primary method of governing the use of the Swiss alps is the restriction on membership to the community. Individuals gain citizenship in a community only by inheritance, from their fathers; citizenship cannot be purchased and community citizenship does not change even when people move. In addition to the rules on community citizenship, there are often other restrictions on the use of the alps such as the types of animals allowed and the dates that the alp is available for use. In most cases individuals graze their private herds on the common alp and retain the full "output" as the increased weight gain of their animals. In other cases, villagers combine their stock on the common alp and hire a manager to care for the herd and process the cheese and other dairy products, which are then divided among these same individuals.

Table 3.2
Characteristics of Common Ownership
In Four Case Studies

Cases	Characteristics					
	Exclude Outsiders	Equal Sharing Rules	Share Access	Share Output	Maintain Homogeneous Membership	Other Private Property
Cree Hunting Territories	Yes	Yes	Yes	Sometimes	No Transfers; Familial Ties	Clothes and Personal Items
Hutterite Farms	Yes	Yes	Yes	Yes	No Transfers; Familial Ties Religious Training	Clothes and Personal Items
Maine Lobster Territories	Yes	Yes	Yes	No	No Transfers; Familial Ties	Boats and Gear
Swiss Grazing Commons	Yes	Yes	Yes	Sometimes	No Transfers; Inherit Citizenship	Land and Barns

Like the lobster territories, the Swiss alps are appropriately viewed as common ownership resulting from private contracting. While the more valuable and lower land is privately owned because of the greater magnitude of the losses from shirking, the relatively infertile alps are held in common because it is not worth delineating rights to small private plots by fencing and policing.

The organization of the alps also points out the distinction between input sharing and output sharing. In cases where there are gains from cooperative production and output is easily divisible, for products like milk and cheese, output sharing is feasible. The use of citizenship to control group size also serves to maintain homogeneity which, as seen in the other cases, can be viewed as a method of reducing shirking losses.

Family Hunting Territories Among the Cree Indians[18]

The Cree Indians live along the eastern shore of James Bay in the subarctic region of northern Quebec. They have well-defined land and resource rights as a result of an agreement with the Canadian government. Hunting, trapping, and fishing is organized into groups comprising several nuclear families of roughly ten to twenty people. These groups effectively own the territorial rights for these activities and share the resources among group members.

The most formal of these territories are the beaver traplines, which delineate hunting areas. These territories are based on pre-white regimes, but have been recognized and mapped by the provincial government since the 1950s. Any member of a family group may use the common property traplines. Similar territories are delineated for hunting geese along the shores of James Bay. For both the beaver traplines and the goose hunting territories there are family members known as the "beaver boss" and the "goose boss."[19] Both bosses inherit the territories from fathers or uncles and must manage the territory in the interest of the group. Bosses manage information about the resource, enforce rules,[20] and oversee sharing of the game among the group. They may not sell rights to the territory and in some cases lose their authority if they have acted against the group's interest.

As with the other cases, the model illuminates the contractual choice in the Cree territories. Like the Hutterite farms, the group members share access to and output from the common property. The members are homogeneous and share a culture that reinforces homogeneity and equal sharing. Their treaties with Canada give the Cree clear ownership of territories, yet they continue to choose common property rules to allocate many of their resources.

Conclusion

The standard economic critique of the commons is incorrect in its assertion that it invariably leads to wealth dissipation. Too often the analytical choice is between perfect private rights and no rights at all. Common ownership, however, implies exclusive rights and is distinct from no rights or open access. Because delineation of rights entails costs, strict private property rights may not be worth defining and enforcing. It may pay, however, to delineate exclusive rights among a group and to establish egalitarian rules for sharing within the group, in other words, to establish common property. In addition to natural resources, common property is often chosen within families, firms, and other organizations. Common property economizes on the costs of pricing at the margin and gives each resource user a partial claim on its value. As shown in the four case studies, common property is best seen as a share contract that can maximize joint wealth.

The policy implications of this contractual approach to common property can be seen in the forest policies of many third-world countries. In India, Nepal, Niger, and Thailand national governments have taken control of what were once traditional village communal forests (Ostrom 1990, 23, 178). Many scholars have documented the "disastrous effects" (Ostrom 1990, 23) of these policies. This outcome should not be surprising since forest nationalization effectively destroys the stable system of common property contracts established by the local villagers. The contracts constrained forest use by members of the community, but nationalization turned common property into open access. Not surprisingly, wealth dissipation has taken the form of severe deforestation and associated side-effects such as soil erosion.[21] These nationalization cases are instructive because they further support the growing recognition that common ownership is not always synonymous with wealth dissipation. Indeed, when viewed as a contractual arrangement that economizes on costs of monitoring variable input usage, on costs of excluding nonmembers, and on costs of dividing output, common property can be a rational alternative to private ownership. Because common property institutions have evolved and survived over long periods of time, economists should not be surprised to find that they provide an efficient institutional mechanism for maximizing the value of resources.

Notes

1. See Berkes et al. (1989) for a survey of this literature. McCay and Acheson (1987) and Ostrom (1990) examine specific cases. Also, see the related papers in this volume.
2. Ciriacy-Wantrup and Bishop (1975), Cheung (1987), McCay and Acheson (1987), Bromley (1989), Eggertsson (1990) and Stevenson (1991) have made this type of distinction.
3. This is the typical production technology assumed in common property analyses (Cheung 1970).

4. I use a static model in order to concentrate on individual effort whereas I ignore questions of investment in, or maintenance of, the fixed asset. Caputo and Lueck (1992) and Ostrom (1990) consider some of these dynamic issues.

5. They are, of course, indirectly affected by incentives to shirk or rush depending on the sharing rule.

6. The formal implications of this are developed in Lueck (1992).

7. Barzel (1989) elaborates on the costs of enforcing rights and the implications for economic organization.

8. See the appendix to this chapter for a formal elaboration of the contracting model for both output sharing and access sharing.

9. For example, output division costs would include the resources spent counting and dividing shared catch from a fishery as well as the resources spent by group members attempting to capture more than their allowed share of the output. The costs of dividing output are often ignored, but are empirically important in many cases. Allen and Lueck (1992), for instance, show how these costs are an important determinant of contract terms in farmland leases.

10. The appendix shows the formal derivation of these contract comparisons.

11. Ambiguous predictions result from the curvature properties of the contract value functions. See Lueck (1992) for an elaboration. In Table 3.1, ambiguity is denoted by the entry (+, −, 0). For instance, the effect of changes in the marginal productivity of effort on the choice between fixed payment and output sharing is unclear because of the competing forces of effort pricing costs and group size. For relatively large groups sharing output, an increase in effort productivity will increase the value of common property relative to fixed payment. Intuitively, this is appealing because bigger groups suffer greater losses from shirking.

12. Because there is no difference between average and marginal shares under egalitarian sharing, costs and production among members must also be identical for infra-marginal units of effort. See appendix for a formal derivation of the homogeneity condition.

13. In general, transfer restrictions are viewed as superfluous at best. The rationale for transfer restrictions is directly tied to the assumption of costly property rights enforcement. For a further discussion of transfer restrictions see Roberts (1993).

14. The size of these territories range from ten to twenty square nautical miles and allow from eight to twelve boats, usually with just one person per boat. Some territories are defined by the perimeter surrounding an island.

15. Hostetler (1983) and Hostetler and Hunnington (1967).

16. Netting (1981) and Stevenson (1991).

17. Forests, rocky wastes, and mountains are also common property. Rhoades and Thompson (1975) noted that this property organization is also typical of the alpine societies of the Andes and the Himalaya.

18. Berkes (1987).

19. The beaver and goose bosses are not necessarily the same person.

20. For example, individuals that waste game or violate other rules may suffer a

lengthy loss of hunting privileges.

21. According to Ostrom (1990) the government of Nepal has denationalized some forests as a result of the resource degradation.

References

Acheson, James M. 1988. *The lobster gangs of Maine*. Hanover: University Press of New England.

———. 1987. The lobster fiefs revisited. In *The question of the commons*, edited by Bonnie J. McCay and James M. Acheson. Tucson: University of Arizona.

———. 1993. Capturing the commons: Legal and illegal strategies. This volume.

Allen, Douglas W., and Dean Lueck. 1992. Contract choice in modern agriculture: Cash rent vs. cropshare. *Journal of Law and Economics* 3 (2). Forthcoming.

Barzel, Yoram. 1989. *Economic analysis of property rights*. Cambridge: Cambridge University Press.

Berkes, Fikret. 1987. Common-property resource management and Cree Indian fisheries in Subarctic Canada. In *The question of the commons*, edited by Bonnie J. McCay and James M. Acheson. Tucson: University of Arizona.

Berkes, Fikret, Davis Feeny, Bonnie J. McCay, and James M. Acheson. 1989. The benefits of the commons. *Nature* 340 (July): 91–93.

Bromley, Daniel. 1989. *Economic interests and institutions*. New York: Basil Blackwell.

Caputo, Michael, and Dean Lueck. 1992. Common property: Dynamic incentives and contract choice. Department of Economics, Louisiana State University, Baton Rouge.

Cheung, Steven. 1970. The structure of a contract and the theory of a non-exclusive resource. *Journal of Law and Economics* 13:49–70.

Cheung, Steven. 1987. Common property rights. *The New Palgrave* 1:504–05.

Ciriacy-Wantrup, S. V., and Richard C. Bishop. 1975. Common property as a concept in natural resources policy. *Natural Resources Journal* 15:713–27.

Coase, Ronald. 1960. The problem of social cost. *Journal of Law and Economics* 3:1–44.

Eggertsson, Thráinn. 1990. *Economic behavior and institutions*. Cambridge: Cambridge University Press.

Hostetler, John A. 1983. *Hutterite life*. Scottsdale, PA: Herald Press.

Hostetler, John A., and Gertrude Enders Hunnington. 1967. *The Hutterites in North America*. New York: Holt, Rinehart, and Winston.

Lueck, Dean. 1992. The contractual nature of common property. Department of Economics, Louisiana State University, Baton Rouge.

McCay, Bonnie J., and James M. Acheson, eds. 1987. *The question of the commons*. Tucson: University of Arizona.

Netting, Robert McC. 1981. *Balancing on an alp*. New York: Cambridge University Press.

Ostrom, Elinor. 1990. *Governing the commons.* New York: Cambridge University Press.

Rhoades, Robert E., and Stephen I. Thompson. 1975. Adaptive strategies in alpine environments: Beyond ecological particularism. *American Ethnologist* 535–51.

Roberts, Russell D. 1993. To price or not to price: User preferences in allocating common property resources. This volume.

Stevenson, Glenn G. 1991. *Common property economics.* Cambridge: Cambridge University Press.

Appendix: A Model of Common Property Contracting

Production is $Y = f(\Sigma x_i)$; where $f'(\cdot) > 0$, and $f''(\cdot) < 0$. Effort cost is $c(x) = c(x_1, x_2, \ldots x_n)$, where $\partial c/\partial x_i > 0$ and $\partial c^2/\partial x_i^2 \geq 0$.

Sharing Output with Common Ownership

Assuming, $\partial x_i/\partial x_j = 0$, each of the $n \geq 2$ individuals in the group simultaneously choose their own level of effort to

$$\underset{x_i}{maximize} \quad \left(\frac{1}{n}\right) f\left(\sum_{i=1}^{n} x_i\right) - c(x_i)$$

where $1/n$ is the share of output owned by each individual. This requires

$$\left(\frac{1}{n}\right) f'\left(\sum_{i=1}^{n} x_i\right) = \frac{\partial c}{\partial x_i}, \qquad i = 1,\ldots,n. \tag{1}$$

Equation (1) implies optimal effort, x_i^*, and is, in effect, a constraint on joint wealth maximization by the group whose problem is

$$\underset{n}{maximize} \quad V = f\left(\sum_{i=1}^{n} x_i^*(n)\right) - c(x^*(n)) - e(n).$$

whose solution implies an optimal group size (n^s).

Sharing Resource Access with Common Ownership

The problem for each member is

$$\underset{x_i}{maximize} \quad f^i(x_i) - c(x_i),$$

$$subject\ to \quad f^i = \left(\frac{x_i}{x_i + \sum_{j \neq i=1}^{n} x_j}\right) f\left(x_i + \sum_{j \neq i=1}^{n} x_i\right)$$

Assuming homogeneous members, $x_i = x_j$, the solution is

$$\left(\frac{n-1}{n}\right)\left(\frac{f\left(\sum_{i=1}^{n}x_i\right)}{\sum_{i=1}^{n}x_i}\right) + \left(\frac{1}{n}\right)f'\left(\sum_{i=1}^{n}x_i\right) = \frac{\partial c}{\partial x_i}, \qquad i = 1,...,n. \qquad (2)$$

The group's problem, which yields an optimal size n^c, is

$$\underset{n}{maximize}\ V = f\left(\sum_{i=1}^{n}x_i^*(n)\right) - c(x_i^*(n)) - e(n).$$

The Choice of Ownership Regime

The comparative statics of contract choice can be derived by examining the curvature properties of the net value functions for each contract. For the case examined in the text consider the first and second partial derivatives of V^S and V^C.

$$\frac{\partial V^C}{\partial d} = 0, \qquad \frac{\partial^2 V^C}{\partial d^2} = 0; \quad and \qquad\qquad (3)$$

$$\frac{\partial V^S}{\partial d} = -1, \qquad \frac{\partial^2 V^S}{\partial d^2} = 0. \qquad\qquad (4)$$

These partial derivatives indicate the functions have the shapes shown in Figure 3.1. Lueck (1992) completed the analysis described by Table 3.1.

Homogeneity as an Enforcement Device

Reconsider the output sharing model by assuming each member has a share, s_i, and individual production functions have a shift parameter, α_i. Each member's effort choice must satisfy

$$s_i\alpha_i\,f'\left(\sum_{i=1}^{n}x_i\right) = \frac{\partial c}{\partial x_i}, \qquad i = 1,...,n. \qquad\qquad (5)$$

The exclusive group (of size n) chooses the optimal share for each member, s_i, and, implicitly, the resulting level of effort. The joint maximization problem is

$$\underset{x_i,\, s_i}{maximize} \quad V = f\left(\sum_{i=1}^{n} x_i\right) - c(x_i),$$

subject to (5) and (6) $\sum_{i=1}^{n} s_i = 1.$ The first-order conditions yield

$$\frac{\alpha_1 f'(\alpha_1 f' - c_1)}{s_1 \alpha_1 f'' - c_{11}} = \frac{\alpha_2 f'(\alpha_2 f' - c_2)}{s_2 \alpha_2 f'' - c_{22}} = \ldots = \frac{\alpha_n f'(\alpha_n f' - c_n)}{s_n \alpha_n f'' - c_{nn}} = -\mu \quad (7)$$

where μ is the Lagrange multiplier for (6). Equation (7) requires that the net gain to each group member be the same at the margin. The condition for input sharing is derived in Lueck (1992).

4

To Price or Not to Price:
User Preferences in Allocating Common Property
Resources

Russell D. Roberts

Introduction

Common property resources, unless access is restricted in some way, are prone to overuse. One way to reduce access is to charge users a fee to use the resource. This chapter provides two reasons why users prefer to leave common property unpriced. First, despite the efficiency gains from reduced access, prices have distributional consequences that are likely to leave users worse off than they were when access was unrestricted. Second, quantity restrictions can achieve efficiency as effectively as prices and can insure that users are made better off rather than worse off by restricted access. The empirical evidence from fisheries is used to explore the distributional effects of quantity and price restrictions.

Why Users Oppose Pricing Access to Common Property

Without entry restrictions or voluntary restraints, fishing grounds are overfished. No one owns the oceans or the fish; they are economic goods with a zero price. As fishermen enter to take advantage of this underpriced resource, the time it takes to find fish increases, and average size of the catch falls. These two effects adjust to produce an equilibrium despite the zero price. In this equilibrium with unrestricted access, the fishery yield is inefficiently low.

The solution is simple—put a price on the seas or the fish. Such fees would be analogous to the suggestion that tolls be put on urban highways. For example, charge a fee for each day a fishing boat is on the water. Choose a fee that reduces the number of boats, reducing the number of fish caught, and maximizing the net yield of the fishery. At this efficient number of boats, the full price of entering the ocean is exactly equal to the cost each fisherman imposes on other fishermen through the creation of congestion and smaller yields. Once the fee is imposed, society is better off. There are fewer boats on the water, but the remaining boats catch more and larger fish. The larger yields outweigh the loss of fewer boats.

Despite the seeming ease of this textbook solution, it is rarely, if ever, used to solve common property problems. Fishing licenses and automobile registration fees are not priced to bring about efficiency. There are no efficient taxes on fish. Tolls for roads, when they exist, are set primarily to pay back capital costs of construction and maintenance rather than reduce congestion optimally.

Why does society throw away resources in such profusion? One answer is that the users of the commons oppose such fees. For example, it can be rational for fishermen to oppose efficient license fees. Fees can make fishermen worse off. This seems unlikely or impossible. If fees are efficient, then surely fishermen must benefit from their imposition. But, in fact, fishermen can be made worse off after efficient fees are imposed.[1]

To see a case where all fishermen are worse off after a fee is imposed, assume that all fishermen have the same skills and fishing abilities. Each employs the same number of boats in competition with the others. When entry is inefficiently priced at zero, there are too many boats on the water catching too many fish. To reduce the number of boats, the profit from adding a boat to the water must fall. Fisherman must be made worse off by the imposition of the fee. If fishermen are made better off, then more people will want to be fishermen and the number of boats on the water will increase. Therefore, to raise the yield to the efficient level, the fee must make fishing less lucrative.

A numerical example may help. Suppose when there is open access to the water, 25 identically skilled fishermen each use four boats per day, for a total of 100 boats on the water. Each boat makes a net profit of $100 per day. Suppose the optimal number of boats is 75. Each of the 25 fishermen must be discouraged from sending a fourth boat onto the water. So the net value from sending a boat out must fall from $100 to say $60 to achieve the necessary reduction in the number of boats. At the efficient level of boats, each catches more fish than it did before and the average size increases. The economic value of this larger catch over and above the costs of operation will be much larger than $100 per boat. But this gain cannot outweigh the size of the fee, since the fee must be high enough to reduce the net gain per boat to $60. If the net effect of the better fishing raises the economic gain per boat to say $150, then the efficient fee is $90. Only with a fee of $90 will the net gain per boat be $60, inducing 75 boats to enter, and the efficient yield is achieved.

If fishermen are identical, as they are assumed to be in this example, they will unanimously oppose the efficient fee, preferring open access even though it is inefficient. Even when fisherman are not identical, it is still possible for *all* fishermen to be harmed by the fee and to unanimously prefer open access to an efficient fee. For a fisherman to be made better off, he must have a differential ability to take advantage of the less crowded seas to increase his share of the catch. Keeping the same numerical example, the efficient fee is $90. Consider the fisherman who had the average gain of $100 when the seas were crowded. Suppose he could catch so many extra fish on the less crowded sea so that his net gains rise above $190, even though the average is only $150. Then even after the $90 fee, such a fisherman will be better off. This outcome is possible for a subset of fishermen. It cannot be true for all, else the fee of $90 is not high enough. Some, if not all, of the fishermen must be made worse off.

This seems paradoxical. How can an efficient change that reduces the number of boats to the efficient level make fishermen worse off? The key is the revenue from the fees. The revenue from the fees *is* large enough to compensate fishermen for their losses with enough left over to make someone (the fishermen, for example) better off. But without this compensation, fishermen are worse off. Whoever receives the revenue captures the gains from the imposition of the fees.

Part of the intuition behind this paradox is that price is playing a purely allocative role. For contrast, consider the case of price controls for a consumer good such as gasoline. A binding maximum price creates a line. Consumers pay both a time and money price, just as they do here. Increasing the money price lowers the time price, just as it does with fishing. But unlike the case of common property, with a consumer good, the sum of the time and money price goes *down*, not up. The full price in time and money goes down because increasing the money price induces an increase in total quantity as the equilibrium moves along the supply curve. This increase in total quantity benefits both suppliers and demanders, and they share the benefits (consumer and producer surplus) from the increased production. There is no corresponding increase in production when we raise the money price of access to common property from zero to a positive amount. The fee does not increase the size of the ocean or the number of fish.

The solution to this problem seems clear. Place an efficient fee on each boat and rebate the fee revenue to fishermen in a lump-sum fashion. This insures that the gains to society caused by pricing the ocean efficiently will accrue to fishermen. It will then be in fishermen's self-interest to ask for regulation. The only problem with this idea is the lump-sum payment. The term "lump-sum" is economic jargon for a payment that does not effect incentives. In fact, there is no such thing in the real world. Every payment affects incentives unless it is random.

At the end of the year, fishermen will have made large contributions to the state's coffers because of the fee. Some fishermen will have paid hundreds and perhaps thousands of dollars. It is going to take a large payment to offset those losses. Suppose everyone gets the same rebate—the total amount of revenue divided by the number of fishermen. Those with the most boat/days will be harmed after the net effects of the fee and the rebate. They will have contributed a much larger share of the toll revenue. To make them better off, they will have to get more than the average rebate. If the fee is on fish rather than boats, you have the same result. The best fishermen will be punished the most by the fees and will have to receive the largest rebate if they are to favor restricted access.

Unfortunately, the only way to give them more than the average is to tie their share, in some fashion, to the size of fees that they have paid. But this will clearly not be lump-sum. By tying the rebate to the size of the fee payments, the effect of the fee is mitigated or eliminated. To achieve efficiency, fishing must become less attractive, so the rebate cannot be tied to being a fisherman or to how productive each fisherman is. It is very difficult to structure the establishment of private property rights in such a way as to have the net gains brought about by efficiency accruing to those who are being harmed. There is both a moral and political consequence to this result. The moral result is that it is difficult to argue for the morality of pricing the ocean if the net effect is to harm the people you want to help in the first place. Not only do you not help them, you make them worse off. Even though a fee is not a zero-sum game, it is hard to argue for a law that creates wealth by impoverishing others.

The political result is that the impetus for the establishment of pricing the ocean is not likely to come from the people who bear the costs of unrestricted common property, the fishermen. In fact, they have an incentive to oppose any improvement and potentially oppose it with much intensity.[2] The beneficiaries of the fee revenue will favor establishing a fee, but this group is likely to be dispersed relative to the concentrated opposition of the fishermen.

The Advantages of Quantity Restrictions

Quantity restrictions can also achieve efficiency but avoid the headache of designing rebates to let users share in the benefits. Rather than using the indirect sanction of price to reduce fishing effort, the number of fishing days or the catch per fisherman can be limited directly. Quotas achieve reduced usage without the gains from less fishing effort being embodied in the fee revenue. With a quantity restriction, the benefits are embodied in the quotas. Whoever gets the quotas captures the benefits. As long as a fisherman gets a sufficiently large share of the quota, he will be better off than with unrestricted access.

The easiest way to see the beneficial effects of the quota over pricing is to consider the case where all fishermen have identical skills, and each has the same number of boats. If each fisherman agrees to reduce his boats from four to three per day, each will be better off. There will be an increased yield per boat that will result in higher total profit.

None of the problems with the pricing system arise. There is no need to set a price and rebate the money. There is no need to determine how to rebate the money in a lump-sum fashion. The commons is used more efficiently and the gains of bigger and more easily found fish accrue to the fishermen. Because everyone is identical, everyone gains an equal share of the total gain.

Now suppose owners are not identical. Some have larger boats than others or catch more fish per boat because they are more skilled. Better fishermen will have to get a bigger share of the quotas to get them to go along with restricting access to the commons. Otherwise, they might be worse off after quotas are imposed, even though there is a net gain to fishermen as a group. If their access is sufficiently limited, the gain from bigger fish might be offset by the reduction in the number of boats or days the individual can use. More successful fishermen in open access must get a bigger quota when access is restricted, else they will oppose restricted access.

A surprisingly simple way to solve this problem is to give each user a pro-rated share of the usage the user would have had in the unrestricted open-access situation. Suppose Joe Fisherman has 10 percent of the boats on the water when there is open access. Give him 10 percent of the new smaller number of boats allowed on the commons with restricted access during the quota situation. Or better yet, if the catch can be monitored, restrict the catch rather than the number of boats. If a fisherman has 10 percent of the catch in open access equilibrium, give him 10 percent of the smaller more efficient yield under restricted access.[3]

This solution, while attractive, is not without problems. If access rights are to be allocated to individuals in proportion to their level of usage in the open access situation, then some agency must determine what this level is or would be. This is not a trivial problem. Access rights are very valuable. If people know that rights are going to be determined by an experiment or a set of observations measuring usage in the open access situation, then they will have an incentive to be heavy users in order to get more access.

Empirical Evidence

I have found no examples where common property access is regulated by price, but two types of quantity restrictions are common on fisheries. The first type tries to handicap fishermen by limiting boat size, net size, the number of fishing days, and so on. The problem with these solutions is that while they can reduce fishing effort, they do so by promoting inefficiency and they create an incentive for fishermen to increase effort on unregulated margins.

An alternative method consistent with the above discussion is the individual transferable quota, or ITQ. "With ITQs, each fisherman is issued an individual quota entitling him to a specific share of the harvestable fish for a season. The quota is usually set by a governmental agency, but fishermen are free to adjust their share by buying, selling, trading, or leasing quota" (Anderson and Leal 1992,

8). The total amount of ITQs can be set to maximize the net yield of the fishery, but whether this occurs depends on the incentives of the bureaucracy setting the quota.

Anderson and Leal (1992) document several examples of ITQs including lake trout in Wisconsin's Lake Superior, wreckfish in the south Atlantic, and surf clams in the mid-Atlantic. Of the eight cases, two distribute quota in proportion to a fisherman's success in a base period of restricted access. As described above, this insures that all fisherman share in the gain from moving to restricted access. Three examples base a portion on catch during a base period but include other factors, and three divide the catch equally.

When ITQs are set proportional to historic usage levels under open access conditions, all current fishermen are better off. If these levels can be measured accurately without the incentive problems mentioned earlier, fishermen should unanimously favor restricted access to open access. This is consistent with the fact that ITQs are typically enforced by state boards staffed by fishermen who establish and enforce the regulations.

The cases of equal division imply a redistribution of the gains from better to poorer fishermen, a potentially important redistribution politically unless fishermen are roughly homogenous. Anderson and Leal have detailed records on one of these cases, the nine fishermen who fish for herring sac roe in Oregon's Yaquina Bay. This ITQ is of particular interest, because it was voluntarily established and is enforced by the fishermen rather than the state. According to Anderson and Leal, two of the nine fishermen caught 30 percent of the catch, while the others had roughly equal shares of 10 percent. Evidently, the gains from reducing overfishing were so large that the better fishermen were willing to share their gains in order to encourage unanimous cooperation. Anderson and Leal document the poor performance before restrictions and improvements afterwards.

Discussion

In this paper I have argued that users prefer quantity restrictions to price restrictions for achieving efficient use of common property. While both can promote efficiency, gains from quantity restrictions can more easily be transferred to users. The historical record and the approach to fishery regulation appear consistent with this hypothesis.[4]

Other authors, however, see a less rosy picture when evaluating the efficiency effects of quantity restrictions. Their basic argument is if the quantity restrictions produce rents, fishermen will pursue other margins than those that are restricted in pursuit of these rents. Ultimately, the efficiency gains will be dissipated.[5] For example, if the restriction is on the number of boats, fishermen will devote too many resources to the beginning of the season in hopes of landing the best fish before others do. In addition, fishermen will buy better and more expensive equipment to improve the productivity of boats. Government agencies will try to limit these forms of competition through further regulations, but these regulations cannot be perfectly specified or enforced. If the restriction is on the number of fish, through ITQs, fishermen will have the incentive to again fish early in the season and devote an inefficiently large amount of effort to fishing early. In addition, fishermen will have the incentive to carelessly dispose of smaller fish that would count against their quota, what is known as high-grading (see Anderson and Leal 1992). The importance of other margins is an empirical question. The claim of this paper is that quantity restrictions can make fishermen better off. The Anderson and Leal findings are consistent with this hypothesis.

In addition to more systematic evidence on the gains from quantity restrictions, this paper suggests a need for more research into the characteristics of the fishermen and their fisheries that lead to the various forms of restrictions.[6] Why are some fisheries regulated with restrictions on boat size; why do others use equal division of ITQs; why do some divide catch proportionally; and why do some remain largely unregulated relying on norms?[7] The analysis presented here suggests a richer theory may result from focusing on the distributional effects of the different forms of regulation.

Notes

1. For a formal proof, see Weitzman (1974) or Roberts (1992).
2. This has also been recognized by Johnson and Libecap (1982) who cite the observation of Scott (1979).
3. As I have shown in Roberts (1992), when users can resell their quota among themselves, proportional allocation of access rights based on historic use makes every user of the commons better off. This results holds no matter how heterogeneous users or how able users are to shift effort to other employment.
4. See Ostrom (1990) or Roberts (1992) for empirical examples other than fisheries where quantity restrictions are used to regulate access to common property.
5. See Townsend and Wilson (1990) in McCay and Acheson (1990).
6. Karpoff (1987) has examined the political competition between the numerous less-skilled fishermen and the high-skilled fishermen who are fewer in number.
7. See Acheson (1993).

References

Acheson, James. 1993. Capturing the commons: Legal and illegal strategies. This volume.

Anderson, Terry L., and Donald R. Leal. 1992. Fishing for property rights to fish. Working Paper 92–16, Political Economy Research Center, Bozeman, MT. Forthcoming in *Taking the environment seriously*, edited by Roger Meiners and Bruce Yandle. May 1993.

Johnson, Ronald N., and Gary D. Libecap. 1982. Contracting problems and regulation: The case of the fishery. *American Economic Review* 72 (December): 1005–22.

Karpoff, Jonathan M. 1987. Suboptimal controls in common resource management: The case of the fishery. *Journal of Political Economy* 95:179–94.

McCay, Bonnie J., and James A. Acheson. 1990. *The question of the commons.* Tucson: University of Arizona Press.

Ostrom, Elinor. 1990. *Governing the commons: The evolution of institutions for collective action.* Cambridge: Cambridge University Press.

Roberts, Russell D. 1992. The tragicomedy of the common. Working Paper, Olin School of Business, Washington University.

Scott, Anthony. 1979. Development of economic theory on fisheries regulation. *Journal of the Fishery Research Board of Canada* 36 (July): 725–41.

Townsend, Ralph, and James A. Wilson. 1990. An economic view of the tragedy of the commons. In *The question of the commons*, edited by Bonnie J. McCay and James A. Acheson. Tucson: University of Arizona Press.

Weitzman, Martin L. 1974. Free access vs. private ownership as alternative systems for managing common property. *Journal of Economic Theory* 8 (June): 225–34.

5

Capturing the Commons:
Legal and Illegal Strategies

James M. Acheson

Introduction

In the literature on common property resources, it is axiomatic that property rights are rules of the game that constrain individual behavior and provide the incentives to behave a certain way. Private property results in conservation of resources while common property leads to over-exploitation (Hardin 1968, 1244ff.; Acheson 1989, 352–53). In addition, the institutional economists point our that since the property rights or rules also determine who gets what, they are often shaped for the benefit of specific individuals or groups rather than for efficiency. As Jean Ensminger (N.d., 1) says, "the underlying assumption is that institutions directly affect economic outcomes (distribution and growth), that individuals realize this, and that they attempt to change institutions to better serve their ends, whether these ends be ideological or materialistic." This chapter describes two strategies used by Maine lobster fishermen to directly affect economic outcomes to better serve their ends.

Property Rights

Because the term "common property" has been used as a catchall term to describe all tenure systems where exclusive, transferable property rights are lacking, it has often confused the discussion of resource allocation and often led to some erroneous conclusions. Recently, however, some progress has been made in developing better conceptual tools and nomenclature (Ostrom 1986, 599–613; Bromley 1989, 187–90; and Cox 1989, 126–34). The following four property regimes expand the range of institutional alternatives and assist in our understanding of the Maine lobster fishery (Berkes and Farvar 1989, 9; Berkes and Kislalioglu 1992, 568–70).

1. Open-access: access to the resource is free and open to all, with no constraints, i.e. there are no property rights.
2. Communal property: the resource is held or controlled by an identifiable community of users different from the government.
3. State property: management of the resource is controlled by the central government of national states.
4. Private property: exclusive rights reside with an individual, groups of individuals or firms, who control access, and who can trade the rights to others.

Since lobster fishing takes place in the open sea, it is difficult to establish private property rights, but this does not mean that the fishery is open access. Two kinds of property rights are in place. The fishery is under communal control in that lobster fishermen maintain lobster fishing territories and limit access to them. Although such territories are defended and enforced by "illegal" means and are not recognized by the state of Maine, they are an institution of long standing all along the Maine coast.

The lobster resource is owned by the state. However, fishermen also lobby in the political arena to influence state management of the lobster fishery. By combining state management institutions with the extra-legal territorial system, the lobster fishermen have generated institutions to effectively capture the benefits of the resources for themselves. Both strategies also help to conserve the lobster.

The Maine Lobster Industry

The Maine lobster fishery is an inshore trap fishery. In 1992 there were an estimated 2,200 full time fishermen and another 7,000 part-time fishermen. Full-time fishermen typically have inboard powered boats between 28 and 40 feet long, and fish between 400 to 600 traps in the mid coast region, where most of my research has taken place. Most of the fishermen own their own boats, which they work alone, or with one helper called a "sternman."

The activities of lobster fishermen vary greatly over the annual cycle. In the mid winter months, catches are low because low water temperatures cause lobsters to go into a state of near hibernation and the stormy weather make fishing difficult. During the "winter fishing" season, lobsters (*Homarus americanus*) are best caught in deep, offshore water, perhaps 3 to 10 miles from the coast. Many fishermen do not fish at this time of year, but rather devote all their time to repairing their gear (Acheson 1988, 15–16).

In the spring, as the water warms, lobsters begin to migrate inshore and can be caught in larger numbers. Thus, there is a spurt of fishing activity during the April and May "spring fishing" season. From mid-June to August, a large percentage of the lobsters are molting or shedding their shells. During this "shedding season" they hide in the rocks close to shore and are not inclined to venture into traps. Again, many fishermen reduce their fishing activity.

The height of the lobster season is late summer and early fall when a new year class of lobsters has molted into legal size, and are inclined to climb into traps while feeding. During this season from mid-August to the first of November, an estimated 65 percent of the total catch occurs. Later in the summer, as the water cools, lobsters migrate again further offshore and by January are in deep water miles from shore.

Along the Maine coast in 1992, there were 17 fishermen's cooperatives and some 95 privately owned lobster dealers, which bought lobsters from fishermen in the harbor where they are located. These dealers and cooperatives, in turn, sell their lobsters to hotels or restaurants, to large out-of-state wholesalers, or to local retail customers.

Illegal Strategies: The Territorial System

The entire coast of Maine is divided into fishing territories, which are owned communally by groups of fishermen. In order to go fishing at all, one must become a member of a "harbor gang," the group of fishermen who fish from a single harbor. Members of a harbor gang can only place traps in the area held by that gang. Interlopers are usually sanctioned by having their lobstering gear surreptitiously destroyed.

Although the territorial system is over 100 years old and the norms concerning territoriality are universally obeyed, this territorial system is not recognized by the state of Maine. From the point of view of state officials, the territory controlled by harbor gangs represents an illegal usurpation of the public domain.

Lobstering territories are relatively small, the largest being no more than 100 square miles. Since lobster fishermen spend their working lives crisscrossing a small area, they come to know it in great detail, but have little knowledge of other areas or the boundaries of those areas. Territorial boundaries are typically relatively small features: a cove, a big rock, or perhaps a tree. Boundaries further offshore are delineated by reference to prominent features on the mainland or islands.

Gaining membership in a harbor gang is no easy task. The amount of resistance a would-be fishermen incurs depends on his own characteristics and on the type of area he is seeking to enter. A "native" boy from an old, established family will experience relatively little difficulty entering mainland harbor gangs—particularly if he comes from a family of fishermen. His entry into the gang will ordinarily be especially easy if he begins part-time fishing as a teenager and takes up full time fishing after finishing school.

People "from away" will have more difficulty in establishing themselves in a harbor gang. Resistance will be especially stiff if an individual begins fishing in middle age and has another source of income. Some of these people are never accepted (Acheson 1979, 261–62).

The most important factor influencing acceptance into a particular gang is the willingness to abide by local fishing norms. A man with a reputation of "meddling with other men's traps" or stealing lobsters will not last long in the business regardless of family history and local ties. Gaining admission to island harbor gangs is even more difficult. Some islands are privately owned in which case fishing rights are granted only to members of the owning family. On permanently occupied islands, such as Monhegan, Matinicus, and Swan's Island, fishing rights are reserved for residents, and it is difficult to buy land (Acheson 1979, 264ff.).

Violation of territorial boundaries brings no certain response. A high status fishermen, with many friends and allies might get away with his incursion for weeks or months, while another man might be sanctioned immediately. If the incursion lasts long enough, however, someone—usually a single person acting alone—will seek to defend the boundary. Usually the interloper is first warned by having two half-hitches tied around the spindle of his buoys, or conspicuously leaving the doors of his traps open. If he persists in fishing in the area of another gang, his traps will usually be cut loose at the buoy line so that they are irretrievably lost. Usually the man or men defending a boundary will not "cut off" any more traps than necessary to force the interloper to move. Touching another man's traps is considered somewhat shameful, and it is certainly illegal. In many cases, the interloper will retreat without a fight, in the knowledge that he has violated a boundary. Sometimes the victim retaliates and a small "cut war" occurs in which the traps of guilty and innocent alike are destroyed. Large scale "lobster wars," involving dozens of fishermen and the destruction of hundreds of traps do occur, but they are more rare than tourist mythology would have one believe.

Trap cutting incidents are kept very quiet. The police or wardens are rarely called since efforts to enforce the law are apt to be ineffective due to the difficulties of getting evidence. After all, traps are not cut off in the presence of witnesses. Moreover, there is a strong feeling that fishermen should handle their own problems and not involve external enforcement agencies.

Types of Territories

There are two different types of territories in the Maine lobster industry. They are what I have termed: "nucleated territories" and "perimeter-defended" areas. In nucleated territories, which exist in mainland harbors, the sense of ownership is strongest near the home harbor of a "gang" and grows progressively weaker with distance from the harbor. Any interloper placing traps close to the harbor mouth is certain to have trouble, but in the middle of bays and offshore, fishermen from as many as five different harbors may engage in mixed fishing. At a distance of perhaps ten miles from the harbor mouth, there is no strong sense of ownership at all. The offshore islands have perimeter-defended areas where boundaries are known to a yard and strongly defended. Here the sense of ownership remains strong up to the perimeter of the island's territory, and little mixed fishing occurs. Entry into the gang in perimeter defended areas is more difficult. The object of maintaining strict boundaries is to reserve a portion of the ocean for the exclusive use of the gang. After all, there is little sense maintaining strict boundaries if anyone can join the harbor gang.

At the turn of the century, virtually all lobstering areas were perimeter-defended areas, but on the mainland, they have been transformed into nucleated areas through the slow progress of boundary movement and easing requirements to join gangs (Acheson 1979, 253–76). The perimeter-defended territories have survived around some of the outer islands because men from mainland harbors have not been able to organize the kinds of effective alliances that allow them to push into the perimeter-defended territories. The islanders, on the other hand, have successfully formed defense alliances because of their small numbers, closely knit kinship system, and the ideology reinforcing their ownership claims. Their willingness to invest in defense efforts is also reinforced by the fact that lobstering provides their sole means of livelihood.

Biological and Economic Effects of Territoriality

The greater restrictions on entry have resulted in fewer boats and fishermen in perimeter-defended areas. There is far less fishing effort as well in these areas. In three nucleated areas, there were a total of 170 boats in 100.4 square nautical miles of fishing area or 0.59 square nautical miles per boat. By way of contrast, in three adjacent perimeter-defended areas, there were only 27 boats with 41.8 square nautical miles of equally good fishing area or 1.55 square nautical miles area per boat (Acheson 1988, 154).

Additionally, in "perimeter defended" areas there is less fishing pressure due to local conservation measures. On Matinicus and Green Island, fishermen have agreed among themselves to limit the number of traps used. In 1984, Swan's Island fishermen successfully lobbied for a trap limit to permit each fishermen to fish only 400 traps. The trap limit does not result in a smaller catch, but it does reduce the fisherman's costs of bait, gas, and maintenance. More importantly, the smaller number of traps enables fishermen to pull their traps more often which means fewer trap losses and fewer "ghost traps" that might permanently incarcerate lobsters. There is less lobster mortality from handling; and molting lobsters, which would have been eaten by other lobsters, can be released. Early in the century, Monhegan Island successfully lobbied the Maine legislature to prohibit fishing from January to June. This conserves the lobster resource by prohibiting fishing during the molting season when trap mortality is high.

Reduced fishing pressure in perimeter-defended areas, is having favorable economic and biological effects. Lobsters are larger in perimeter defended areas. The mean carapace length of 9,089 lobsters measured in nucleated and perimeter-defended areas in the same region of the coast was 89.0 mm in the perimeter-defended areas compared to 87.9 mm in the nucleated areas (Acheson 1975a, 200–03). (Test results indicate this difference in means was significant at the 0.005% level.)

The difference in mean size has an influence on the number of lobsters that survive to become breeding stock and thus on the well-being of the fishery itself. Only 6% of all female lobsters less than 90 mm in length become sexually mature; a very large percentage become mature between 90 mm and 100 mm; and virtually all females are sexually mature by 105 mm (Krouse 1973, 170–71). Because of less fishing pressure, the percentage of lobsters between 90 mm to 100 mm is much higher in the perimeter-defended areas than in the nucleated areas. Of the lobsters caught in the perimeter-defended areas sample, 1.9% were over 98 mm, but only 0.8% over 98 mm in the nucleated areas were this large. Moreover, 2.7% of the lobsters caught in perimeter-defended area were females with eggs as opposed to only 1.2% in the nucleated areas.

One of the standard measures of the health of a fishery is stock density (i.e. the number of lobsters on a given unit area of sea bottom). Stock density is indicated by catch per unit of effort. Measures of catch per trap per day (Acheson 1975a, 201) show that for all seasons of the year, catch per unit of effort was substantially higher in perimeter-defended areas than nucleated areas. Perimeter-defended areas produced 0.244 and 0.471 pounds of lobster per trap per day, compared to 0.053 and 0.267 pounds per trap per day from nucleated areas in the fall and summer, respectively.

Data in Table 5.1 summarize the productive superiority of perimeter-defended areas over nucleated areas. Not only do perimeter-defended area fishermen catch more lobsters per trap hauled, but the larger size of the lobsters caught translates into more premium "dinner lobsters" selling for a higher price per pound. A sample of eight lobstermen from perimeter-defended areas showed that they earned an average gross income of $22,929 in the mid-1970s from lobster fishing, while fishermen from nearby nucleated areas earned only $16,499.[1]

In summary, it is easier to enter nucleated areas than perimeter-defended areas. This results in a higher number of boats per unit of fishing area, and hence, relatively more fishing effort per unit of area. In such nucleated areas, lobsters are smaller, and catches, stock density and average incomes of fishermen are lower than they are in perimeter-defended areas where fishing effort has been lowered by local level conservation measures.

Table 5.1
Lobster Catch Figures
In Nucleated vs. Perimeter-Defended Areas

	Nucleated Areas	Perimeter-Defended Areas
Number of Lobsters Caught	6,180	3,169
Number of Lobsters Caught/Trap Hauled	0.68	1.13
Mean Pounds of Lobsters Caught/Trap Hauled	0.81	1.23
Mean Weight of Lobsters (in pounds)	1.18	1.20

Entering the Political Arena

Despite a history of successfully restricting entry into the lobster fishery, lobster fishermen have had a long history of lobbying for regulations. This has occurred several times in the past, and the last five years has again seen fishermen playing a very active political role. The result has been a set of new regulations with far reaching consequences for lobster conservation.

A short history of regulation is in order. The commercial lobster fishery began in the 1840s when the advent of the lobster smack (boats with circulating seawater tanks) made it possible to ship lobsters to cities along the eastern seaboard. Shortly thereafter, very large numbers of lobsters began to be canned, and by the 1870s there was fear among the canners and fishermen that the lobster fishery might crash. According to Martin and Lipfert (1985, 43), "There was general agreement by the seventies that something ought to be done about all this, but a consensus on what was necessary was almost impossible to reach because of conflicting vested interests." Fishermen wanted one thing; canners something else, and sellers of live lobsters had other aims. Somehow the state of Maine was persuaded to began imposing some regulations on the industry. In 1872 the taking of berried females (female lobsters with eggs attached) was prohibited, and in 1874 fishing was prohibited during the summer shedding season and lobsters under 10.5 inches (25.4 mm) carapace length could not be taken. In 1932, a legal maximum size was also established, largely at the urging of biologist Francis Herrick, who convinced fishermen and the legislature that large lobsters are prolific breeders. These laws have been revised, but from the 1870s to the present, size limitations and protection of the breeding stock have remained the main focus of regulations (Acheson 1992).

Since 1976 and the passage of the Fisheries Conservation and Management Act, the federal government has had the authority to manage the fishery beyond the 3 mile zone, but most of the regulations have been promulgated by the state of Maine and this remains true today.

At present, Maine requires all people who want to catch lobsters to have a lobster fishing license, which can be obtained by all for a nominal fee. All traps and equipment must be marked with the fisherman's license number, and his buoys must be marked with a distinctive combination of colors registered with the state. According to 1992 regulations, lobsters smaller than 3.25 inches (80 mm) or larger than 5 inches (12.7 mm) carapace length may not be harvested. In addition, it is still illegal to take "berried" lobsters and lobsters over 5 inches on the carapace. A law has been passed allowing fisherman to mark berried lobsters by cutting a v-shaped notch in one of their tail flippers, and once notched, the lobster may not be legally harvested. Both the so called "oversized" lobster and "v-notched" lobsters are considered proven breeding stock. In addition, since 1984 it has been required that all traps be equipped with a vent, which will allow small, illegal sized lobsters to escape.

While we know little about the strategies and maneuvers giving birth to regulations in the past, we are able to obtain a clear picture about the conditions motivating current industry efforts to influence the regulation of their industry.

The tradition of regulation has been fueled by a long-standing fear that the lobster fishery is facing demise. These fears are expressed in a variety of publications beginning with a poem written by Holman Day in 1901 entitled "Good-by Lobster." In the past few years, these concerns continue to be expressed in articles with titles such as "Where Have All the Lobsters Gone?" (Keiffer 1973); "A Fishery Under Fire," (Kreis 1986); and "For A Lot of Mainers, Lobstering Life is Losing Allure," (Kleiman 1991, C1).

The crisis atmosphere is partly engendered by the fishermen themselves who, not surprisingly, advertise the difficulties of their business while minimizing any successes. But disaster stories also seem popular with the press, and the fisheries bureaucracy.

The current crisis atmosphere cannot be explained by recent drops in catches. Between World War I and World War II, the lobster catch dropped precipitously for reasons that are still not completely clear (Acheson 1992). However, in recent decades, the lobster catch has proven remarkably stable. Since 1947, when the modern record-keeping system was introduced, the total Maine lobster catch has fluctuated from a low of 15.9 million pounds in 1948 to a high of 30.2 million pounds in 1991. In most years the catch hovers around 20 million pounds. Moreover, catch per trap per day has remained stable since 1968 at approximately 0.2 lobsters (Thomas et al. 1983).

Nevertheless, the past 15 years have witnessed virtually all lobster biologists advocating a change in the regulations to save the industry. In general, they argue that the industry may be poised on the brink of disaster because the breeding stock is at dangerously low levels and because there are not enough eggs in the water. The main solutions proposed by the biologists were to increase the legal minimum size to 3.5 inches carapace length thereby allowing a much larger number of females to survive to breeding size. They propose abolishing the "notched tail" law because cutting notches in the tail presumably leaves the lobster prone to infection. They also advocate abolition of the oversize law (maximum legal size law) because there are few such lobsters and only Maine has such a law.

Lobster fishermen are generally not in favor of these proposed regulations, but their attitudes towards management have undergone considerable change in the past few years. A 1973 lobster survey (Acheson 1975b, 654–56) revealed fishermen were against placing a moratorium on fishing; against any tax on traps even though many believed that there were too many traps in the water; and overwhelmingly against raising the legal minimum size to 3.5 inches. Fishermen were divided on the question of whether to prohibit taking lobsters over 5 inches in carapace length. They generally supported a limit on the number of lobster traps, and there was mixed support for a limit on the number of licenses issued. This last result is not surprising since fishermen have been limiting entry into harbor gangs for decades. Basically, they wanted the law to exclude those who had traditionally been excluded and allow those who had always been permitted to go fishing to continue. However, there was broad support for a law that would prohibit adult "part-timers" from fishing, but allow children of fishermen to fish on a part-time basis.

In the mid-1970s, there were no attempts to introduce legislation to change the legal size limits since there was no support in the industry for such legislation. One bill was introduced into the state legislature to limit traps and licenses, but it was defeated by groups of well organized fishermen.

In the 1980s, fishermen became more inclined toward legislative management. In 1986 and 1987, 61 full-time fishermen were interviewed regarding proposed legislation for the industry and revealed near unanimity on many issues. The strong ambivalence towards government action and the range of opinion on most issues concerning management that was so marked in the mid-1970s no longer existed. Virtually all agreed that there were too many traps in the water and too many fishermen and therefore favored limited entry and limited number of traps. Many spontaneously noted that a trap limit and license limit had to be combined, for they recognized that limiting only one would do no good if the other were allowed to increase. In addition, the fishermen interviewed all approved of the passage of the 1984 law requiring escape vents on traps to allow undersized lobsters to escape.

There was also a reversal of attitudes regarding other regulations. Of the 61 fishermen interviewed, 59 favored the 5-inch maximum size law, but opinion was divided on the question of raising the legal size to 3.5 inches. Thirty-eight of the 61 fishermen wanted to see the legal size raised and thus benefit the industry in the long run, because they felt this would increase the number of eggs in the water. Those who disagreed argued that this measure would cut their catches and income and would likely have no beneficial effect on conservation. None of the interviewed fishermen wanted to see the "punched tail" abolished. In their view, this law maintains the breeding stock and ensures that millions of females carrying eggs are not only returned to the water but are protected so they can breed again.

These preferences have been expressed recently by fishermen in the form of activities to influence legislative efforts to regulate their industry. In the spring of 1986, bills were presented in the Maine legislature to increase the legal minimum size measure, abolish the 5-inch maximum size measure, and introduce trap limits for various classes of licenses. There was also a bill that would establish lobster hatcheries. However, no change was proposed for the v-notch law. Intense lobbying activity by fishermen and industry leaders persuaded the legislature to postpone action on all these matters until the next legislative session when the results of a study, mandated by the legislature, would be available.

Throughout the early 1980s, federal and state bureaucracies continued their efforts to have enacted a federal fisheries management plan that would increase the minimum size in 1/32-inch increments over a period of 5 years to a minimum limit of 3.5 inches and abolish the v-notch law and the 5-inch oversize measure. Lobster fishermen, however, have opposed these measures.

In an effort to come to grips with federal fisheries management plans, Eddie Blackmore, President of the Maine Lobstermen's Association, proposed an unusual compromise. He and the MLA support the 3.5-inch measure which many fishermen felt was not necessary, if the federal and state governments maintained the 5-inch oversize measure and the notched-tail law. The Maine legislature passed a bill that went into effect in 1988 incorporating all features of this compromise. It included not only rules which the biologists and managers thought were important but those which the fishermen thought were important as well.

Explaining the Shift

Though fishermen are generally reluctant to enter the political fray, they have done so periodically. Why are they increasingly willing to support regulation now? The literature on institutional economics provides some insight. One of the axioms of institutional economics is that institutions evolve when the benefits of organizing collectively outweigh the costs (Ouchi 1980, 129; Williamson 1975). In particular, individuals and groups will apply more effort to defining and enforcing property rights when the benefits and costs change (Demsetz 1967; Anderson and Hill 1975). In the case of the Maine lobster fishery, changes in the economic and legal environments have provided the impetus.

Despite the successful passage of a state management plan, all is not well with the industry. The problems are not due so much to a shortage of lobsters but to rising costs for fishermen and declining lobster prices. The real costs of everything from bait to gas and boats has risen dramatically in the past few years. In 1975, a three-year-old wooden boat might have cost about $32,911 (1991 prices) fully equipped. In 1991, that same boat would cost over $80,000. On the other side of profits, the real price of lobsters has been falling. In August 1979, lobsters were bringing $4.40 (1989 prices) per pound, but by August 1989 the real price had dropped to $1.75. In 1990, the average price per pound was $2.59 at the Pemaquid Harbor Cooperative compared to $3.24 (1990 prices) in 1982.[2]

Not unlike experiences in the agricultural sector, this economic pressure has generated a great deal of agitation from fishermen for changes in regulations which would bring relief. The industry first approached the U.S. Congress for trade regulations which would reduce imports. The result was the so called Mitchell Bill, which went into effect in 1990, prohibiting the importation of live lobsters under the U.S. federal minimum size and ostensibly ending "unfair competition" by Canadians.[3]

Since 1991, the Maine Lobstermen's Association has been lobbying heavily to stop the incremental increase in the minimum size limit to 3.5 inches. They were never much in favor of the increase which they felt produced larger and less salable lobsters. They went along with it only as a means of retaining the oversize rule and the "punched tail" law. In March of 1991, their lobbying efforts with the U.S. Congress again resulted in action. The New England Regional Fisheries Management Council agreed to postpone the last two 1/32-inch increases in the minimum size measure.

The other main reason of fishermen entering the regulatory arena is that the Fisheries Management and Conservation Act of 1976 gave the federal government control over the fishery from the 3 miles line to 200 miles from shore. (Before 1976, management of the lobster fishery was solely in the hands of state officials.) In the mid-1980s it became apparent that the New England Fisheries Management Council was moving toward a 3.5-inch minimum size and abolishing the maximum size and notched-tail rule. From the point of view of many fishermen, this was the worst combination possible. The Maine lobstermen had little choice but to enter the fray to ward off efforts by very aggressive bureaucrats and devise bills the industry "could live with."

The lobbying efforts of fishermen are having results, but those successes come at enormous costs in time and negotiating effort. Leaders of fishing organizations, such as Eddie Blackmore of the Maine Lobstermen's Association, can have a good deal of influence on the shape of legislation when they have the active support of men in the fishing industry. But the changes in regulations which we recently have seen in the Maine lobster industry, are the result of literally years of long, painful negotiations. In these negotiations, all the active players (the state bureaucracy, National Marine Fisheries Service, Regional Council, and the fishermen) have had to compromise. None of the parties to the agreement got all that they wanted and they are not likely to get all they want in this current effort to influence regulations surrounding the industry.

Not all lobbying efforts succeed. In 1991, for example, there were a number of bills pending in the Maine legislature and before the New England Regional Fishery Management Council. These bills, which underwent several incarnations in the spring months of 1991, would have limited entry into the industry, prohibited fishing during the molting season in mid summer and limited the number of traps fishermen could use. All failed despite the enormous lobbying effort expended on them.

Conclusion

Ownership rights over the lobster resource is affected by two different property regimes. The state has one bundle of rights over the lobster, which stem from its right to control resources in the public domain. These rights are asserted by maintaining and enforcing management regulations and licensing procedures. The second regime consists of "traditional" communal rights over the resource held by groups of fishermen in given territories.

Both the government and fishermen have enormous influence over the kinds of ownership and management rights employed by the other. Maine lobster fishermen obey the laws concerning licensing, size regulations, laws protecting berried lobsters, and so on. The state of Maine could also annihilate the entire territorial system if it so choose by vigorously enforcing the laws concerning trap cutting. It chooses not to do so. But the point should not be lost that the territorial system (i.e., communal ownership rights) exists only because of the benign neglect of the state.

Fishermen, for their part, have exerted a great influence over the entire lobster management process. What passes for state control of the resource is, in great part, nothing short of control by the fishing industry working through the political process. It is what Pinkerton (1987) calls "co-management of the industry with the State of Maine and Federal Government."[4] (The fact that fishermen have influenced these regulations no doubt makes them more palatable and lowers enforcement costs.)

The territorial system is perhaps best described by what F. G. Bailey (1969, 176–81) calls an encapsulated system. That is, it is a political system within a larger political system. Both the territorial system and the legislation have made a mutual accommodation to each other.

At present, the political environment surrounding lobster management is undergoing change. In the past, fishermen sought to conserve the lobster resource, and their share of the catch, by limiting entry through the territorial system. In the late 1980s and early 1990s, they have entered the political arena with more force. Their lobbying efforts are stimulated by a desire to preserve the lobster and fend off the efforts of aggressive bureaucrats.

The case of the Maine lobster industry calls into question one of the central axioms underlying the common property model—namely the proposition that the users of common property resources will have great difficulty in generating institutions to conserve those resources on which their livelihood depends, if they can conserve them at all (Acheson 1989; Hardin 1968, 1244). This case study shows that under certain conditions users of common property resources can effectively generate such institutions.

There are, of course, enormous costs in maintaining the territorial system including traps lost, conflict, guarding boundaries, threats of fines and even jail sentences. But there are other costs involved in lobbying efforts including years of negotiations. There are also benefits. The lobster fishery of Maine may be one of the best examples of successful management in the world. There are very few instances where catches have remained stable for fifty years (McGoodwin 1990, 145). This highlights the success of the institutions developed by the Maine fishermen.

Notes

1. While the sample is small, the difference is statistically significant. See Acheson (1975a, 203).
2. James Wilson (pers. com. 1991), Professor of Resource Economics, University of Maine, points out that this is the first recession in which the real price of lobster has fallen. Also see Greenlaw (1991).
3. The Canadians are now shipping their small lobsters to Japan and Europe, thus raising the fear that they will take these markets away from American fishermen.
4. This is not unlike other industries where private agreements exist conterminously with state regulations and where industry representatives influence the regulations.

References

Acheson, James M. 1975a. The lobster fiefs: Economic and ecological effects of territoriality in the Maine lobster industry. *Human Ecology* 3(3): 183–207.

———. 1975b. Fisheries management and social context: The case of the Maine lobster industry. *Transactions of the American Fisheries Society* 104(4): 653–68.

———. 1979. Traditional inshore fishing rights in Maine lobstering communities. In *North Atlantic maritime cultures,* edited by Raoul Andersen. The Hague: Mouton, 253–76.

———. 1988. *The lobster gangs of Maine.* Hanover and London: University Press of New England.

———. 1989. Economic anthropology and the management of common property resources. In *Economic anthropology*, edited by Stuart Plattner. Palo Alto: Stanford University Press.

———. 1992. The Maine lobster industry. In *Climate variability, climate change, and fisheries,* edited by Michael Glantz. Cambridge and New York: Cambridge University Press.

Anderson, Terry L., and P. J. Hill. 1975. The evolution of property rights: A study of the American West. *Journal of Law and Economics* 18(1): 163–79.

Bailey, Frederick G. 1969. *Stratagems and spoils*. New York: Schocken.

Berkes, Fikret, and M. Taghi Farvar. 1989. Introduction and overview. In *Common property resources*, edited by Fikret Berkes. London: Belhaven Press.

Berkes, Fikret, and Mina Kislagioglu. 1992. Community management and sustainable development. In *La Recherche Face a la Peche Artisanale*, edited by J. R. Durand, J. Lemoalle, and J. Weber. Symposium International. Paris: ORSTOM-IFREMER.

Bromley, Daniel W. 1989. *Economic interests and institutions*. London: Blackwell.

Cox, Susan. 1989. Multi-jurisdictional resources: Testing a typology for problem-structuring. In *Common property resources*, edited by Fikret Berkes. London: Belhaven Press.

Demsetz, Harold. 1967. Towards a theory of property rights. *American Economic Review* 57:347–59.

Ensminger, Jean. N.d. *Making a market: The institutional transformation of an African society*. Cambridge: Cambridge University Press. Forthcoming.

Greenlaw, Skip. 1991. Lobster industry: What is the problem. *Commercial Fisheries News* (March): 14bff.

Hardin, Garrett. 1968. The tragedy of the commons. *Science* 162:1243–48.

Keiffer, Elizabeth 1973. Where have all the lobsters gone? *New York Times Magazine* (November 18): 36–37.

Kleiman, Dena 1991. For a lot of Mainers, lobstering life is losing allure. *New York Times* (May 1): C1, C6.

Kreis, Donald. 1986. A fishery under fire. *Maine Times* (September 26): 1.

Krouse, Jay S. 1973. Maturity, sex ratio, and size composition of the natural population of American lobster, *Homarus americanus*, along the Maine coast. *Fisheries Bulletin* 71(1): 165–73.

Martin, Kenneth, and Nathan R. Lipfert. 1985. *Lobstering and the Maine coast*. Bath, ME: Maine Marine Museum.

McGoodwin, James R. 1990. *Crisis in the world's fisheries*. Stanford: Stanford University Press.

Ostrom, Elinor. 1986. Issues of method and theory: Some conclusions and hypotheses. In *Common Property Management*. Washington DC: National Academy Press, 599–613.

Ouchi, William. 1980. Markets, Bureaucracies and Clans. *Administrative Science*

Quarterly 25:129–41.

Plante, Janice M. 1986. Inside lobster hatcheries. *Commercial Fisheries News* (August): 1.

Pinkerton, Evelyn 1987. Intercepting the state: Dramatic processes in the assertion of local co-management rights. In *The question of the commons*, edited by Bonnie J. McCay and James Acheson. Tucson: University of Arizona Press, 344–69.

Thomas, James, C. C. Burke, G. A. Robinson, and J. R. Parkhurst. 1983. Catch and effort information of the Maine commercial lobster (*Homarus americanus*) fishery, 1967–1981. *Lobster Informational Leaflet* No. 12. Boothbay Harbor, ME: Maine Department of Marine Resources Lobster Research Program.

Wilson, James A. 1991. Letter to the author, March 1991.

Williamson, Oliver. 1975. *Markets and hierarchies: Analysis and antitrust implications.* New York: The Free Press.

6

The Politics of Changing Property Rights: Dismantling a Commons From Within

Jean Ensminger and Andrew Rutten*

Economic growth has brought dramatic changes to pastoral societies.[1] One of the many indirect effects of economic growth is greater sedentarization.[2] Sedentarization in turn increases the threat of overgrazing. Although in the past such systems were routinely changed to prevent overgrazing, pastoralists have recently had less in restructuring property rights.

The roots of their failure lie in the economic and political changes brought on by economic growth. Economic growth has increased the gains to be had from dismantling the commons while also making it harder to reach agreement about

* Reproduced by permission of the American Anthropological Association from *American Ethnologist*, vol. 18, no. 4 (November 1991). Not for sale or further reproduction. We wish to thank Lee Alston, Yoram Barzel, Victor Goldberg, Robert Higgs, Gary Miller, Rodney Smith, Michael Taylor, and several anonymous reviewers for their comments on earlier drafts. Jean Ensminger also thanks the following institutions for generous research support: Fullbright-Hays, the Ford Foundation, the National Science Foundation (BNS-7904273), the Rockefeller Foundation and the National Institutes of Health (SSP 5 R01 HD213427 DBS). Finally, the National Museums of Kenya and the Institute of Development Studies at the University of Nairobi provided much appreciated institutional support during two field stays in Kenya.

how to distribute those gains. Sedentarization has increased the costs of maintaining common grazing, and growing economic diversification within pastoral societies has created groups that want very different property rights. At the same time, the replacement of local government by national government has changed the balance of power within, as well as between, groups. To illustrate the changing economics and the politics of common property in pastoral societies, we examine the case of the Galole Orma of Kenya.

The Orma of northeastern Kenya are riverine pastoralists. They are an Islamic, Eastern Cushitic-speaking people of the Oromo language group. Together with the Boran and others, the Orma were part of the greater Oromo expansion of the late 1500s which overran much of southern Ethiopia and northeastern Kenya. The current homeland of the Orma is Tana River District, Kenya, on the west bank of the Tana River, with particularly heavy concentration in the Tana River delta and some settlements in Lamu District to the east of the Tana. The Orma depend largely upon cattle, with lesser numbers of small stock (sheep and goats) and virtually no camels. They increasingly supplement their pastoral production with farming along the flood plains of the Tana River and the many seasonal rivers which cross-cut the territory from west to east.

The Galole Orma inhabit the middle portion of the Tana River district along the banks of the east-west Galole River, which flows in the Tana at Hola. In 1979, 39 percent of the Galole households were settled in villages with shops and were strongly integrated into the market economy as commercial beef producers. The other 61 percent were less involved in the market economy and were to some extent nomadic. The nontown households were generally more nearly self-sufficient in meeting their subsistence needs, which for them still consisted primarily of milk and stock products. Strikingly, by 1987, 63 percent of the Galole had settled in market towns. While we often think of sedentarization as being synonymous with a transition to farming, this was not the case with the Orma. Although floodplain agriculture along the seasonal Galole River continues to increase, it is quite unreliable, and virtually all households are still practicing pastoralists.

During this period, Orma income, like that of many Kenyans, has grown. Among African countries, Kenya has had a relatively high rate of economic growth. From 1965 to 1980 growth averaged 6.4 percent per year, while from 1980 to 1987 it averaged 3.8 percent per year (World Bank 1989). The Orma shared in this, as reflected in the 37 percent growth in their real per capita income between 1980 and 1987 (Ensminger 1992), despite livestock losses of 70 percent during the 1984 drought.

The Orma illustrate the influence of growth on property rights in pastoral economies. The Orma, like most African pastoralists, developed a complex system of property rights. Until recent times, land tenure consisted of shared grazing open to the entire ethnic group. Unlike grazing land, wells, which were redug seasonally at select locations in dry river beds, were owned not in common, but by the person who first dug the spot and his patrilineal descendants. As people began to settle, these options were no longer effective, and the Orma had to develop new methods of preventing the overuse of land, which they did by imposing restrictions on the access to the commons near sedentary villages. These restrictions functioned quite effectively in the absence of third-party enforcement until the mid-1980s. But by the mid-1980s the broad support for the restrictions had begun to break down, owing to the diverging interests of some commercially oriented sedentary livestock producers and others (cf. Johnson and Libecap 1982; Libecap 1989). This trend was compounded by other groups' pressure on Orma land. The relatively sedentary producers have been aided by their ability to use the national government's policies in favor of sedentarization to enforce restrictive property rights against the nomadic, subsistence-oriented producers. The result has been a gradual dismantling of the commons to the benefit of the sedentary producers.

The framework that we use to analyze these changes process is derived from the new institutional economics (Eggertsson 1990; North 1981, 1990), a perspective premised on the assumption that institutions influence choices, that people realize this, and that people try to structure institutions to their own ends (cf. Bates 1981, 1989).[3] While some institutions exist primarily in order to channel behavior according to religious and ideological norms, here we are concerned with more explicitly economic phenomena. From this perspective, the analysis of institutions is a three-step process. The first step is to analyze different possible institutions and determine how they distribute costs and benefits across society. The second is to assess current ideologies concerning the legitimate distribution of costs and benefits. Together these determine who will want which institutions. The third step is to consider the politics of institutions, or the way in which the political system treats the desires of the different groups involved. Politics determines how the various groups control the outcomes.[4]

The new institutionalism should appeal to anthropologists for several reasons.[5] Not only do the new institutionalists examine subjects of interest to anthropologists, ranging from the evolution of cooperation (Axelrod 1984; Schofield 1986; Taylor 1982, 1987) to the conditions under which markets will evolve (North 1977), but more important, while they retain the general economic approach to human behavior, they relax many of the particular assumptions that have bothered anthropologists: costless transacting, perfect rationality and information, and narrow economic self-interest (Goldberg 1981, 378). This leads them to depart significantly from neoclassical analyses by emphasizing the importance of institutions and ideology (Higgs 1987, 1989; Hinich and Munger 1992, N.d.); North 1981, 1990; Siegenthaler 1989). The resulting focus on the details of institutional structure gives much of this work a distinctly anthropological flavor (Cheung 1973; Ellickson 1991; Ostrom 1990). Of course, it does not yet (and may never) provide anything like a general theory of social institutions. However, it can add much to our understanding of the recent history of pastoral property rights in Africa.

The conclusions that we reach using this approach cut across existing scholarly boundaries. Like many economists and proponents of the "tragedy of the commons" theory (Hardin 1968; Hardin and Baden 1977), we believe that the viability of pastoral societies is related to the incentives provided by their systems of property rights and politics. Tragedy theorist believe that common ownership of land coupled with private ownership of livestock and the lack of a strong state provides incentives to degrade the environment. Unlike these scholars, however, we do not see common property as necessarily problematic in pastoral societies. Like many anthropologists (McCay and Acheson 1987), we believe that the record shows too many successful common property systems to allow for this analysis. Yet unlike some anthropologists (Peters 1987), we do not believe that this is grounds for rejecting rational choice. Rather, we believe that economists and tragedy theorists are wrong because they have failed to create proper models of pastoral common property systems. Their mistake simply proves the new institutionalists' claim that neoclassical economists fail to consider institutions adequately. Finally, unlike many of the property rights analysts (Demsetz 1967; cf. Williamson 1985 on contracts), we make no claims about the optimality of property rights or about their compatibility with long-run economic growth (Binger and Hoffman 1989; North 1981, 1990). Indeed, we argue that the role of politics makes such claims problematic. Political choices depend on the political structure as well as on what people want (Bates 1981); how choices are made can determine which choices are made (Riker 1980, 1986). This is precisely why institutional change does not necessarily enhance economic performance.

There are obvious similarities between our conclusions and those of neo-Marxists and other contemporary analysts of the state (see, for example, Evans, Rueschemeyer, and Skocpol 1985).[6] Like them we eschew the classical Marxist notion of class as analytic category and focus instead on conflict among groups within classes. We also agree with them that the state cannot be viewed simply as a passive agent of class domination. Instead, we see the state as both an autonomous actor and an entity subject to capture by groups, including the various factions within any class.

But in spite of these similarities, there are real differences in our approaches. Neo-Marxists begin with groups (although not necessarily the classes of Marx and Engels) and analyze their interactions;[7] we begin with individuals (albeit individuals who are embedded in a specific social and institutional context) and work up. Thus, while we acknowledge the importance of groups, we believe that it is more fruitful not to take them as given. Instead, we explicitly consider the conditions under which individuals will come together as members of groups and the conditions under which they will not do so (or will cease participating in groups they have formed).[8] For example, in the Galole case, we find that preferences for particular property rights are based not on simple class interests so much as on economic interests and kin alliances.

Our approach is especially useful for analyzing the path of institutional change. For example, it allows us to explain why common property systems worked so well in the past but are giving way to alternatives. A new institutional analysis goes a long way toward explaining the nature and time of institutional changes. These changes reflect changes in transaction costs, relative prices and burden sharing in enforcement. Our approach does not, however, account for preferences.

Property Right, Politics and Economic Growth

Property rights, politics and economic growth are inextricably intertwined. Much has been made of the role of property rights, rules over the control of resources, in determining the path of economic growth. Unfortunately, little has been made of the role of economic growth in determining the long run viability and adaptability of property rights. Indeed, it is often assumed that property rights automatically adjust to changing economic circumstances (Netting 1982; North and Thomas 1973). The advantages to such adjustments are obvious, but the adjustments are also obviously not automatic. To understand why they are not, we must examine how economic growth changes the effectiveness and adaptability of property rights.

Effective property rights are essential to the long-run viability and adaptability of a society. They allow people to take advantage of the gains from cooperation. When property rights are not completely specified or enforced, people are giving up (sometimes obvious) gains from cooperation. Despite these losses, incomplete property rights need not be irrational, paradoxical or imperfect. There are good reasons why property rights are not always perfectly specified or enforced (Barzel 1989). Most important, it is costly to specify, monitor and enforce them. Goods have many characteristics; to be complete, rights would have to be established and enforced over every valuable characteristic of every good. However, in the real world, it is costly not only to determine which goods are valuable and should be protected, but also to police compliance and punish offenders. Because of these costs, which economists call transaction costs, property rights are never completely specified and enforced, nor would it be cost-effective to do so.[9] Therefore, all other things being equal, goods and characteristics that are not controlled will be substituted for those that are.

Since property rights must be tailored to particular economic circumstances, changes in circumstances will change the effectiveness of particular property rights. By increasing the use of goods over which there are no property rights, growth can increase the cost of not having property rights. Perhaps the best example of this is the air and water pollution around cities; until recently, the levels of pollution were so low that property rights were not needed. Growth can also affect property rights that exist and are enforced. If growth raises the benefits from cheating, either by increasing the value of the good or by lowering the chance of getting caught, it may promote cheating. Much of the recent increase in ivory poaching, for example, has been related to ivory's increasing value. Finally, the strengthening of institutions such as courts and of infrastructure such as roads that often accompanies growth can change the transaction costs incurred in enforcing property rights. Thus, where a lack of roads once made it difficult to enforce property rights in land, a better infrastructure may open privatization as an alternative to common tenure.

So far, we have ignored the question of what property rights people want. Economists usually assume that people will always want those property rights that maximize net output. Otherwise, the reasoning goes, people will be foregoing gains; the prospect of capturing these gains will provide a powerful incentive for restructuring property rights. But this argument ignores the role of ideology and politics in determining property rights.

Ideology shapes preferences in property rights by making people consider more than their own narrow gains when evaluating various systems of rights. In particular, people may be interested in ensuring that economic rewards are distributed fairly within society. Economists admit that some people are motivated by more than their own narrow self-interest, but they deny that these people affect the structure of property rights. They argue that when even a few people are selfish, competition forces everyone to be selfish by rewarding selfishness. Thus, competition gives everyone a powerful incentive to ignore such factors as fairness.[10] While this reasoning may apply to property rights, such as contracts, that are developed in competitive markets, many important property rights are not subject only to market pressures.[11] In some of these settings, ideological considerations may be salient.

Ideology is likely to be particularly important when it comes to those property rights that are determined politically. Indeed, there is good reason to believe that politics does not simply mimic the market, even when people are narrowly self-interested. To the extent that this is true, political considerations will affect the choice of property rights. The result may be property rights that decrease economic performance.

Politics is the process by which the desires of the members of a group are turned into collective choices. The political structure determines how much influence each member will have over any particular outcome. Political problems occur only if individuals disagree over policy; when everyone agrees, the collective choice is obvious. The changing of property rights is likely to cause extensive disagreement, for property rights are never neutral in their economic effects, and changing them creates winners and losers. As long as nobody wants to be a loser, there will be disagreement over which property rights ought to be changed or chosen.

Unfortunately, extensive disagreement complicates the analysis of collective decisions. Indeed, formal investigations of political decisions have found that such decisions depend crucially on the political structure: for the same configuration of individual wants, it is usually possible to get many different decisions by changing the political mechanism (Riker 1980). Radical changes in outcomes are caused not only by such changes in the political system as the replacement of a monarchy by a democracy, but also by keeping the system the same, but making relatively minor changes in procedure, such as reordering the sequence in which exactly the same issues are voted on (Riker 1986). Clearly, then, analysis of the details of the institutional structure, whether formal or informal, is crucial to understanding politics.

In a variety of ways, economic growth decreases the ability of the political system to resolve conflicts over property rights. Increasing specialization and division of labor bring with them increasing economic differentiation, with each group wanting the property rights that favor them. Growth also creates winners and losers. Since changing from a losing to a winning economic strategy may itself be costly, losers have an incentive to turn to politics to reverse their loses more cheaply.

Growth changes the political structure as well. Especially in developing nations, national government tends to expand at the expense of local government. With improvements in transportation and communication, national governments have been able to increase their power. The coalitions that control national politics are often very different from those controlling local governments.

What are we to conclude from this? The complexity of the world makes it hard to design property rights that promote economic performance while fulfilling socially desirable dictates regarding distribution. Because they are costly to negotiate, monitor, and enforce, property rights will not be complete, but will focus on a few valued characteristics where compliance is easily enforced. Such schemes are particularly sensitive to changes in the relative cost of not complying with the restrictions on those characteristics. When property rights, for whatever reason, result in large economic losses, the losses create an incentive to change the rights. Whether and how the rights are changed will depend not only on the economic incentives but also on ideological perspectives and the political structure. Since there is no guarantee that ideology or political structures will themselves depend primarily on economic considerations, the resulting property rights may be inefficient.

The Political Economy of Nomadic Pastoralism

The political economy of pastoral societies is distinguished by their reliance on common property in land, by the individual ownership of livestock, and by the lack of a strong state. Many scholars see these features as the source of pastoralists' recent problems. Given each individuals' desire to build a larger herd, common property, by failing to provide incentives to conserve on land, leads to the tragedy of the commons (Hardin 1968), the destructive overuse of land. According to the tragedy theorists, the lack of a strong state limits the ability of pastoral societies to enforce any collective decisions, and it thus hinders the development of more effective property rights. Neither conclusion is warranted. A deeper analysis shows that these features do not necessarily have such effects. Indeed, when correctly analyzed, the pastoral common property system appears to be an effective response to economic circumstances.

The benefits of common property in grazing land come from the peculiar ecology of arid regions in Africa. These regions are characterized by erratic and unevenly distributed rainfall, a climatic condition ensuring that a small area of land cannot support cattle over the long run. Moreover, common property obviates the need to monitor private rights to the large parcels of land necessitated by ecology. These benefits do not explain how traditional systems avoided the tragedy or why some of them are now succumbing to it. We need a model of common property that explains when common property will be tragic and when it will not (cf. Barzel 1989).

The key to such a model is a more complete characterization of the pastoral production process. In the tragedy model, the only inputs into the production of cattle are cattle and land. When land is free, pastoralists have an incentive to overuse the land by increasing the number of livestock they put on it. In fact, land is not the only factor whose limited availability constrains production. Raising real livestock requires several inputs besides land, notably water and labor. As a result, pastoralists do not necessarily have an incentive to use more and more land simply because it is free. Generally, they will only do so if the value (including insurance) of doing so exceeds the cost. While the marginal cost of land is almost nothing, the marginal value may be even lower. Whether it is depends on the cost of the other inputs needed to produce cattle.

Stocking levels will depend in part on the cost to the pastoralist of each of the inputs. Moreover, the marginal cost of inputs depends on property rights. If property rights can be established over one of the other inputs, then the cost of using it can be raised enough to make overusing unowned inputs such as land uneconomical. Indeed, it may be cheaper to establish and enforce property rights over these other inputs than over land. When this is so, then it may be economically sensible to structure property rights so that land is free.

Such protective mechanisms are found in most pastoral areas. Among any pastoral group, several different sorts of rights in property are likely to coexist. Some resources belong to individuals, some to lineages, and still others to everyone; some are usufruct, some leasehold, and some freehold. In addition, most pastoralists have rules that govern the use of resources during emergencies, such as droughts or epidemics. Taken together, these factors make it seem unlikely that the tragedy model, based on oversimplified assumptions about individual freehold rights in livestock and common rights in land, applies to real pastoral systems.

Not surprisingly, water is the subject of many complex rights. Without water, even free land, is worthless to a pastoralist. In arid regions, access to dry-season water is easily controlled, since there are only a limited number of sources. In these areas, dry-season water sources are often not owned in common (see Gulliver 1972, 23 for the Turkana; Helland 1980 for the Boran; Lewis 1961, 34 for the Somali). And some herders control inputs besides water. For example, in those areas where the cattle of different owners are allowed to mingle, owners need to be allowed access to the annual roundup; in areas where production is commercialized, access to the market is controlled (Dennen 1976).

The recent history of Botswana provides striking evidence of the efficacy of ancillary controls (Hitchcock 1985; Peters 1984). In Botswana, development planners noted that a lack of water limited the number of cattle. To solve this problem, they began a program of sinking boreholes. As planned, the program dramatically increased the amount of water available to pastoralists, and led to an increase in the number of cattle they raised. It also had the unplanned effect of leading to a destructive overuse of land. Yet this was the predictable consequence of relaxing the constraint—the limited access to water—that was keeping the value of land low. Thus, the failure of the borehole program was not an example of the tragedy of the commons, but of the tragedy of making common what had once been private property.[12]

Many precolonial African pastoral societies were distinguished not only by the holding of common property in land but also by statelessness. Most pastoral groups had some body that made collective decisions, such as a council of elders; however, few had a central body to enforce those decisions. Like common property in land, this system was economically sensible. However, it would appear to have left pastoral polities with no power to enforce collective decisions. Yet innumerable anthropological studies of stateless societies show that statelessness does not necessarily imply disorder. Statelessness means not the absence of enforcement but the decentralization (or privatization) of enforcement (Eggertsson 1990, ch. 9; Taylor 1982). Instead of relying on third-party specialists to enforce collective agreements, the citizens of stateless societies must rely on one another.

Decentralized private enforcement will not work unless ordinary citizens want to enforce collective decisions.[13] They must also have the means to do so, and they must know who has broken the rules and thus must be punished. Recent work in game theory suggests that these conditions can be met when people deal with each other repeatedly (Axelrod 1984; Taylor 1982, 1987): when people play a game over and over, they can punish offenders by refusing to deal with them in the future; moreover, in small groups it is relatively easy to determine who cheats and who does not (Hechter 1987).

Perhaps the most important consequence of decentralized enforcement is to limit the range of possible political decisions. Anyone who was not happy with a collective choice could refuse to enforce it (Bailey 1965), and as a result, choices that favor one part of the collectivity at the expense of another without acceptable compensation are unenforceable. Thus, the need for broad support may limit the degree of collectively induced inequality. This need not, as some theorists have argued (Taylor 1982), imply equality. After all, people may accept unequal outcomes as long as they are the result of fair play within accepted rules. However, it does seem unlikely that people will accept inequality that is based on manipulation of the political system. Thus, ceteris paribus, decentralization implies that inequalities are less likely to be based on political decisions than on economic or ideological motivations.

Economic Growth and the Emergence of Conflict

Growth has dramatically altered pastoral economies by making commercial production economically feasible and rewarding. In many pastoral societies, this has increased diversity, with some people becoming commercial producers, traders, farmers, and wage-laborers, while others continue to focus on subsistence pastoral production. As a result, there is now less agreement about what forms of property rights are appropriate. A growing share of pastoral output is being sold on the market, not kept for domestic consumption. The needs of commercial beef producers are very different from those of subsistence-oriented nomads. Therefore, the two groups want very different property rights systems.

The emergence of a commercial sector can be traced directly to the changes associated with economic growth, including an increase in the relative and absolute size of the urban population. Since city dwellers cannot grow their own food, their food needs must be met by commercial production by those who remain in agriculture. Growth has also resulted in improvements in the infrastructure (roads, telecommunications, public transport, government and banking facilities), even in pastoral areas. Moreover, the spread of stores, along with the increased use of money and credit, make it possible for pastoralists to use the proceeds from their sales to purchase goods they desire. All in all, these changes make it economic for some pastoralists to specialize in producing for national and international markets.

Nevertheless, the pastoralists in any given society are not all equally interested in producing for the market. Those who have the appropriate access to stock, skill, and labor, and who prefer decentralized political authority, may still migrate and avoid dependence on the market for subsistence foodstuffs as much as possible. The factors related to settlement and involvement in commerce include a facility with the language of trade, kin relations with traders or other well-off sedentarists, access to credit, job opportunities, the availability of arable riverine land, a household age structure that makes movement difficult, infirmities that make access to health care facilities important, and fear of losing land that is not settled. The fact that different populations have very different land tenure needs makes it increasingly difficult to reach agreement over property rights.[14]

Economic Growth and the Resolution of Conflict

In addition to heightening conflict over collective decisions, growth has changed the methods of resolving those conflicts. The methods first began to change with the appearance of the modern state in nomadic areas. Over the past fifty years, the national governments of Africa have exercised increasing sovereignty over nomadic areas (cf. Ensminger 1990). The extent to which they exercise control varies greatly, but in most areas there is now an effective, if limited, national presence, a presence that has resulted in several different changes, each with important implications for the resolution of the conflict. In most areas the overall effect has been to bias collective decisions towards policies that favor commercial producers at the expense of subsistence producers.

One of the most important changes has been the development of a new method of enforcing political decisions. We argued above that the lack of third-party enforcement in stateless societies imposed limits on the substantive political decisions that could be made. These limits disappeared when the state replaced the members of the group as the enforcer of collective decisions. With a third party enforcing collective decisions, the group is no longer forced to consider only decisions that can be agreed upon by fairly broad consensus and thus privately enforced. As a result, a smaller group can dominate decision making with the concessions previously necessary to acquire broad support.

Having said this, however, we must note that even modern states do not rule by formal constraints and third-party enforcement alone. In fact, as North (1990) argues, much enforcement of contracts and property rights comes from informal constraints. In many contexts people will not break the law even when they know they can get away with it, for they believe in its legitimacy and justice. Thus, the degree of ideological support for particular property rights and other institutions will greatly affect compliance and, therefore, economic performance. It is hence often in the interest of those attempting to dominate decision making to act cautiously and bring others around to their perspective even when they have the government's police forces at their disposal. A loss of ideological support cannot be entirely compensated for by third-party enforcement.

The replacement of local by national government has other implications. One is to increase the importance of national-level politics. Those who determine what policies the state enforces will be able to get decisions that favor them. National government also opens the door for the state to decide policy without considering the desires of local residents. However, for the same reason that a minority may not wish to substitute force for ideological legitimacy by imposing a totally self-interested policy, so the state may acquiesce in some degree to local interests. Another consequence of accepting state government is the recognition of the state's monopoly over legitimate force. This has in some cases diminished the pastoralists' ability to protect grazing land from incursions by outsiders.

Acceptance of the national government also increases the vulnerability to its urban bias (Lipton 1977), resulting in the passage of a variety of laws that are inconsistent with the continued viability of the more subsistence-oriented households. Some laws, such as those establishing game preserves, irrigation schemes, and private ranches, may benefit outsiders at the expense of local groups. Others, however, favor some members of the local group at the expense of others; for example, compulsory schooling laws penalize nomads more than sedentary producers, and taxes serve primarily to fund social services used disproportionately by sedentarists.

So far, our discussion of the process of changing property rights has been rather abstract. To make it more concrete and to provide more detailed evidence, we turn to a single case, that of the Galole Orma of northeastern Kenya.[15] The history of property rights among the Orma show clearly their relations to growth and politics.

The Historical Orma Solution to the Commons Problem

Although the limited historical accounts of the Orma for the last few centuries provide few precise details of land tenure practices, there is every reason to believe that land was held in common and stock owned individually, as was the case among most East African pastoral groups until recent decades. Orma lineage rights over water were—and are—similar to those found among the Boran (Helland 1980, 65), from whom the Orma separated several centuries ago.

In the earliest accounts, it appears that the Orma relied on military expansion to reduce overcrowding of commonly held grazing land. In the consequent absence of shortage, no commons problem existed. The Orma were of course not alone among pastoralists in using such a strategy. Among others, the Somali and the Maasai were known to be expanding their territories at the time of the British pacification efforts in the late 19th century. In fact, these three groups eventually met in military adventures over Orma territory.

Until the 1860s, the Orma were exceptionally successful militarily. Originating in Ethiopia, the Oromo began expansion in the early 1500s and made it as far as northern Tanzania in less than a century. The Orma's fierce military posture also discouraged foreigners, including the usually aggressive Arabian coastal traders, from penetrating their territory (Lobo 1984, 66; New 1873, 161). However, beginning in the 1850s, the Maasai and the Somali, also in an expansionary posture, made serious attacks upon the Orma from the south and the north, respectively.

As long as the Orma were successful militarily, they had little need to develop mechanisms for regulating grazing. Moreover, the defeats of the mid-19th century so decimated both the Orma and their stock that repopulation, even of their much reduced territory, took a long time. Therefore, pressure on the commons was not an issue in the first half of this century. In the 1960s, however, the Orma began to face problems of land pressure. These problems took the form of both external encroachment by other ethnic groups and internal disagreement over changes in property rights as a consequence of economic growth.

External Encroachment on Orma Territory

The nationalization of government has increased the encroachment of outsiders on Orma land. Part of this increase comes from the activities of the national government itself. A variety of development projects are land intensive, and in Kenya, as elsewhere, pastoral lands are a natural source of land for these projects. In addition, the national government prohibits the Orma from defending their territory militarily. As a result, the Orma are increasingly susceptible to encroachment, especially by Somali pastoralists.

The Orma have lost large amounts of territory to development projects, especially irrigation projects along the Tana River (including Hola, Bura, and the Tana Delta Rice Project), game reserves (including Tsavo, the Tana River Primate Reserve, and the Kitui Reserve), non-Orma commercial ranches (especially Galana), and group and cooperative ranches. The Orma have been essentially powerless to stop any of the encroachment upon their territory for agriculture, irrigation, commercial ranches, or game reserves. The government considers all of these land uses more economically productive than pastoralism and has therefore given them national priority in this and other parts of Kenya. Even if the Orma had powerful representatives in Nairobi, it is unlikely that they would be successful in stopping these encroachments.

The Orma have had relatively more success in drawing the attention of the government to encroachment by other pastoral groups. In particular, they have taken advantage of the hostility between Kenya and Somalia to push for the removal of the Somali from their territory. For example, in 1980 there was an influx of marauding bandits believed to be Somali (commonly referred to as *shifta*) who were believed to be Somali.[16] The Orma used the situation to attempt to rid their territory of all foreign ethnic groups: Somali, Wardei, and even Boran. Accusations that all of these groups were harboring *shifta* in their settlements were rampant at the time. Following each attack by bandits on Orma villages, the Orma made retaliatory raids on Somali settlements, raids constituting the equivalent of ethnic warfare. Ultimately, however, the Orma were no match militarily for the Somali. Consequently, when the Orma were inundated with large numbers of Degodia Somali in the drought of 1980, they had no recourse but to turn to the government for help in ordering these outsiders out of their territory. The government of Kenya did take action on their behalf, permitting the Orma Chief, under the authority of the "chief's act," to order any foreign stock out of his location (the subunit of the district) and to refuse any other livestock permission to cross into it.

Earlier, the Orma had also attempted to force the Somali out by making it difficult for them to get water. The Orma complained that the Somali and Wardei residing in the northern part of Orma territory at this time refused to acknowledge Orma ownership of wells and merely used (and destroyed them) at will. When chastised for such behavior their response was that the Orma did not own the wells, since "Only God can own a well." The Somali were probably making a strained effort to appeal to a common institutional structure in the form of Islam, which is shared by all of the groups involved. This state of affairs represented the breakdown of the Orma's primary institutions for regulating common pasture: military action and the ownership of wells. At this point the Orma had little choice but to resort to a higher authority, as the Wardei and Somali made it very clear that they did not consider themselves bound by Orma institutions.

The experience with the influx of Somali and Wardei had several consequences for the Orma system of property rights. More than ever before, the Orma realized the vulnerability of their situation, and began taking steps to secure their property. This they did by cultivating the sentiment of local Kenyan officials against the Somali. They also took steps to guard their territorial claims more directly. For example, in one remote nomadic area far from any shops, villagers were reported to be afraid to leave their camp for fear that if they vacated the area the Somali would move in. Thus people began to settle in part to secure their rights to land. This particular crisis was eventually resolved when the rains came at the end of 1980. The Somali did leave Galole territory, but the Orma were much changed by the experience. Furthermore, the Somali returned in even larger numbers during the drought of the mid-1980s.

The external threats to Orma property rights are potentially more costly to the Orma than the internal threat. Consequently, we should not ignore the effect of the external threat when we consider the internal dynamics of change that ensued. In evaluating the relative effects of internal and external pressures on the commons, one must bear in mind that the dismantling of the commons began in the early 1960s, long before the recent wave of Somali encroachment. However, while the processes of economic growth and Orma settlement would ultimately have precipitated a change in property rights on their own, the Somali crisis may have aided in overcoming ideological resistance to the system that resulted. With this in mind, we turn now to the internal situation, which may cast more light on changing property rights in other contexts.

Internal Pressure on Property Rights

The Galole Orma began to sedentarize in the Wayu area in the late 1940s and early 1950s. In the 1950s, they had a small shop, school, dispensary, mosque, chief's office, and road to the district headquarters. The process was at first extremely gradual and the area so naturally fertile, that a reasonably good-sized population could remain there through wet and dry seasons with few detrimental consequences for either the ecology or the well-being of the livestock. By the 1960s, however, the population was great enough that the Orma were beginning to feel some pressure on the local resources.

In the case of the Galole Orma, sedentarization is not synonymous with a transition to agricultural production. While the chief did experiment with large-scale agricultural commercial agriculture in the 1960s, large scale farming did not develop until the 1970s. Even today it is at best an opportunistic strategy, as it depends on river flooding, which yields reasonable harvests only one season in four, or roughly every other year.

Settling is incompatible with East African pastoralism because rainfall tends to be highly localized; pastoralists need to be as mobile as possible in order to purse the rains and grazing and to match population density with resource availability. The wealthy sedentary households solve this problem by keeping only small milking herds in the village and hiring herders to take the majority of their stock to remote and highly mobile cattle camps.

The Orma are attracted to settlement for a variety of reasons. For those with commercial interests, settlement greatly facilitated access to information, transportation, and buyers and sellers. Others were attracted by some combination of the school, mosque, dispensary, shops, availability of arable land by the river, presence of wealthy kin, opportunities for employment, and relative ease of a settle lifestyle. Whatever their reasons for settling, however, all households were forced to depend on purchased foodstuffs for a great deal of their subsistence, as access to milk (the dietary mainstay) was greatly reduced with sedentarization; in other words, everyone was forced into a highly commercial production strategy— they sold stock and purchased grain.

As stocking pressure increased over the entire territory, there was nothing to stop the nomads from using the lush grazing in the settled area, thus leaving insufficient grazing for the sedentarists' milking herds during the dry season. Early in the 1960s, the sedentary elders, including the resident government chief, proclaimed that a small area around the permanent village of Wayu was off-limits for wet-season grazing to any stock but that owned by the local villagers. The Orma term for the area was laf sera, or roughly, "prohibited land" (cf. Behnke 1985).

In the 1960s and 1970s, the restricted area was not large enough to represent a serious threat to the nomads. Conflict was relatively easily avoided, and incursions, although they definitely occurred, were not serious enough to jeopardize the resource base of the settled households. But over the years, the settled villagers gradually increased the restrictions on this grazing area by limiting the period recognized as "dry season," and by increasing the size of the territory to include all grazing land within a day's walk from the center in all directions. By 1985 the restricted area was substantial and was out of bounds to outsiders year round. As always, nomads still had the option of settling at any time and thus enjoying access to the restricted grazing but there were costs. All settlers were obliged to send at least some of their children to school and to contribute to harambee (self-help) fundraising, the primary means of taxation.

Significantly, by 1985 the new property rights system was being enforced largely by the state. Up to the early 1980s, trespassers were reported to the elders by herdboys and such sanctions was were employed worked through traditional Orma institutions controlled by the elders. The chief (a state civil servant) never arrested herders for trespassing on the restricted grazing area. By the mid-1980s, however, the chief was commonly using his police to arrest both Orma and Somali encroachers. Typically, the offenders were detained briefly and fined. While the majority of the settle Orma, rich and poor alike supported the chief in this policy, the Orma nomads clearly did not, and some settled households were sympathetic to the nomads' cause. In order to understand the breakdown of the elders' ability to enforce the restricted grazing and thus the need for third-party enforcement by the state, we must analyze the increasing differentiation that occurred among the Orma during the 1970s and 1980s. Much of the differentiation can be related to economic growth and the diverse economic interests that resulted.

Over the 1970s and 1980s there were significant changes in relative prices, changes favoring the commercial production of livestock and increasing the value of the land around permanent settlements. For example, between 1980 and 1987 the profits from livestock production on Orma land rose 116 percent, while overall inflation was 93 percent, (Ensminger 1991, 1992). Since sedentary households have better access to transportation, markets, and price information, increased commercialization tends to result in increased sedentarization. As the sedentary population grew, so too did the value of land, in turn promoting the demand for restrictions on land around permanent settlements.

Changes in the relative costs of maintaining distant cattle camps also fostered the sedentarists' demand for land. As the demand for education increases, the pool of young men available for work decreases, raising not only the direct cost of labor but the transaction costs (here agency costs) as well. As the labor of sons is replaced by hired herders in the remote cattle camps, the quality of herding declines, leading to significant losses. Herd owners especially complained that this was a problem during the 1984 drought and accounted for much of the 70 percent livestock loss at that time. Such labor problems are less severe among hired herders living in settled villages, where they are under the watchful eye of the herd owner on a daily basis. Thus, in 1987 the sedentarists began trying to expand the restricted areas around the settled villages to accommodate their cattle camps.

The alienation of Orma land to irrigation schemes, game reserves and a variety of ranches has also dramatically reduced the Orma's access to dry-season water sources such as the Tana River. As the access to alternative water sources declines, the relative value of land around the sedentary villages, which have their own water supplies, increases. Finally, the social and economic services available in the sedentary villages all enhance the relative benefits of settlement and the value of land in the area.

These changes in relative prices have widened the gap in economic interests between the sedentary and the nomadic herders and have possibly persuaded some sedentarists to overcome their ideological misgivings about restricting access to the commons. Over the years the settlers used two forms of ideological reasoning to justify more restrictive property rights. Initially, the Orma appealed to custom, which gives preference to the needs of milk herds over those of ureni, or cattle camps (cf. Hogg 1990 for the Boran). Conceivably, even the nomads could have accepted this, especially given that the costs to them were initially small. Later, the sedentarists argued that they had sedentarized in order to send their children to school and that therefore they had to prohibit the nomadic herders (who could go elsewhere) from using the only resources which were within the reach of the villagers' herds. This explanation appealed to the national "ideology," as compulsory schooling was the law (albeit not seriously enforced) as of the late 1970s. The sedentarists knew, therefore, that by so arguing their case they could claim the backing of the national government.

By 1987 the situation had gone so far that neither of these claims to ideological legitimacy was tenable. First of all, for some years the children of many households excluded from the restricted grazing had already been going to school. Second, in 1987 some wealthy commercial households were lobbying for an extension of the restricted grazing zone to encompass an area large enough to accommodate their cattle camps in the dry season. In part, they proposed this as the most effective strategy to counter the Somali threat to their territory. Together with similar initiatives in other villages along the Galole River, this movement threatened to create a nearly continuous restricted zone east to west across the entire Orma frontier. Such a change would probably force all Galole nomads to sedentarize. While the proposal was still in the negotiation phase in late 1987, the fact that it was even seriously considered by a substantial number of sedentarists is highly significant, indicating either that the norms regarding the acceptable distribution of costs and benefits across society had changed considerably over the years or that the wealthy sedentary households felt confident that their will could prevail in the face of significant ideological objection. The latter is possible only under conditions of third-party enforcement, such as now prevail.

The growing gap between the subsistence nomads and the sedentary commercial pastoralists, rich and poor alike, is not the only form of economic differentiation that has rent Orma society. Had it been the only one, the decentralized enforcement sanctioned by the sedentary elders might still be working. However, with the sedentary community serious cleavages developed, some clearly economic and others less clearly so. Most notably, a number of wealthy sedentary households, many of whom settled only recently as a consequence of the 1984 drought, had close family members who were nomads and whose interests they supported. Many families practiced a divided strategy, with part of the household sedentarized and part nomadic, and thus had mixed interests. Moreover, a limited number of wealthy shopkeepers and poor tea-kiosk owners did considerable business with both the nomads and the Somali and supported them politically. Clearly, the lines of conflict in this dispute were not based on class interests so much as on economic interests and kin loyalties.

For most Orma, the external threat to grazing posed by the Somali encroachment precipitated a crisis that may have greatly enhanced the sedentarists' ability to overcome ideological resistance to changing property rights. While some change would have been necessary even in the absence of the external threat, it might not have come as fast nor have taken the form that it did, had historical circumstances differed.

Enforcement by the state offered the advantage of harsher sanctions (and thus greater protection for the now valuable land) while obviating the need for broad-based political support of the new property rights. In other words, it is now possible for a smaller group to implement institutional changes that favor them. The composition of this group changes over time, in part as a response to changes in relative prices.

Conclusions: Property Rights and Development

The relation between economic growth and property rights is complicated. Growth changes the costs and benefits of any system of property rights and the distribution of those costs and benefits. However, property rights are not always restructured only in response to purely economic considerations; the long-run viability and desirability of certain property rights also reflect ideology and politics. In addition, perceptions of fairness affect people's willingness to comply with any particular system and thus affect the transaction costs of that system. Which property rights are actually chosen depends on how rights are chosen as well as on which rights are desired. People choose many, if not most, important property rights collectively, using a combination of formal and informal political institutions. The extent to which different groups can affect the choice of property rights depends on the political institutions used to make choices.

The case of the Orma illustrates the interaction of economics, ideology, and politics in the evolution of property rights. The timing of the move away from common to more private property rights among the Orma is not coincidental. Economic growth created a situation in which new property rights were necessary, desired by some factions, and were more affordably enforceable than they had previously been. Since the 1960s, the Orma, like many other pastoralists in Africa, have faced increased overgrazing. Overgrazing could be reduced by altering property rights. However, the various groups did not agree on what rights to adopt. The disagreement was largely driven by the commercial producers' desire to protect their gains. And as the Orma were fighting over property rights, the central government of Kenya was getting closer and closer. Those who had most contact with the government were in a favored position to use the new institutions to their advantage. The costs of enforcing more exclusive control of the range would previously not have been paid for by the economic savings of the new property rights. Once the costs of enforcement could be at least partially shifted to the central government, however, the new rights became more economically attractive to some interested groups. The presence of a large population of ethnic Somali probably did not dramatically alter the situation's final outcome, but it may have considerably forced the issue, so that the lingering ideological resistance to a solution costly to the nomads was more easily overcome. Thus, by 1985, most Orma agreed that it was legitimate for the state to use force against their own members: the chief commonly used his police to arrest encroachers on restricted grazing, Orma and Somali encroachers alike, and the vast majority of the settled Orma population (63 percent of the population) considered this policy appropriate.

The Orma case should be instructive for many other parts of the developing world. The issue of who pays for the enforcement of new rights is especially important in understanding changing property rights in developing countries. The central bureaucracies of developing nations are reaching further and further into the remote areas. As they do, forms of property rights that could not be economically enforced locally may become economical because enforcement is subsidized by the central state, as is the case for the Orma. But the changing economics of enforcement implies nothing about the effect of economic performance of the new property rights, about their ecological soundness, or about their equity. In such circumstances, economic growth may well create certain windfalls, not only economic ones but also political windfalls in the form of privileged access to the central state. This being the case, those with better access may be able to manipulate the enforcement agencies to their own ends, thus creating new property rights favorable to them.

Notes

1. By economic growth, we mean growth in the total output of society regardless of distribution.

2. Some might argue that many of the changes we describe in this article may in fact have been driven by population pressure rather than economic growth. Indeed, population pressure can induce many of the changes in property rights that we not here, and for many of the same intermediate reasons (increasing land value, for example). In this particular case, however, we feel that a strong argument can be made that economic growth in itself accounts for much of the change. The 1980 human population for the Galole Orma area under study was approximately 2,232, while the 1987 population was approximately 2,414, representing an increase of

only 8.2 percent over seven years. Population growth was greater than this, however, and resulted in net emigration to nearby large towns. For our purposes, the livestock population is actually the more significant variable, and this population actually declined over the period (by approximately 24 percent) because of the severe drought of the mid-1980s.

3. By institutions we mean here "the rules of the game in a society or, more formally, . . . the humanly devised constraints that shape human interaction" (North 1990, 2).

4. Typically, economists and political scientists consider institutional change to be a two-stage process, for they assume, usually, implicitly, that people will automatically want those institutions which ensure the greatest economic return (see, for example, Gilligan, Marshall, and Weingast 1989). We modify the approach to allow alternative distributional preferences, in order to be more consistent with empirical reality. By so doing we greatly broaden the potential range of analysis to which this approach may be applied.

5. The new institutional economic as practiced by economic historians should be of particular interest to anthropologists. See the 1989 symposium issue of the *Journal of Institutional and Theoretical Economics* (Furubotn and Richter 1989); Eggertsson (1990); Higgs (1987, 1989); Libecap (1989); and North (1981, 1990). Among the new institutionalists, the economic historians are the most akin to anthropologists: they focus for example, on the processes of institutional change and development, and many are sensitive to the importance of ideology and the political process.

6. For further discussion of the similarities and differences between the neo-Marxists' positions and positions similar to ours, see Bates (1983, 134–47); Levi (1988, 185–204); North (1986); Przeworski (1985); and Roemer (1982).

7. There are of course exceptions, the most obvious being Jon Elster (see Elster 1985).

8. Our position here is extremely close to that of Skocpol, who puts it as follows:
> Marxists may be right to argue that classes and class tensions are always present in industrial societies but the political expression of class interests and conflicts is never automatic or economically determined. It depends on the capacities classes have for achieving consciousness, organization, and representation. Directly or indirectly, the structures and activities of states profoundly condition such class capacities. Thus, the classical wisdom of Marxian political sociology must be turned, if not on its head, then certainly on its side. (1985, 25)

9. For an especially clear discussion of transaction costs, see Goldberg (1989, ch. 1.3).

10. The question of the economic desirability of various property rights is complex in this instance. Property rights that distribute rewards relatively equitably may in fact lead to higher output than those that do not, for the greater legitimacy afforded by a more equitable distribution may reduce "cheating"

sufficiently that the overall performance is better. In other words, the savings in transaction costs (from reduced negotiating, monitoring, and enforcing) exceed the losses in underused potential.

11. However, a growing body of literature suggests that people take fairness into account even in markets (see, for example, Kahneman, Knetsch, and Thaler 1986).

12. Ironically, many of the boreholes eventually fell into disrepair, themselves the victims of a tragedy of the commons.

13. This does not mean that enforcement must be unanimous or that all members of society must be equally involved. For example, there may be differences related to age, gender, wealth, economic strategy, and political status. Nevertheless, it is a characteristic of decentralized enforcement that the enforcing group be quite broadly distributed throughout society.

14. In no way are we suggesting that until recently pastoral societies were undifferentiated. We are arguing, however, that such differentiation has increased in the economic realm and that as a result there is less agreement regarding property rights.

15. This study is based on research with the Galole population of the Orma. The Orma are divided into three groups, from north to south: the Hirman, the Galole, and the Chaffa. For simplicity, we hereafter refer to the population in question merely as the "Orma."

16. The bandits should not be confused with the political movement of the same name in the late 1960s.

References

Axelrod, Robert. 1984. *The evolution of cooperation.* New York: Basic Books.

Bailey, F. G. 1965. Decisions by consensus in councils and committees with special reference to village and local government in India. In *Political systems and distribution of power,* edited by Max Gluckman and Fred Eggan. New York: Frederick A. Praeger, 1–20.

Barzel, Yoram. 1989. *The economic analysis of property rights.* New York: Cambridge University Press.

Bates, Robert. 1981. *Markets and states in tropical Africa.* Berkeley: University of California Press.

———. 1983. *Essays on the political economy of rural Africa.* New York: Cambridge University Press.

———. 1989. *Beyond the miracle of the market: The political economy of agricultural development in Kenya.* New York: Cambridge University Press.

Behnke, Roy. 1985. Open-range management and property rights in pastoral Africa: A case of spontaneous range enclosure in South Darfur, Sudan. Pastoral Development Network Paper no. 20f. London: Overseas Development Institute.

Binger, Brian, and Elizabeth Hoffman. 1989. Institutional persistence and change: The question of efficiency. *Journal of Institutional and Theoretical Economics* 145:67–84.

Cheung, Steven N. S. 1973. The fable of the bees: An economic investigation. *Journal of Law and Economics* 16:11–34.

Demsetz, Harold. 1967. Toward a theory of property rights. *American Economic Review* 57:347–59.

Dennen, R. Taylor. 1976. Cattlemen's associations and property rights in land in the American West. *Explorations in Economic History* 13:423–36.

Eggertsson, Thráinn. 1990. *Economic behavior and institutions*. New York: Cambridge University Press.

Ellickson, Robert. 1991. *Order without law: How neighbors settle disputes*. Cambridge: Harvard University Press.

Elster, Jon. 1985. *Making sense of Marx*. New York: Cambridge University Press.

Ensminger, Jean. 1990. Co-opting the elders: The political economy of state incorporation in Africa. *American Anthropologist* 92:662–75.

———. 1991. Structural transformation and its consequences for Orma women pastoralists. In *Structural adjustment and African women farmers*, edited by Christina Gladwin. Gainesville: University of Florida Press, 281–300.

———. 1992. *The making of a market: The institutional transformation of an African society*. New York: Cambridge University Press.

Evans, Peter, Dietrich Rueschemeyer, and Theda Skocpol, eds. 1985. *Bringing the state back in*. New York: Cambridge University Press

Furubotn, E. G., and R. Richter, eds. 1989. Symposium issue. *Journal of Institutional and Theoretical Economics* 145:1–245.

Gilligan, Thomas, William Marshall, and Barry Weingast. 1989. Regulation and the theory of legislative choice: The Interstate Commerce Act of 1887. *Journal of Law and Economics* 32:35–51.

Goldberg, Victor. 1981. Bridges over contested terrain: Exploring radical accounts of the employment relation. In *Management under differing value systems*, edited by Gunter Dlugos and Klaus Weiermair. Berlin: Walter de Gruyter, 375–403.

———. 1989. *Readings in the economics of contract law*. New York: Cambridge University Press.

Gulliver, P. H. 1972. *Family herds*. London: Routledge, Kegan Paul.

Hardin, Garrett. 1968. The tragedy of the commons. *Science* 162:1243–48.

Hardin, Garrett, and John Baden, eds. 1977. *Managing the commons*. San Francisco: W. H. Freeman.

Hechter, Michael. 1987. *Principles of group solidarity*. Berkeley: University of California Press.

Helland, Joan. 1980. *Five essays on the study of pastoralists and the development of pastoralism*. Sosialantropologisk Institutt, Univeritetet I Bergen, occasional paper no. 20. Bergen: Sosialantropologisk Institutt, Univeritetet I Bergen.

Higgs, Robert. 1987. *Crisis and leviathan.* New York: Oxford University Press.
————. 1989. Organization, ideology and the free rider problem: Comment. *Journal of Institutional and Theoretical Economics* 145:232–37.
Hinich, Melvin, and Michael Munger. 1992. A spatial theory of ideology. *Journal of Politics* 4 (1): 5–30.
————. N.d. *Ideology and a general theory of politics.* Ann Arbor: University of Michigan Press. Forthcoming.
Hitchcock, Robin. 1985. Water, land and livestock: The evolution of tenure and administration patterns in the grazing areas of Botswana. In *The evolution of modern Botswana,* edited by Louis Picard. London: Rex Collins, 84–121.
Hogg, Richard. 1990. The politics of changing property rights among Isiolo Boran pastoralists in northern Kenya. In *Property, poverty and change: Changing rights in property and problems of pastoral development,* edited by P. T. W. Baxter with Richard Hogg. Manchester: Department of Social Anthropology, University of Manchester, 20–31.
Johnson, Ronald, and Gary Libecap. 1982. Contracting problems and regulation: The case of the fishery. *American Economic Review* 72:1005–22.
Kahneman, Daniel, Jack Knetsch, and Richard Thaler. 1986. Perceptions of unfairness: Constraints on wealth seeking. *American Economic Review* 76:728–41.
Lewis, I. M. 1961. *A pastoral democracy.* London: Oxford University Press.
Levi, Margaret. 1988. *Of rule and revenue.* Berkeley: University of California Press.
Libecap, Gary. 1989. *Contracting for property rights.* New York: Cambridge University Press.
Lipton, Michael. 1977. *Why poor people stay poor: A study of urban bias in world development.* London: Maurice Temple Smith.
Lobo, Jeronimo. 1984. *The itinerario of Jeronimo Lobo,* edited by M. G. Da Costa, trans. Donald M. Lockhart. London: The Hakluyt Society.
McCay, Bonnie, and James Acheson, eds. 1987. *The question of the commons: The culture and ecology of communal resources.* Tucson: University of Arizona Press.
Netting, Robert. 1982. Territory, property and tenure. In *Behavioral and social science research: A national resource,* edited by R. M. Adams, N. J. Smelser, and D. J. Treiman. Washington, DC: National Academy Press, 446–501.
New, Charles. 1873. *Life, wanderings, and labours in eastern Africa.* London: Hodder and Stoughton.
North, Douglass C. 1977. Non-market forms of economic organization: The challenge of Karl Polanyi. *Journal of European Economic History* 6:703–16.
————. 1981. *Structure and change in economic history.* New York: Norton.
————. 1986. Is it worth making sense of Marx? *Inquiry* 29:57–63.
————. 1990. *Institutions, institutional change and economic performance.* Cambridge: Cambridge University Press.

North, Douglass C., and Robert Paul Thomas. 1973. *The rise of the western world: A new economic history.* New York: Cambridge University Press.

Ostrom, Elinor. 1990. *Governing the commons: The evolution of institutions for collective action.* New York: Cambridge University Press.

Peters, Pauline. 1984. Struggles over water, struggles over meaning: Cattle, water and the state in Botswana. *Africa* 54:29–49.

———. 1987. Embedded systems and rooted models: The grazing land of Botswana and the "commons" debate. In *The question of the commons: The culture and ecology of communal resources,* edited by Bonnie McCay and James Acheson. Phoenix: University of Arizona Press, 171–94.

Przeworski, Adam. 1985. Marxism and rational choice. *Politics and Society* 14:379–409.

Riker, William. 1980. Implications from the disequilibrium of majority rule for the study of institutions. *American Political Science Review* 74:432–46.

———. 1986. *The art of political manipulation.* New Haven: Yale University Press.

Roemer, John. 1982. *A general theory of exploitation and class.* Cambridge: Harvard University Press.

Schofield, Norman. 1986. Anarchy, altruism and cooperation: A review. *Social Choice and Welfare* 2:207–19.

Siegenthaler, Hansjor. 1989. Organization, ideology and the free rider problem. *Journal of Institutional and Theoretical Economics* 145:215–31.

Skocpol, Theda. 1985. Bringing the state back in: Strategies of analysis in current research. In *Bringing the state back in,* edited by Peter Evans, Dietrich Rueschemeyer, and Theda Skocpol. New York: Cambridge University Press, 3–37.

Taylor, Michael. 1982. *Community, anarchy and liberty.* New York: Cambridge University Press.

———. 1987. *The possibility of cooperation.* New York: Cambridge University Press.

Williamson, Oliver. 1985. *The economic institutions of capitalism: Firms, markets, relational contracting.* New York: Free Press.

World Bank. 1989. *World development report 1989.* New York: Oxford University Press.

7

Analyzing Institutional Successes and Failures: A Millennium of Common Mountain Pastures in Iceland

Thráinn Eggertsson*

Introduction

Throughout their history, the island economies of the North Atlantic have relied to a large extent on common property resources both in agriculture and in the fisheries. It is well established that the sharing of resources need not always lead to a full-scale dissipation of wealth, the *tragedy of the commons*, when certain conditions are met.[1] However, it is also well known that communities often fail to establish institutions for restricting entry to the commons, and, even when they

* Reprinted with permission from *International Review of Law and Economics*, vol. 12, no. 4, (December 1992) 423–37. I thank my research assistant, Thorarinn Petursson, for valuable help. I am also thankful of various Icelandic scholars for sharing their thoughts and research findings with me. The paper was originally presented in Copenhagen at the 1991 meeting of the European Association of Law and Economics. I have received valuable comments from David Haddock, Arthur Denzau, and two anonymous referees. The paper has also benefited from comments by workshop participants at the University of Iceland, the Copenhagen School of Business, Washington University, University of Illinois at Urbana-Champaign, and Indiana University at Bloomington.

exist, these institutions are often fragile structures, vulnerable to pressures from population growth, technological change, and shifts in political power and processes.[2] Therefore, it is of considerable interest to examine the evolution of property rights to natural resources in the North Atlantic communities, such as Iceland, Greenland, and the Faroes, and investigate whether institutions did emerge in these societies that effectively regulated entry and prevented the dissipation of their natural resources. The present study is concerned with the law and economics of Icelandic agriculture, specifically with the institutions that for more than a thousand years have regulated the use of the country's extensive common mountain pastures.

Icelandic agriculture dates back to the rapid settlement of the country in the 9th century A.D.[3] In their ships the settlers brought with them cattle, sheep, horses, goats, pigs, geese, chickens, and dogs and found that the local environment invited the raising of livestock rather than the cultivation of fields. The conditions for grazing were ideal, and, as there were no wild mammals, except the fox, the herds could graze unattended in mountain pastures during the summer months.[4] In Iceland the farmland and home pastures are primarily in locations all around the coast. Rising above the farmland are the mountain pastures, while a third of the country's 103,000 square kilometers is wilderness with no vegetation (Thoroddsen 1919, 1–30). The mountain pastures are sometimes continuous green areas but often include cliffs, rocks, sands, and wasteland interspersed with vegetation, and, therefore, the grazing animals often must roam far and wide (Thoroddsen 1919, 175–213).

The early settlers appear to have claimed land as far as the wilderness of glaciers, sands, and lava in the interior and initially appropriated the mountain pastures that in Icelandic are called *afréttir* (singular *afréttur*). In fact, some mountain pastures always have remained exclusive private property, but generally the ownership of the afréttir evolved into communal property. No documentation, however, exists that throws light on how the pastures were divided among the different communities (Thoroddsen 1919, 184).

In spite of considerable scholarly interest in the question of the commons, the institutional arrangements of the *afréttir* in Iceland have not been studied by economists, as far as we know. It is almost trite to argue that reliance on common property arrangements may end in a tragedy, and Icelandic society certainly had its share of tragedies. Long-term economic decline, probably beginning in the 13th century, hit bottom in the 18th century, when the Icelanders came close to extinction.[5] Furthermore, at the beginning of the twentieth century the country's green areas are conservatively estimated to be one-half of their size at the time of the settlement in the 9th century and the annual production of vegetation only one-third of the 9th century level (Fridriksson 1986, 32–33). Historians have blamed centuries of economic decline on foreign rule, adverse external trade relations, volcanic eruptions, pests and plagues, and cooling climate, but the role of the system of property rights in agriculture has received little attention.[6]

In this paper we limit our attention to the structure and consequences of property rights in the communal mountain pastures. We are concerned with the following questions:

- Why were the afréttir used communally and not divided into exclusive plots for each user?
- Was the environment of the Icelandic farm districts likely to encourage collective action, and how were the afréttir regulated?
- Are the rules governing afréttir an example of a tragic solution to the commons problem rather a first best or second best solution?

We proceed in our examination by first briefly introducing certain theoretical concepts before turning to each of the questions above. The theoretical analysis draws on recent work by others (Ostrom 1990; Field 1986 and 1989; Roberts 1993). The empirical part is based on various published documents, such as the old law codes, records of deeds and judgments, regulations from various periods, a computer search of the Icelandic Sagas, studies by historians and by experts on agriculture, climate and vegetation, and, finally, personal interviews in Iceland with agriculturalists, natural scientists, and historians.

We find a) that joint utilization of the mountain pastures is economically rational, when allowance is made for transaction costs (costs of exclusion and internal governance), b) that the social and economic environment of Icelandic farm districts was suitable for collective action, and there is evidence, extending back through the entire history of the country, of elaborate rules for preserving the jointly used afréttir, c) that open access problems in the common mountain pastures are not an important explanation of centuries of economic decline in Iceland.

A Note on Theory

The economics of property rights and, generally, the economics of institutions involve several levels of analysis. A useful initial approach, that I have referred to as the *naive model*, ignores the supply side and only considers the demand for property rights (Eggertsson 1990, 249–77). The naive approach suggests that institutions which restrict access to a common property resource tend to emerge when there are net aggregate gains to the community from internalizing the external effects that are associated with open access (Demsetz 1967). The theory predicts that, given measurement and enforcement costs (transaction costs), an institutional structure will emerge that maximizes the value of the resource. The theory also suggests that overuse and dissipation of a valuable resource will occur when the costs of measurement and enforcement exceed the potential gains from restricting access.

A complete model of institutions requires that we add a supply side to the naive model and, thereby, introduce issues concerning the provision of property rights. Property rights are the output of political processes (and also of subtle social processes that are not well understood) and depend not only on the distribution of power and on the institutions for collective action in the community of users but, in many instances, also on the interests, choice set, and institutions of an external authority. For instance, it has been suggested that property rights designed by external authorities, remote from the actual and potential users, are less likely to be efficient in the neoclassical sense than rules set by the users themselves (Ostrom 1990; Libecap 1989).[7]

In sum, the full model of institutions is based on three constructs:

- the preferences of the relevant individuals,
- their opportunities, and
- the system (and processes) of collective action.

Finally, it should be emphasized that the redistribution of wealth is an important consideration in a full theory of institutional change: new property rights always alter the distribution of wealth, and high transaction costs often render it impractical for those who gain from new institutions to compensate the losers. In many groups unanimity (or near unanimity) is required to alter basic property rights, and, when transaction costs are high, only new institutions that make (almost) no one worse off will be considered (Roberts 1993).

The Economic Logic of Afréttir

The mountain pastures in Iceland, the afréttir, are a case of joint utilization of a natural resource. Why is it that a natural resource is sometimes divided among individual owners and users and sometimes shared by two or more independent economic units? If we ignore for the moment the question of both political processes and redistribution, the structure of ownership is best explained with three types of production functions: the production (or transformation) function of conventional price theory, the exclusion function, and the internal governance function.

Let us consider cost minimization in terms of the three production functions and briefly illustrate the relevant relationships with reference to a formal model that is due to Field (1986). The cost of exclusion simply refers to the cost of excluding outsiders from the resource (for instance, the cost of fencing and monitoring borders), and the return on exclusion for the insiders takes the form of greater output per unit of input in regular production. Internal governance cost is the cost of preventing free-riding by the insiders who are prone to overuse the resource and dissipate the rent from it. The return on internal governance is the greater net output that results when overexploitation is prevented.

In other words, to minimize the cost of producing any level of output from the natural resource involves a three-fold allocation problem: the allocation of the variable input(s) a) to regular production, b) to exclusion, and c) to internal governance. As always, costs are minimized when the marginal return on the variable input is equal in all uses.

Let us assume that the identical N members (individuals or firms) of a community of potential users of a natural resource, that measures R physical units, agree to divide R into whatever number, m, of equal plots (commons) that will minimize aggregate costs and maximize the community's net wealth. Then the number of insiders on each plot, n = N/m, can be expressed as a function of governance cost, G; exclusion cost, E; and a vector representing all other variables, including conventional production costs, A. In equation (1), a change in E or G represents a parametric shift in the exclusion and governance cost curves.[8]

$$n = F(E, G, A) \tag{1}$$

$$\text{and} \quad \delta n/\delta E > 0, \quad \delta n/\delta G < 0$$

First, note that n, the degree of exclusivity, depends in part on the regular production function of neoclassical economics. In fact, if there are no exclusion and internal governance costs, then n (the number of firms jointly using each subdivision of R) and m (the number of commons) is determined solely by the economies of scale in production.[9] Let us assume here that we have constant returns to scale.

If we also assume that the cost of exclusion is a function of the total length of the borders of R, then it is clear that the total exclusion cost reaches the maximum level when R is divided into N units with one firm in each, and is at the minimum level when there is only one firm and all N individuals join together. Let us now consider the implications of shifts in the exclusion function. Other things equal, an upward shift in the cost of exclusion lowers the marginal return on exclusion activities below the marginal returns on the variable input in production and internal governance. In the Field (1986) model, a new equilibrium is established by shortening the borders, which implies that now R is divided into larger commons and n is larger than before. Similarly, an innovation that lowers the costs of exclusion (such as low-cost electric fences) moves the solution in the direction of exclusive individual ownership.

Finally, consider the question of internal governance and assume that the cost of preventing any given loss of output from excessive utilization is a direct function of n, the number of insiders. Again, an upward shift in cost of internal governance lowers the marginal return on the variable input allocated to monitoring excessive use by the insiders, and equality of marginal returns is established by reducing n, the number of insiders that use each plot.

We are now ready to consider the logic of ownership in the afréttir in terms of the costs of exclusion, internal governance, and production. The discussion is restricted to the grazing of sheep in the mountain pastures, which has been their most important use. For several reasons exclusion costs for individual plots in the afréttir would be high.

First, individual plots would have to be large. The vegetation is often scattered, and the herds of each farmer require a relatively large area to feed on during the summer. Furthermore, as the subarctic vegetation of the highlands is sensitive to climatic changes, grazing conditions vary from one year to another which requires mobile grazing. Second, the cost of monitoring the area would be high. As the flocks did not require protection against wild animals, the monitoring of borders could not be an inexpensive byproduct of shepherding. Third, in historical Iceland, the cost of fencing in the highlands was prohibitive because of the length of the borders, the rugged terrain, and the lack of material for fencing.[10] However, nature itself often formed natural enclosures with rivers, lakes, wasteland, mountains and glaciers, but in most cases such natural fences enclosed vast areas, sometimes the highland pastures of several farm districts.[11] Therefore, we conclude that the high exclusion cost in the afréttir indicates that n, the number of insiders in each afréttur, should be relatively large, other things equal. However, it should be noted that high exclusion costs in themselves do not rule out that a large afréttur with natural enclosure be privately owned by a rich farmer, the church or even the crown, and the grazing rights sold to a number of independent farmers.

The internal governance of an afréttur involves efforts to protect the grazing capacity of the resource by regulating the time of usage and the number of sheep, and by controlling other uses that would reduce the output of vegetation. In the case of joint usage, there is also the internal governance problems of protecting the property right of each farmer in his variable input, the sheep, as the animals mingle in the pastures. In the following section that deals with the regulation of the afréttir we argue that, provided the farm districts were capable of collective action, the technical problem of internal governance in the afréttir was relatively uncomplicated and the corresponding costs low, which also suggests a large n and a large number of commoners.

Consider now the production costs of using the afréttir. The driving of the sheep into the mountains in summer and back again in the fall, and especially the search for the animals in the vast pastures, are activities that involve positive economies of scale; aggregate costs are lower when the farmers of a district join in these activities rather than when they are performed in isolation. Further, the joint movement of the flocks of a whole district to and from the afréttir would minimize trampling and trespassing on private farmland.

Finally, we note that the relatively low return on fencing in Icelandic agriculture gave rise to various spillover problems that could be handled at a relatively low cost by collective action. For instance, unless some measures were taken, external costs would be imposed on farmers whose unfenced farmland bordered on an afréttur, as the animals could easily stray over onto their land. Costly spillover effects could also be expected if some farmers in a district did not drive their sheep into the afréttir in the summer but let their flocks graze on their unfenced home pastures during the summer, as the sheep might invade the fields of their neighbors.

In sum, the theory suggests that the joint use of the mountain pastures (rather than individual plots) is consistent with the minimization of costs, particularly if the farm communities can overcome the problems of collective action and establish effective institutions for internal governance and the control of spillover effects. We now proceed to examine briefly the basic pattern of utilization of the afréttir and then, in the following section, turn to a more detailed examination of the institutions that regulated their use.

The Icelandic Sagas, that deal with events in the 9th to the 11th centuries but were written one to three hundred years after the events they describe, are the earliest sources of information about the organization of sheep raising in Iceland. Sheep raising is also mentioned in passing in the Sturlunga Sagas, which contain contemporary accounts of the civil war in the 13th century, and in the Bishop Sagas, but the most important source are the extensive law codes of the Icelandic Commonwealth (930–1262 A.D.) preserved in two main manuscripts called *Grágás* (which translates "Gray Goose").[12]

When they lost their independence in the 13th century to Norway (and later to Denmark), the Icelanders received new laws in 1281.[13] The new law code of 1281 was amended in 1294, 1305, and 1314 and is referred to as *Jónsbók*. *Jónsbók* only made modest changes in the laws of *Grágás* relating to the afréttir and served, with some amendments, as the legal framework in this area into the 20th century.[14] The laws of *Jónsbók* regarding the afréttir were finally all preempted with special legislation, No. 42/1969.[15]

Grágás, the ancient law code of the Commonwealth, refers to the afréttir as property jointly owned by two or more individuals and proceeds to enumerate regulations that (in our terminology) relate to exclusion, internal governance, and spillover effects (Finsen 1974, 1:113–22). In the Icelandic Sagas fleeting references to the organization of sheep farming confirm that already in the first centuries of Icelandic history the alternative use of home pastures in the winter and mountain pastures in the summer and the celebrated search of the mountains for the animals in the fall had become an essential part of the country's farming practices.[16]

However, accounts in the Icelandic Sagas offer little detail of the exact structure of property rights in the afréttir. Sources from the 13th century onward suggest that, over time, many of the afréttir (but not all) had become communal property of or were managed by one or more local farm communities, called *hreppar* (singular *hreppur*), but no documentation exists that describes the transfer of rights from private individuals to the hreppar (Thoroddsen 1919, 184–5).[17]

The hreppur is an ancient organization of self-government for the primary rural community. The origins of hreppar are not known, but they already existed in 1096, when the tithe was introduced in Iceland. *Grágás* requires that all communities have their hreppur, and each hreppur must be a community of at least 20 adjacent farmers in good standing (Björnsson 1972, 11–32).[18] In *Grágás*, and later in *Jónsbók* of 1281, hreppar are assigned the task of collecting the tithe and maintaining the poor, but the law does not mention that the hreppar oversee the afréttir. However, this is probably an omission because the 1294 and 1305 amendments of *Jónsbók* give the hreppar an active role in regulating the afréttir system, and later court documents confirm that they exercised this authority (Björnsson 1972, 66; Sigurdsson et al. 1857–1952).

In recent centuries district authorities have published detailed rules governing afréttir in their area. For instance, in 1792 a lengthy regulation was issued for the afréttir in a county of western Iceland, Borgarfjardarsýsla.[19] The *Local Government Legislation* of 1872 required that regulations for afréttir be formally drawn up and published by all districts. These regulations, embodying ancient customs, are found in the *Official Gazette* of the years following.[20]

The evidence shows clearly that the Icelandic afréttir have been used jointly by independent economic units throughout the country's history, but the evidence also shows that the afréttir are not a case of open access; the use of the resource system has been regulated by small communities of farmers. We now turn to an examination of the nature of these regulations.[21]

The Regulation of Afréttir

The provision and enforcement of rules for preserving a jointly used resource, such as the afréttir, have the characteristics of a public good, although the resource itself is not a public good.[22] Therefore an explanation of the structure of the property rights in common resources that emerges in alternative situations must be based on a comprehensive theory of collective action that so far is not available. In a major research project, Ostrom (1990) has examined common-pool resource problems in countries throughout the world.[23] She finds that the users of common-pool resources frequently have been successful in overcoming the temptation to free-ride and act opportunistically and have organized themselves to solve the commons problem, but in other instances cooperation has failed and resources have been wasted on a large scale. Ostrom seeks to account for the factors that contribute to a successful resolution of the common-pool problem, and, at the risk of simplifying her complex theoretical framework, it can be said that she considers factors that affect both the demand for institutions and their supply and associates the emergence of effective institutions with positive net benefits for the individuals involved.

Ostrom's major insights relate to the determinants of the supply side. Several factors are seen to lower the cost of collective action for small communities that rely on common-pool resources. They include:

1. a clearly defined and stable set of actual and potential users, and a high visibility of users, implying low monitoring costs;
2. low discount rates used by potential appropriators, implying continuity, limited alternative opportunities, and a high return on investment in reputation, implying low gains from cheating; and
3. comparable interests in the resources by the relevant individuals or homogeneity. (Ostrom 1990)[24]

In the case of afréttir most of the factors that contribute to a satisfactory resolution of the commons problem seem to be present. Both the resource and the potential group of users are clearly defined. The afréttir were of critical importance for the farm community which was extremely stable, as was the technology used until the 19th century. Alternative opportunities were few, the farming families had to live with each other for generations, the afréttir had no highly valuable use other than as meadows for grazing, and all the farmers were involved in similar activities. Finally, potential users were compulsory members of a local governance institution, the hreppur, that was fairly autonomous and a flexible instrument for supplying and enforcing rules.

It would be surprising, therefore, to find that the afréttir had been unregulated commons with open access. In fact, we find that they have always been regulated by a detailed body of rules, and cooperation among the users has supplied the collective goods of exclusion, internal governance, and internalization of spillover effects. Let us consider each of these collective goods in turn.

Exclusion

The need to restrict entry to the afréttir by outsiders was recognized already in the law codes of the Commonwealth (930–1262), and the laws concerning the afréttir were replicated with relatively minor changes in *Jónsbók* of 1281 and remained partly in effect into the 19th and 20th centuries. *Grágás* proclaims the exclusive rights of a group of individuals to an afréttur and states that outsiders require the permission of all the owners of an afréttur before they can use it for grazing. Violations were punishable with a fine (Finsen 1974, 1:113–115).[25] An individual who wanted to trade his grazing rights in an afréttur to an outsider had to call for an evaluation of aggregate grazing capacity of the pastures and the establishment of individual shares. He was then free to use the share (or the stint) himself or sell it in part or wholly to outsiders.

As both the afréttir and the home pastures generally were not fenced, the exclusive rights of farmers with land bordering on an afréttur had to be protected from intrusions by the unsupervised grazing herds of the mountain pastures. The law books show a great concern for this issue. They require that the flocks be driven into the middle of the afréttur (and not left near the borders).[26] Further-more, the law enumerates various legitimate responses that are open to owners of adjacent land, when flocks of animals from an afréttur invade their property. Also, those who own farmland next to an afréttur have the right to graze their flocks in the afréttur all year long (except for two weeks in the summer), presumably as a form of compensation for trespassing.

Sometimes the afréttir of different communities merge and have no natural boundaries. Various customary rules have evolved to cope with problems that arise in such situations—for instance, the problem of handling wayward animals from neighboring afréttir when the sheep are rounded up in the fall.[27] Note also that the virtual absence of fencing made it costly for a farmer to protect his fields and home pastures from the wandering sheep of his neighbors, particularly in the summer. The law demanded, therefore, from Grágás onward, that all farmers drive their sheep into the afréttir for the summer or face penalties. Only in exceptional cases, and with the permission of the local authorities, could a farmer be exempted from this rule.

Internal Governance

The internal governance of the afréttir involves two important issues: the preservation of the grazing capacity of the afréttir from overuse by the insiders, and the protection of exclusive individual property rights to the sheep when flocks belonging to a substantial number of different owners mingle unattended in the mountain pastures. We discuss overgrazing in some detail in the last section of the paper, but at this point we note that the law has been conscious of the problem of overgrazing since Grágás.

According to Grágás and later Jónsbók, any insider in an afréttur could call for an independent evaluation of the grazing capacity of the pasture. The criterion for optimal usage of an afréttur appears to predate, with modest success, the marginal revolution in economics: the arbitrators were instructed to find the maximum number of sheep that could use the pastures without affecting the average weight of the flock—"let them find that number, which in their judgment does not give fatter sheep if reduced but also fills the afréttur," says Grágás (Finsen 1974, 1(2): 115).[28] Once the maximum number of animals had been determined, each user of the afréttur was given a quota on the basis of the value of his farm. A farmer who exceeded his quota paid for each additional sheep a penalty to his fellow users that was twice the rent to an outsider for using the pasture, according to Jónsbók.

The basic method for enforcing the property rights of the individual farmers in their sheep, when the flocks were rounded up in the fall, relied on marks on their ears.[29] Each owner of sheep was required to mark all the members of his flock in the same way before it was sent to the afréttur. Each ear is given a separate mark, which can give rise to a large number of combinations, and the authorities kept careful records of the marks. Some marks were more special than others; the Crown ear-marked its sheep by cutting off both ears, a dangerous mark in the hands of the unscrupulous, as the possessor of such a mark could steal sheep and easily remark the animals without leaving traces of their former marks (Thoroddsen 1919, 330–33).

Economies of Scale

The use of vast, unfenced mountain pastures suggests important economies of scale in driving the animals up to the mountains in early summer and in searching the afréttir and driving the flocks down again in the fall, but to realize these gains collective action is required. Furthermore, as the sheep often have to be driven through private farmland on the way to and from the afréttir, trespassing and trampling is minimized if all users of each afréttur join forces.

Grágás and *Jónsbók* required the farmers to drive their flocks to the afréttir in a given week in June and round them up and drive them back before a specific week in September.[30] In 1281, when the law codes of *Jónsbók* were confirmed by the Assembly (Althing), demands were made that each district be allowed to set its own dates on the basis of local circumstances. These demands were met in the Amendments of 1294 and the right to set the dates given to the overseers of the hreppar (Thoroddsen 1919, 205–06).

Rounding up the sheep, often in formidable mountain terrain of a vast scale, and driving them back to the farm district can be major task. In large and rugged afréttir the first search might take a week or ten days, and there were usually at least two sequential search expeditions.[31] The sheep were driven to a fixed place in each district, a public fold, called *rétt*, and distributed to their owners according to the marks of the ears.

Rounding up the sheep from the afréttir and distributing them to their owners constitute a highly structured activity based on ancient custom, overseen by the management of hreppar and by specially appointed individuals. In the more recent centuries the duties of each sheep-owner were spelled out in a special document, the *mountain bill*, that was circulated in the district (Björnsson 1972, 184–8; Thoroddsen 1919, 197–207). Each individual who owned some minimum number of sheep was required to provide one or more persons with supplies, and/or there was a toll to be paid.[32] The arrangements have been compared with military conscription: each search group was assigned a leader, in the south of the country called *fjallkóngur* (mountain king), who was given authority comparable to the authority of a military officer (Thoroddsen 1919, 201). Early judgments show that some farmers were not satisfied with their share in the costs of the roundups or even tried to free-ride, but they could be taken to court and fined.

The Afréttir: A Tragedy?

The history of agriculture in Iceland is a sad story of long-term economic decline extending from the 13th century (or earlier) and into the 19th century (Thoroddsen 1919, 1921). The decline is correlated with a drastic reduction in the country's vegetation which, over time, shrank both in terms of area and productivity. A leading Icelandic botanist maintains "that it is very likely that the primary production of Icelandic vegetation during the 15th century had dropped to half of the amount it was around the time of the settlement" (Fridriksson 1986, 33).[33]

A drastic reduction in plant production was likely to affect the size of the population, which relied heavily on animal products that in turn were directly related to the output of the natural grassland. Fridriksson (1972) has made a bold attempt to estimate the maximum population that the country's vegetation could support from the time of the settlement until the 19th century, when new technology and new industries rescued the population from the Malthusian bind. Fridriksson concludes that at the time of the settlement the surface area of vegetation was sufficient to support about 70,000–80,000 individuals, but the carrying capacity of the land declined with time, and, at the beginning of the 18th century, the usable crop of the pasture and the hay crop could, in an average year, support only about 55,000 individuals.[34] These figures are roughly consistent with the estimated actual population.

There does not exist a direct enumeration of the Icelandic population at the time of the Commonwealth, but estimates based on a count of tax-paying farmers in 1095 and other information usually place it around 70,000–80,000. The first census was taken in 1703, and then the population numbered 50,358, but a small-pox epidemic in 1707–1709 left the country with only some 34,000 inhabitants (Baldursson 1975, 23). A study by Bishop Hannes Finnsson, published in 1796, that examines the country's annals for evidence of famines reports isolated years of hardship as early as in the middle of the 11th century, famines of rising severity in the 13th and 14th centuries, and further deterioration in the 17th century, culminating in the disasters of the 18th century when the population was nearly erased (Finnsson 1970).

To what extent is this history of decline caused by the practice of the commons, the sharing of the country's mountain pastures? In the paper's second part we argued that the joint utilization of the mountain pastures in Iceland, an arrangement operating for more than a thousand years, was rational economically if we allow for transaction costs. In the previous section we first considered the decision environment of the farmers in terms of categories suggested by Ostrom (1990) and concluded that the environment was favorable for collective action to emerge. Furthermore, a search of historical data showed that, already in the Age of the Commonwealth, the farming communities had developed conventions and governance structures that should have prevented large-scale dissipation of wealth in the afréttir. In sum, our study suggests that the afréttir were a relatively efficient resource system and did not represent a case of serious overcrowding and rent dissipation.

In addition to the rules that governed the commons, indirect evidence suggests that, at least in some districts, the limited capacity to feed the sheep in the winter may have eased pressures of excessive summer grazing in the mountain pastures. As late as the first part of the 20th century, the sheep were not primarily fed on hay in the winter but left to graze on the farmland, and the hay from the relatively small fields was used as a last resort, when winter grazing became impossible.[35] Only in the 20th century did new technology, that lowered the cost of cultivating the farmland and making hay, begin to relieve the oppressive constraint of winter grazing (Fridriksson 1972, 793–6).

Why then was there economic decline? We make the case that, once Iceland had been settled in the 10th century, erosion of the vegetation and economic deterioration was the only prospect facing the nation, given the natural environment of the country and the agricultural technology of the times.[36] Erosion of the sensitive vegetation in Iceland is directly related to deforestation, and deforestation was an unavoidable consequence of the only type of agriculture that was practicable in the country at the time. It is estimated that it took about 200–300 years of clearing, grazing, and charcoal-making to reduce drastically the country's extensive areas of scrub birch and willow and introduce the treeless modern landscape. In this northerly terrain the destruction of the woodlands released a relentless, long-term (and irreversible at the time) process of erosion of the soil that was accelerated by a cooling climate and frequent volcanic eruptions (Fridriksson 1987).

Notes

1. For instance, see Ostrom (1990).
2. For the problems of contracting for property rights in various environments, see Libecap (1989).
3. Medieval texts say that the settlement of the country was completed in 60 years from about 870 to 930 A.D. See Benediktsson (1974). For an account in English of the early history of Iceland, see Jóhannesson (1974).
4. See Thoroddsen (1919, 1921). Thoroddsen's volume is still the best available history of Icelandic agriculture.
5. The economic history of the country is reflected in the average height of the population: "From the age of the settlement down to the 16th century stature remained more or less constant, or about 172 cm. In the 18th century, it fell to 167 cm, and about the middle of the 20th century it rose again to 176.8 cm. In other words, in a period lasting 400 years at the outside, or in the course of 16 generations, the mean stature of the population first falls about 5 cm and then rises 10 cm again, a variation of 1 cm a generation on the average" (Steffensen

1958, 44).

6. The drop in temperatures "happened most frequently during the 13th and 14th centuries and during the so-called little ice age in the period between 1600 and 1900" (Fridriksson 1986, 32). "In these periods the average air temperature may have been 1.5 to 2°C lower than it is today in good years, which may have caused a 50% drop in primary production of the grassland compared with the yield as it had been in good years" (Fridriksson 1986, 35).

7. The rules governing afréttir in Iceland were not imposed by an external authority; they appear to be homespun although presumably reflecting foreign models.

8. Note that we present here only a brief and simplified version of the formal model found in Field (1986).

9. Note that it is assumed that N, the total number of firms (or individuals), is a constant.

10. For instance, native wood for fencing was not available. In early Iceland some sod and stone fences were erected but mostly to protect home fields. The law code Jónsbók of 1281 states that farmers who do not fence have no valid claims for compensation when their in-fields are invaded by their neighbors' livestock. It is interesting to note that farmers protested this clause in the Assembly (Althing) when Jónsbók was accepted as law and managed to get the clause abolished in 1294 (except they still had to enclose their storages of fodder). See Thoroddsen (1919, 99).

11. A dramatic example of a natural enclosure is the mountain range Breidamerkurfjall in southeastern Iceland. To get there the sheep had to be driven over snowcapped mountains as the afréttur is surrounded by glaciers (Thoroddsen 1919, 192).

12. For the definitive editions, see Finsen (1974). The main manuscripts of Grágás are called Konungsbók (Codex Regius) and Stadarhólsbók.

13. We omit to mention the law code Járnsída that served the Icelanders only from 1271 to 1281.

14. For the standard edition see Halldórsson (1970). It includes the amendments of 1294, 1305, and 1314. For instance, the Jónsbók laws of the afréttir were modified by the new Law of Local Government (Sveitarstjórnarlögin) of May 4, 1872.

15. Lög um afréttarmálefni, fjallskil o.fl. (Laws regarding afréttir and related matters) Nr. 42/1969.

16. The Icelandic Sagas also refer to the practice of driving the flocks from the mountains to a public fold where the sheep were distributed to their owners. For instance, see Svarfdaela saga (1987, 1801). For a computer search of the Sagas for references to sheep farming, I used a special program developed by Örnólfur Thórsson and associates at the University of Iceland.

17. Historians stress that initially the ownership rights of the hreppar over the afréttir were not clear. See Björnsson (1972, 30). Gudmundsson (1981, 69) argues

that initially the afréttir were owned jointly by the farmers of the local community and managed on their behalf by the overseers of the hreppar. In time this distinction became blurred, and eventually it became common for the hreppar to augment the size of the local afréttir by purchasing additional pastures, for instance, from the church that was a big landowner.

18. The legislative body of the Commonwealth could, in exceptional cases, allow fewer than 20 farmers to form a hreppur (Finsen 1974, 1:171). In the Census of 1703, the hreppar numbered about 163, and the country's population was 50,358. The average population of a hreppur was some 309 persons and about 80 percent of the hreppar had a population of 100 to 500 individuals. During the Commonwealth the number of hreppar is estimated at about 150 (Björnsson 1972, 93, 126).

19. See Stephensen and Sigurdsson (1853–1889, 6:16–27).

20. For instance, in the *Official Gazette*, Section B, there is in 1885 a regulation for the afréttir in the hreppar between the rivers Thjórsá and Hvítá in the county Árnessýsla. The regulation constitutes 96 paragraphs and covers 20 pages in the Gazette (pp. 93–113). These rules are remarkably similar to the laws of *Grágás* and *Jónsbók*, except that they are more elaborate and also cover new areas.

21. It should be noted that many afréttir have always been exclusively owned, for instance, by rich farmers or the church, but often rented to the farmers of the district who used the pastures communally. (Unfortunately, we have no records of the extent and evolution through time of private ownership.) It is not unreasonable to expect that an exchange between the owner and the users of the afréttur is vulnerable to holdups from either side. However, the relationship was apparently governed (at least in some cases) by enforceable long-term (implicit) contracts. For instance, in a legal case from 1584 two farmers in a district in northwestern Iceland sued other farmers of the region for not driving their sheep to the afréttur owned by the two farmers, who thereby lost their revenue from the *lamb toll*. The former users of the afréttur claimed in turn that the output of vegetation on the afréttur was unsatisfactory, and they had, therefore, decided to take their sheep elsewhere, to another privately owned mountain pasture where they duly had paid the lamb toll. The justice ruled against the users, as the law requires farmers to continue using their *customary* afréttur. The judgment also refers to a failure by the dissatisfied farmers to find the proper channel for their complaints and have the quality of the afréttur measured by a third party. See *Althingisbækur Íslands* (1912–1982, 2:50–52).

22. Pasture land, per se, is not a public good because the consumption possibilities by one individual depend on the benefits enjoyed by others. For individual users, however, the provision and the enforcement of rules for governing common pastures is a public good.

23. In her study of common-pool resources, CPRs, Ostrom (1990, 26) "focused entirely on small-scale CPRs, where the CPR is itself located within one country and the number of individuals affected varies from 50 to 15,000 persons who are heavily dependent on the CPR for economic returns."

24. The list is not exhaustive. See Ostrom (1990, ch. 6).

25. Surviving court documents show that the legal system enforced exclusive rights to the afréttir. For instance, a judgment rendered at Hjardarholt in 1592 concerns the complaint of three hreppar, which shared an afréttur, that farmers from other hreppar had invaded their mountain pastures. The judgment favored the plaintiffs. See *Althingisbækur Íslands* (1912–1982, 2:334). The rule that an outsider must get permission from all owners of an afréttur before he can use it was also enforced. For instance, see a ruling by Thórdur Gudmundsson, justice for southern and eastern Iceland, in a case from 1596 where the plaintiff was the church in Reykholt. In his judgment the justice quotes a paragraph from *Jónsbók* corresponding to the passage from *Grágás* that we mention above (*Althingisbækur Íslands* 1912–1982, 3:420–21).

26. This requirement is still present in the regulation for Borgarfjardarsýsla from 1792. See Stephensen and Sigurdsson (1853–1889, vol. 6). Note that the requirement could not be taken literally in the case of vast afréttir that spanned half the way across the country. See Thoroddsen (1919, 198–99).

27. For instance, in parts of the district Árnessýsla (Thoroddsen 1919, 191). A good example of these customs is found in the regulations for the afréttir of hreppar in Árnessýsla from 1895 that reflect ancient customs (*Stjórnartídindi* 1985, sec. B: 85–121).

28. My translation.

29. Ear marks are mentioned already in *Heidarvígssaga* that many consider the oldest of the Icelandic Sagas, probably written in the early 13th century (dealing with events of the 10th century). In the Saga, Styr, the main character, is enjoying a meal at the home of a neighbor and is served the head of sheep, a traditional Icelandic dish. "And, as they sit at the table, one of Styr's men takes the head in his hand and remarks how enormously fat the sheep is. Styr turns and looks at the head and says: "This is an astoundingly great head but do others see what I see, there are no marks on the ears?" (My translation.) See *Svarfdaela saga* (1987, 1334).

30. The law allowed the farmers to leave their animals behind in the afréttir for the winter, but in most cases that was not a practical consideration.

31. Descriptions of the customs and adventures of roundups in the afréttir in all districts of the country, in the late 19th and early 20th century, written by the farmers themselves are available in five volumes (Sigurjónsson 1948–1952).

32. Some local regulations from the 19th century show that the most difficult areas to search were to be given to those representing rich farmers, except where the search required scaling cliffs, which was assigned to the fittest (Thoroddsen 1919, 201).

33. Fridriksson (1972, 786–87) estimates that the annual rate of erosion of fertile land in the last 1000 years has been about 20 square kilometers a year, in total about half of the area of vegetation in the country. In addition, the average output of the remaining fertile land fell.

34. Fridriksson (1972, 792) makes clear that the tenuous relationship between fertile land and population "was subject to periodic distortion due to epidemics, affecting sometimes animals and sometimes men, and in both ways contributing to human depopulation."

35. Fridriksson (1972) estimates that in the early 18th century the country's total hay crop was equal to only 10 percent of the usable crop from the mountain and home pastures. In the 11th century the proportion was only 5 percent, according to Fridriksson (1972, 785), due to a larger output from the pastures and smaller hay fields.

36. McGovern et al. (1988, 228) refer to a transported continental agricultural system at the edge of the climatic tolerance limit. Our dire prediction does not allow for the possibility that economic decline could have been averted by a large-scale diversification into fishing (or perhaps other activities) in the Middle Ages.

References

Althingisbækur Íslands (Records of the Icelandic Althing). 1912-1982. 15 vols. Reykjavík: Sögufélagid.

Baldursson, Gudni. 1975. Population. In *Iceland 874–1974,* edited by Valdimar Kristinsson and Jóhannes Nordal. Central Bank of Iceland.

Benediktsson, Jakob. 1974. Landnám og upphaf allsherjarríkis (The settlement and the origins of the commonwealth). Vol. 1 of *Saga Íslands,* edited by Sigurdur Líndal. Reykjavík: Hid íslenska bókmenntafélag.

Björnsson, Lýdur. 1972. *Saga sveitarstjórnar á Íslandi* (The history of local government in Iceland). Vol. 1. Reykjavík: Almenna Bókafélagid.

Demsetz, Harold. 1967. Toward a theory of property rights. *American Economic Review: Papers and Proceedings* 57:347.

Eggertsson, Thráinn. 1990. *Economic behavior and institutions.* Cambridge: Cambridge University Press.

Field, Barry C. 1986. Induced changes in property rights institutions. Department of Agricultural and Resource Economics, University of Massachusetts, Amherst.

———. 1989. The evolution of property rights. *Kyklos* 42:319.

Finnsson, Hannes. [1796] 1970. *Mannfaekkun af Hallaerum* (Fall in population from famine). Reykjavík: Almenna bókafélagid.

Finsen, Vilhjálmur. [1852, 1879, 1883] 1974. *Grágás.* 3 vols. Reprint. Odense: Odense University Press.

Fridriksson, Sturla. 1972. Factors affecting productivity and stability of northern ecosystems. *Ecology* 53:785.

———. 1986. Factors affecting productivity and stability of northern ecosystems. In *Grazing research at northern latitudes,* edited by Ólafur Gudmundsson. NATO ASI Series A: Life Sciences, vol. 108. New York: Plenum Publishing.

————. 1987. *Thróun lífríkis Íslands og nytjar af Thví* (The evolution of the Icelandic ecosystem and its utilization). Vol. 1 of *Íslensk thjódmenning,* edited by Frosti Jóhannesson. Reykjavík: Thjódsaga.

Gudmundsson, Gunnar F. 1981. *Eignarhald á afréttum og almenningum. Sögulegt yfirlit* (Ownership of mountain pastures and commons. A historical survey). Reykjavík: Sagnfraedistofnun Háskóla Íslands.

Halldórsson, Ólafur. 1970. *Jónsbók.* Odense: Odense: University Press.

Jóhannesson, Jón. 1974. *A history of the Icelandic commonwealth.* Translated by Haraldur Bessason. Winnipeg: University of Manitoba Press.

Libecap, Gary D. 1989. *Contracting for property rights.* Cambridge: Cambridge University Press.

McGovern, Thomas H., G. F. Bigelow, T. Amorosi, and D. Russel. 1988. Northern islands, human error, and environmental degradation: A view of social and ecological change in the Medieval North Atlantic. *Human Ecology* 16:225.

Ostrom, Elinor. 1990. *Governing the commons: The evolution of institutions for collective action.* Cambridge: Cambridge University Press.

Roberts, Russell D. 1993. To price or not to price: User preferences in allocating common property resources. This volume.

Sigurdsson, Jón., et al., eds. 1857-1952. *Diplomatarium Islandicum: Íslenskt fornbréfasafn.* 16 vols. Copenhagen: S. L. Möller; Reykjavík: Félagsprentsmidja. [Editor's note: This series spans 95 years and has many different editors too numerous to list.]

Sigurjónsson, Bragi, ed. 1948–1952. *Göngur og réttir.* 5 vols. Akureyri: Nordri.

Steffensen, Jón. 1958. Stature as a criterion of the nutritional level of Viking Age Icelanders. In *Árbók hins íslenska fornleifafélags, fylgirit* (Yearbook of the Icelandic Archeological Society, Supplement) edited by Kristján Eldjárn. Reykjavík.

Stephensen, Oddgeir, and Jón Sigurdsson, eds. 1853–1889. *Lovsamling for Island* (The laws of Iceland). 21 vols. Copenhagen: Höst og Søn.

Stjórnartídindi (The Official Gazette of Icelandic Government). Various years. Sections A and B. Reykjavík: Government of Iceland.

Svarfdaela saga. 1987. In *Íslendinga sögur* (The Icelandic Sagas). Reykjavík: Svart á hvítu.

Thoroddsen, Thorvaldur. 1919, 1921. *Lýsing Íslands* (A portrait of Iceland). Vol. 3, *Landbúnadur á Íslandi* (Icelandic agriculture). Parts 1 and 2. Copenhagen: Hid íslenska bókmenntafélag.

8

Covenants With and Without A Sword:
Self-Governance is Possible

Elinor Ostrom, James Walker, and Roy Gardner*

> And Covenants, without the sword, are but words, and of no
> strength to secure a man at all. (Hobbes 1960, 109)

Contemporary political theories frequently presume that individuals cannot make credible *ex ante* commitments where substantial *ex post* temptations exist to break them, unless such commitments are enforced by an external agent. Hobbes justified the necessity of Leviathan on the frailty of mere words. For Hobbes, a contract that involves a promise by at least one of the parties to perform in the future is called a "covenant" (Hobbes [1651] 1960, 87). When both parties promise future performance, it is a "covenant of mutual trust" (Hobbes 1960, 89).

* We thank the American Political Science Association for permission to reprint this article from the *American Political Science Review,* vol. 86, no. 2 (June 1992). We also thank the many individuals, too numerous to list, who gave valuable comments. Financial support from the National Science Foundation (Grant SES–4843901) and the United States Department of Agriculture (Cooperative Agreement 43–3AEM–1–80078) is gratefully acknowledged. The assistance of Dean Dudley in the Experimental Lab is also much appreciated. All data are stored on permanent NovaNet disk files. Send inquiries to Professor James M. Walker, Department of Economics, Ballantine 901, Indiana University, Bloomington, IN 47405.

A covenant of mutual trust in a state of nature is void in Hobbes's view if either has a reasonable suspicion that the other will not perform.

> For he that performeth first, has no assurance the other will perform after; because the bonds of words are too weak to bridle men's ambition, avarice, anger, and other passions, without the fear of some coercive power; which in the condition of mere nature, where all men are equal, and judges of the justness of their own fears, cannot possibly be supposed. (Hobbes 1960, 89–90)

On the other hand, a covenant made "where there is a power set up to constrain those that would otherwise violate their faith" is likely to be fulfilled (Hobbes 1960, 89–90). Thus, Hobbes argued for the necessity of a "coercive power, to compel men equally to the performance of their covenants, by the terror of some punishment, greater than the benefit they expect by the breach of their covenant" (Hobbes 1960, 94).

The weakness of mere words and the necessity of external agents to enforce contracts is also a foundation upon which the powerful edifice of noncooperative game theory has been constructed. John Nash (1950, 1951) distinguished between cooperative and noncooperative games. In cooperative games, players can communicate freely and make enforceable agreements; in noncooperative games, they can do neither. Some theorists particularly stress the inability to make enforceable agreements:

> the decisive question is whether the players can make enforceable agreements, and it makes little difference whether they are allowed to talk to each other. Even if they are free to talk and to negotiate an agreement, this fact will be of no real help if the agreement has little chance of being kept. An ability to negotiate agreements is useful only if the rules of the game make such agreement binding and enforceable. (Harsanyi and Selten 1988, 3)[1]

In other words, communication without a change in the payoff function does not eliminate a Nash equilibrium, the major solution concept used in noncooperative game theory. Not all Nash equilibria are efficient. Equilibrium payoffs are lower in a finitely repeated, full-information dilemma game, than if the participants could make credible *ex ante* commitments. Hobbes's state of nature has frequently been represented as a social dilemma game.[2]

The assumption that "a sword" wielded by "an external enforcer" is necessary before individuals can make credible *ex ante* commitments in social dilemma situations has important implications for common-pool resources. Common-pool resources (CPRs) are natural or man-made resources from which: (a) yield is subtractable and (b) exclusion is nontrivial (but not necessarily impossible).[3] Because CPRs can be represented as social dilemmas, particular policy recommendations follow almost immediately. Ophuls (1973, 228) argued, for example, that "environmental problems cannot be solved through cooperation . . . and the rationale for government with major coercive powers is overwhelming." His conclusion was that "even if we avoid the tragedy of the commons, it will *only* be by recourse to the tragic necessity of Leviathan" (Ophuls 1973, 220).

Empirical evidence suggests, however, that individuals facing social dilemmas in many cases develop credible *ex ante* commitments without relying on external authorities. *Appropriators* from CPRs, such as fishers, irrigators, or herders, have repeatedly shown their capacity to organize themselves, to establish credible commitments, to monitor each others' behavior, and to impose sanctions on those who break their commitments.[4] Self-organized CPR institutions have been devised without reference to central authorities and sustained over long periods of time without enforcement by external agents.[5] Experimental studies have repeatedly found that individuals placed in laboratory social dilemmas, who are allowed to communicate, consistently achieve better outcomes than are predicted by noncooperative game equilibrium. While findings concerning the positive effect of communication in laboratory settings—covenanting without a sword—lead to optimistic predictions about the capacities of individuals to solve social dilemmas, many cases of self-organized arrangements in field settings rely on internal sanctioning mechanisms (Ostrom 1990).

Past research has produced three anomalies from the standpoint of predictions derived from both Hobbes's state-of-nature theory and noncooperative game theory:

- In one-shot social dilemma experiments, communication alone leads to substantial improvement in outcomes.[6]
- In repeated social dilemma experiments, repeated communication alone leads to substantial improvements in joint outcomes.[7]
- In field settings of repeated social dilemmas, participants invest substantial time and effort monitoring and imposing sanctions on one another.[8]

The results from field settings show that participants in social dilemmas do not rely entirely on communication. They closely monitor each other and impose sanctions on those who do not conform to the rules they have devised. If communication alone were a fully reliable mechanism to overcome the gap between *ex post* temptations and *ex ante* promises, then one should not observe time and effort being devoted to monitoring and sanctioning efforts in the field. Thus, prior research has generated interesting puzzles. Given that social dilemmas lie at the foundation of the theory of the state and the theory of collective action, it is important to explore the independent and interactive effects of: (1) communicating (or, to use Hobbes's term, covenanting), (2) sanctioning (or, the sword), and (3) communicating with options to sanction (covenants with a sword).

In this paper we undertake this exploration. We manipulate experimental treatments to examine: (1) communication alone (one-shot and repeated), (2) sanctioning alone, and (3) communication combined with the possibility of sanctioning. We construct a common constituent game which is the basis for all these manipulations. This game, an n-person CPR appropriation game, is described and solved in the next section.

Game-Theoretical Predictions

The CPR Constituent Game

We will first specify the class of constituent CPR games from which we draw our designs. Assume a fixed number n of appropriators with access to the CPR. Each appropriator i has an endowment of resources e which can be invested in the CPR or invested in a safe, outside activity. The marginal payoff of the outside activity is normalized equal to w. The payoff to an individual appropriator from investing in the CPR depends on aggregate group investment in the CPR, and on the appropriator investment as a percentage of the aggregate. Let x_i denote appropriator i's investment in the CPR, where $0 \leq x_i \leq e$. The group return to investment in the CPR is given by the production function $F(\Sigma x_i)$, where F is a concave function, with $F(0) = 0$, $F'(0) > w$, and $F'(ne) < 0$.

Initially, investment in the CPR pays better than the opportunity cost of the foregone safe investment $[F'(0) > w]$, but if the appropriators invest all resources in the CPR the outcome is counterproductive $[F'(ne) < 0]$. Thus, the yield from the CPR reaches a *maximum net level* when individuals invest some but not all of their endowments in the CPR.[9] This environment is much richer and more complex than the ubiquitous repeated Prisoner's Dilemma game. While no formal game or laboratory experiment ever captures all the nuances of field settings, this n-person, CPR game is a far more realistic environment in which to investigate the questions we have posed than many of the dilemma games previously explored.

Let $x = (x_1, \ldots, x_n)$ be a vector of individual appropriators' investments in the CPR. The payoff to an appropriator, $u_i(x)$, is given by:

$$u_i(x) = we \quad \text{if } x_i = 0$$
$$w(e - x_i) + (x_i/\Sigma x_i)F(\Sigma x_i) \quad \text{if } x_i > 0. \quad (1)$$

Equation (1) reflects the fact that if appropriators invest all their endowments in the outside alternative, they get a sure payoff (we), whereas if they invest some of their endowments in the CPR, they get a sure payoff $w(e - x_i)$ plus a payoff from the CPR, which depends on the total investment in that resource $F(\Sigma x_i)$ multiplied by their share in the group investment $(x_i/\Sigma x_i)$.[10] Let the payoffs (1) be the payoff functions in a symmetric, noncooperative game. Since our experimental design is symmetric, there is a symmetric Nash equilibrium, with each player investing x_i^* in the CPR, where:

$$-w + (1/n)F'(nx_i^*) + F(nx_i^*)((n - 1)/x_i^* n^2) = 0. \tag{2}$$

At the symmetric Nash equilibrium, group investment in the CPR is greater than optimal, but not all yield from the CPR is wasted.

Compare this deficient equilibrium to the optimal solution. Summing across individual payoffs $u_i(x)$ for all appropriators i, one has the group payoff function $u(x)$,

$$u(x) = nwe - w\Sigma x_i + F(\Sigma x_i) \tag{3}$$

which is to be maximized subject to the constraints $0 \leq \Sigma x_i \leq ne$. Given the above productivity conditions on F, the group maximization problem has a unique solution characterized by the condition:

$$-w + F'(\Sigma x_i) = 0. \tag{4}$$

According to (4), the marginal return from a CPR should equal the opportunity cost of the outside alternative for the last unit invested in the CPR.

It is worth noting that both the Nash equilibrium investment and the optimum group investment do not depend on the endowment parameter e, as long as e is sufficiently large. Out of equilibrium, however, larger e means players are capable of making larger mistakes. If the time required to converge to an equilibrium is large, then the Nash equilibrium may be an inappropriate behavioral theory for CPRs with high endowments.

Finite Repetition of a CPR Constituent Game

Denote the constituent game by X and let X be played a finite number of times. Typically, a repeated game has many equilibria to choose from. Two equilibrium refinement principles are subgame perfection and subgame consistency. An equilibrium is subgame perfect if it prescribes equilibrium play on every subgame. An equilibrium is subgame consistent if it prescribes identical play on identical subgames. If the constituent game has a unique equilibrium, then the finitely repeated game has a unique subgame perfect and subgame consistent equilibrium (Selten 1971). Thus, equation (2) characterizes a finite sequence of equilibrium outcomes. This prediction is based on the assumption of a finite game of complete information. Our subjects know the game is finite.[11] Although we do not have complete control over our subjects' understanding of their decision task, we make all information readily available to them. Failure to induce complete information on the part of our subjects jeopardizes the uniqueness of this refined equilibrium (Kreps et al. 1982).

Communication and the Constituent Game

When the constituent game X has a unique equilibrium x^*, neither repetition nor communication creates new equilibrium outcomes. Let c denote a communication strategy, in the communication phase C, available to any player. As long as saying one thing and doing another has no payoff consequences, then any strategy of the form (c, x^*) is an equilibrium of the one-shot game (C, X), and finitely repeated x^* is a subgame consistent equilibrium outcome of one-shot communication (C, X, X, . . . , X) or repeated communication (C, X, C, X, . . . , C, X). In this situation, subgame consistency is deaf to covenants. However, as we show below, communication makes a big difference in behavior.

Sanctioning and the Constituent Game

Our sanctioning institution is represented formally using the following construction. Let s be a matrix of 0s and 1s, where $s_{ij} = 1$ means that player i has sanctioned player j, and $s_{ij} = 0$ means that i has not sanctioned j. Row i of the matrix s codes all of player i's sanctioning behavior. As before, let x be a vector of individual investments in the CPR and $u_i(x)$ be i's payoff function in the game without sanctioning. Player i's payoff function in the game with sanctioning, $u_i(x, s)$, is given by:

$$u_i(x, s) = u_i(x) - f1 \sum_j s_{ij} - f2 \sum_j s_{ji}. \qquad (5)$$

The parameters f1 and f2 represent the cost of fining and the cost of being fined, respectively.[12] The sum $\sum s_{ij}$ is the total number of fines j levied by player i, costing him f1 each; the sum $\sum s_{ji}$ is the total number of times player i is fined, costing him f2 each.

Adding this sanctioning mechanism to our constituent game X produces a game X–S with a unique subgame consistent equilibrium. In a one-shot game with a unique Nash equilibrium x^*, any sanctioning activity is costly and cannot lead to higher payoffs. Thus, the equilibrium of the one-shot game with sanctioning is the pair $(x^*, S^*) = (x^*, 0)$, i.e., the equilibrium sanctioning matrix is the 0-matrix. At equilibrium, no one sanctions. Now suppose that the one-shot CPR game with sanctioning is to be repeated a finite number of times T. This finitely repeated game has a unique subgame consistent equilibrium given by strategy 1:

Strategy 1: In every round, play $(x^*, 0)$.
In the event of any deviation from prescribed play,
resume playing $(x^*, 0)$ after the deviation.

This equilibrium follows from backward induction. At the last round T, no deviation is profitable. At the next to last round T–1, given that no deviations will occur in the last round, then no deviation is profitable, and so on. Repeating the game should not lead to sanctioning either. There is, however, compelling evidence that backward induction must be learned through repeated play.

Besides the unique subgame consistent equilibrium, there are many imperfect equilibria as well. Let $z_i < x_i^*$ be the same for all i. Consider the repeated game strategy, strategy 2:

> Strategy 2: In every round except T, play $(z, 0)$.
> In the event of any deviation,
> play $(x_i = e, s = I)$ for one round,
> then resume playing $(z, 0)$.
> If no deviation took place in round $T - 1$,
> play $(x^*, 0)$ in round T.

This represents a trigger strategy. All players agree to invest less than they would according to strategy 1. If some player cheats, then every player dumps all his resources into the CPR ($x_i = e$) and every player issues one sanction for one round. Then play returns to normal.

In the final round, everyone plays the one-shot Nash equilibrium. We claim that strategy 2 represents an imperfect equilibrium. To show this, it suffices to show that no deviation from prescribed play pays. Let $F(ne)$ be a very large negative number. For f1 and f2 large enough, a player who deviated optimally for one round would gain some positive amount, depending on the level of z_i, but in the next round would lose $(1/n)F(ne) + f1 + f2$ due to punishment from over-investment and sanctions, as in strategy 2. This threat we call the *dire threat*, as it is the worst threat imaginable for one round in our design. Given such a threat, it does not pay to deviate, even for one round. Finally, if a punishment is not called for in the last round, the endgame equilibrium is played in that round. This shows that strategy 2 is an equilibrium. Its imperfection lies in the fact that the trigger punishment—dumping all tokens into the resource, everybody placing a fine—is too harsh to be credible at the end of the game.[13]

There is a large set of equilibria along the lines of strategy 2, involving variation of the length of punishment (1 or more rounds), the base level of investments z_i, and the direness of the one-period threat (dump not quite all tokens in the CPR, levy fines with some probability). In particular, by varying f1 and f2, we hoped to allow the subjects to find equilibria of the family strategy 2 which involve punishments of the form (z_i, I)—that is to say, reduced investment in the CPR, but sanctions for everyone if a deviation occurs (see Jankowski 1990).

Communication, the Constituent Game, and Sanctioning

We investigate the combination of communication with sanctioning in two ways. Our first design allows for a one-shot communication period, which is then followed by a sequence of constituent games with a sanctioning mechanism imposed. In our second design, we impose a one-shot communication period in conjunction with an opportunity for the subjects to choose whether or not they want a sanctioning mechanism. In both designs, the payoff functions are still given by (5) since communication per se has no payoff consequences and sanctioning does. Without loss of generality, let c be a communication strategy. Then appending c to strategy 1 yields a subgame consistent equilibrium, and every subgame consistent equilibrium has the same payoffs as does strategy 1. In addition, as in repeated X–S, imperfect equilibria exist yielding higher payoffs than equilibria which are subgame consistent.

The Laboratory Decision Environment

Design

In our experimental investigation we have operationalized this CPR environment with eight appropriators ($n = 8$) and quadratic production functions $F(\Sigma x_i)$, where:

$$F(\Sigma x_i) = a\Sigma x_i - b(\Sigma x_i)^2 \qquad (6)$$
$$\text{with } F'(0) = a > w \text{ and } F'(ne) = a - 2bne < 0.$$

For this quadratic specification, one has from (4) that the group optimal investment satisfies $\Sigma x_i = (a - w)/2b$. The CPR yields 0% on net when investment is twice as large as optimal, $\Sigma x_i = (a - w)/b$. Finally, solving (2), the symmetric Nash equilibrium group investment is given by:

$$\Sigma x_i = (n/(n + 1))(a - w)/b. \qquad (7)$$

This level of investment is between maximal net yield and zero net yield, approaching the latter as n gets large. One additional constraint that arises in a laboratory setting is that the x_i be integer-valued. This is accomplished by choosing the parameters a, b, d, and w in such a way that the predictions associated with Σx_i are all integer valued.

In particular, we use the parameters shown in Table 8.1. These parameters lead to the predictions that: (a) 36 tokens invested in Market 2 yields the level of investment that maximizes group earnings and (b) each subject investing 8 tokens in Market 2 is a unique Nash equilibrium. At this equilibrium, subjects earn approximately 39% of maximum net yield from the CPR. Once again, note that the Nash equilibrium and optimal investment are not affected by the level of endowments.

Subjects and the Experimental Setting

The experiments reported in this paper used subjects drawn from the undergraduate population at Indiana University. Students were volunteers recruited from principles of economics classes. Prior to recruitment, potential volunteers were given a brief explanation in which they were told only that they would be making decisions in an "economic choice" environment and that the money they earned would be dependent upon their own investment decisions and those of the others in their experimental group. In all experiments reported here, subjects were randomly recruited from a pool of subjects with prior experience in a CPR decision environment. All experiments were conducted on the NovaNet computer system at Indiana University. The computer facilitates the accounting procedures involved in the experiment, enhances across experiment subject control, and allows for minimal experimenter involvement.

Table 8.1
Experimental Design
Baseline Parameters
For a Given Decision Period

	Experiment Type	
Experiment Characteristics	**Low Endowment**	**High Endowment**
Number of Subjects	8	8
Individual Token Endowment	10	25
Production Function: Market 2[*]	$23(\Sigma x_i) - .25(\Sigma x_i)^2$	$23(\Sigma x_i) - .25(\Sigma x_i)^2$
Market 2 Return/unit of output	$.01	$.01
Market 1 Return/unit of output	$.05	$.05
Earnings/Subject at Group Maximum[**]	$.91	$.83
Earnings/Subject at Nash Equilibrium	$.66	$.70
Earnings/Subject at Zero Net Yield	$.50	$.63

[*] Σx_i = the total number of tokens invested by the group in Market 2. The production function shows the number of units of output produced in Market 2 for each level of tokens invested in Market 2. Market 2 represents a CPR because the total output from Market 2 (and each subject's share of that output) is a function of the investment levels of all subjects.

[**] In the high endowment design, subjects were paid in cash one-half of their "computer" earnings. This maintains potential experimental profits at near equal levels across designs. Amounts shown are potential cash payoffs.

Organization and Overview of Results

The results will be organized around four major headings. First, we represent the state of nature with the minimal institution baseline game (no covenants/no swords). We then present findings from three environments with institutional configurations: (1) an imposed communication mechanism, (2) an imposed sanctioning mechanism, and (3) an imposed communication mechanism with either an imposed sanctioning mechanism or an opportunity to choose a sanctioning mechanism. Figure 8.1 gives an overview of the experimental design. Table 8.2 presents a summary of results across designs, focusing on the average net yield from the CPR (Market 2) as a percentage of maximum possible net yield.[14]

Figure 8.1
Experimental Design

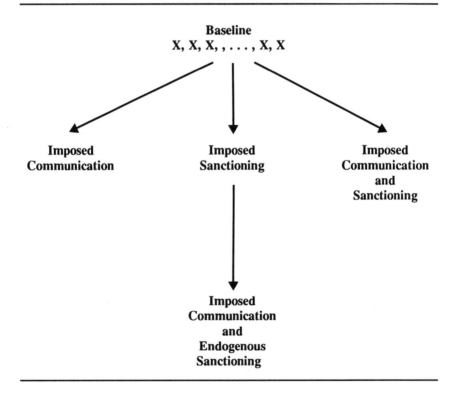

Table 8.2
Summary Results
Average Yield as Percent of Maximum

Experimental Design	Round					
	1–5	6–10	11–15	16–20	21–25	26+
Baseline 10TK[a]	51.5	34.7	34.4	35.6	37.1	29.6
Baseline 25TK	−42.5	−12.4	10.3	32.0		
One-Shot Communication 25TK	−40.9	−12.7	74.1	45.4	42.5	58.6
Repeated Communication 10TK	32.6	27.3	97.2	98.4	100.0	
Repeated Communication 25TK	32.5	−14.4	74.1	75.0	68.9	
Sanction 25TK	−35.7	−39.6	40.1	38.8	28.7	
One-Shot Communication 25TK Sanction	−0.7	−27.0	86.8	86.3	82.5	77.8
One-Shot Communication 25TK No Sanction Chosen[b]	46.4	41.2	91.7	61.9	14.7	
One-Shot Communication 25TK Sanction Chosen[b]	−16.9	−05.1	92.5	91.6	89.9	93.8
One-Shot Communication 25TK Sanction Chosen[c]			96.8	97.0	96.7	90.4

[a] TK corresponds to tokens per subject

[b] Communication and sanctioning choice occurred after round 10.

[c] Communication and sanctioning choice occurred after round 1; table displays this data beginning in round 11 for comparison purposes.

The Baseline Game: No Covenants and No Swords

For comparison with the designs discussed later, the baseline experiments can be represented as an iterated series (of 20 rounds) of the constituent game X. At the beginning of each experimental session, subjects were told that: (1) they would make a series of investment decisions, (2) all individual investment decisions were anonymous to the group, and (3) they would be paid their individual earnings (privately and in cash) at the end of the experiment. Subjects then proceeded at their own pace through a set of instructions summarized below:[15]

Subjects faced a series of decision rounds in which they were endowed with a specified number of tokens, which they invested between two markets. Market 1 was described as an investment opportunity in which each token yielded a fixed (constant) rate of output and that each unit of output yielded a fixed (constant) return. Market 2 (the CPR) was described as a market which yielded a rate of output per token dependent upon the total number of tokens invested by the entire group. The rate of output at each level of group investment was described in functional form as well as tabular form. Subjects were informed that they would receive a level of output from Market 2 that was equivalent to the percentage of total group tokens they invested. Further, subjects knew that each unit of output from Market 2 yielded a fixed (constant) rate of return.[16]

Subjects knew with certainty the total number of decision makers in the group, total group tokens, and that endowments were identical. Subjects knew that the more the group invested in Market 2, the lower the average and marginal returns from Market 2 would be. They did not know the exact number of decision rounds.

In the baseline experiments, subjects participated in a series of 20 decision rounds. After each round, subjects were shown a display that recorded: (a) their profits in each market for that round, (b) total group investment in Market 2, and (c) a tally of their cumulative profits for the experiment. During the experiment, subjects could request, through the computer, this information for all previous rounds. Subjects received no information regarding other subjects' *individual* investment decisions or the number of rounds.

As shown in Table 8.2, in the first 10 rounds, the low endowment treatment leads to an average net yield of 43%. In the high endowment treatment, net yield averages −28%. This shows the importance of the endowment treatment out of equilibrium. In the last five rounds of the baseline experiments, the two treatments are very close, 36% and 32%, respectively. These percentages are fairly close to the 38% predicted by the subgame consistent equilibrium, evidencing strategic learning on the part of the subjects.

Several characteristics of the individual experiments are important. Investments in Market 2 are characterized by a "pulsing" pattern in which yield is reduced, at which time investors tend to reduce investments in Market 2 and yields increase. For the high endowment experiments, the low points in the pulsing pattern were at yields far below zero. There was some tendency for the variance in yields to decrease over the course of the experiments. At the aggregate level, the Nash prediction best describes our data. However, at the individual level we observed no experiment in which individual investments stabilized at the Nash equilibrium.

To sum up, as predicted by both Hobbes's state-of-nature theory and subgame consistent equilibrium, individuals acting independently in a CPR without communication or sanctioning do not solve the collective-action problem they confront.

Covenants Without a Sword—Communication Alone

Prior experimental evidence strongly supports the conclusion that communication in social dilemmas increases the frequency with which players choose and sustain joint income maximizing strategies, even when individual incentives conflict with such strategies. In this section we examine the results from several types of communication experiments.

One-Shot Communication

Our first communication design was parallel to that of the high endowment baseline game for the first ten repetitions of the constituent game.[17] At the end of the tenth round, the subjects were informed that they would have a single opportunity of ten minutes to discuss the decision problem. The instructions are given below.

> Some participants in experiments like this have found it useful to have the opportunity to discuss the decision problem you face. You will be given ten minutes to hold such a discussion. You may discuss anything you wish during your ten-minute discussion period, with the following restrictions. 1) You are not allowed to discuss side payments. 2) You are not allowed to make physical threats. 3) You are not allowed to see the private information on anyone's monitor.

After this opportunity to communicate, the subjects returned to the constituent game which was then repeated up to 22 more times. The structure of the one-shot communication experiment is:

$$X, X, X, \ldots, X, C, X, X, \ldots, X.$$

The subgame consistent and subgame perfect equilibrium outcome for the one-shot communication game is for each individual to invest 8 tokens in the CPR, the same as in the baseline. The maximum net yield is obtained if a total of 36 tokens are invested. Subjects are not allowed to invest fractional tokens and the symmetric strategy to obtain the maximum return is half-way between everyone investing 4 tokens and investing 5 tokens. If the subjects were to decide to invest either 4 or 5 tokens each, they would obtain 99% of maximum net yield in either case.

The transcripts of the discussion during the communication round reveal that subjects perceived their problem as involving two tasks: (1) determining the maximal yield available and (2) agreeing upon a strategy to achieve that yield. In all three groups, an agreement was reached; but no group found the optimal solution. Averaging over all experiments, yields were negative throughout the first

10 rounds (−27%). Once communication was allowed, net yields jumped to an average of 74% for the five rounds immediately following the communication time-out, then gradually decayed thereafter. The average net yield in the post-communication phase was 55%. Defining a *defection* as a Market 2 investment by an individual greater than that agreed upon, we observe a defection rate of 25% during the decision rounds following communication. These results suggest that a single communication period enables participants to begin the process of adopting a joint strategy. However, the inability to communicate more often limits the durability of their agreements.

Repeated Communication

Our second design involves repeated communication in both the low and high endowment settings. At the outset, the constituent game was repeated for 10 rounds. After round 10, the subjects read an announcement similar to that for one-shot communication but informing them they would have an opportunity for discussion after *each* subsequent round. The subjects left their terminals and sat facing one another.[18] The structure of the repeated communication experiment is:

$$X, X, \ldots, X, C\text{–}X, C\text{–}X, \ldots, C\text{–}X.$$

These experiments provide strong evidence for the power of repeated face-to-face communication. Subjects successfully used the opportunity to: (a) calculate coordinated yield-improving strategies, (b) devise verbal agreements to implement these strategies, and (c) deal with nonconforming subjects through verbal statements. When allowed to communicate repeatedly, subjects greatly enhanced their joint yield and sustained this enhancement. In the *low* endowment environment, net yields averaged 99% of optimum in the repeated communication phase with a 5% defection rate.[19] The *high* endowment CPR game is a more challenging decision environment than the low endowment environment. While the subgame consistent equilibrium outcomes of the two games are identical, the disequilibrium implications of the 25-token (high endowment) game change considerably. With 25 tokens, as few as three subjects investing all of their tokens can essentially ruin the CPR (bring returns below w), while with 10 tokens it takes seven out of eight subjects to accomplish this much damage. Net yields in the repeated communication phase averaged only 73% of optimum, with a 13% defection rate.

Repeated communication enabled subjects to discuss defections and to significantly cut the defection rate on agreements. In all communication experiments, subjects offered and extracted promises of cooperation, thereby increasing their joint yield significantly above that obtained prior to communication. Discussions went well beyond discovering the level of investments that would generate maximum yields. A striking aspect of the discussion rounds was how rapidly subjects, who had not had an opportunity to establish a well-defined community with strong internal norms, were able to devise their own agreements and verbal punishments for those who broke those agreements. These verbal sanctions had to be directed at unknown defectors, since subjects' decisions were anonymous. Subjects detected defection solely through aggregate investments. In many cases, statements like "some scumbucket is investing more than we agreed upon" were a sufficient reproach to change defectors' behavior. However, verbal sanctions were less effective in the 25-token environment.

The evidence from the one-shot and the high endowment designs suggests why individuals in many field settings may not rely only on face-to-face communication. When repeated discourse is infeasible or when the actions of one or a few individuals can be a strong disequilibrating force, individuals who have the capacity to agree to sanction one another, as well as communicate with one another, might well want to reinforce their covenants with their own swords. While subgame consistency predicts that individuals in such settings would not sanction one another, endogenous sanctioning is frequently observed in field settings. We now turn to an examination of whether sanctioning behavior will occur in our laboratory environment and its effects on behavior.

Sword Without Covenants—Sanctioning Alone

Experiments in this design began like high endowment baseline experiments with the exception that after each round, subjects received *individual* data of all decisions.[20] This information was given by subject number, thus maintaining anonymity. Our sanctioning mechanism required that each subject incur a cost (a fee) in order to sanction another. In our first sanctioning design, after round 10, subjects were given an announcement summarized below.

> Subjects were informed that in all remaining rounds each would be given the opportunity to place a fine. Each subject could levy one fine at a specified fee. The subject fined would pay a fine of a specified amount. It was possible for a single subject to be charged multiple fines. After each round, each subject filled out a fining form. These forms were collected and tallied by the experimenter, who then reported the results privately to each subject. Note that any subject who was fined did not know the identity of those who imposed the fine. At the end of the experiment, the experimenters subtracted from subjects' total profits the total of all fees and all fines.

The actual fees ranged from 5 to 40 cents, and fines from 10 to 80 cents. The fee/fine ratio was either .25 or .50. After subjects read the announcement, questions regarding the implementation of the procedure were answered. No discussion was held on why the subjects might want to use the procedure or its possible consequences. This created an experimental setting as close as possible to the noncooperative assumptions of no communication and no capacity to engage in enforceable agreements. Structure of the imposed sanctioning design is:

$$X, X, \ldots X–S, X–S, X–S, \ldots, X–S, X.$$

The principle results from our sanctioning experiments are summarized as follows.[21] Across all eight experiments, net yield rose from −38% before the imposition of sanctioning to 37% after. When one subtracts the costs of fees and fines, however, average net yield increased to only 9%. Thus, sanctioning alone is not an efficient institution. Besides these quantitative results, we draw the following qualitative conclusions:

1. significantly more sanctioning occurs than predicted by subgame consistency, and the frequency is inversely related to cost;
2. sanctioning is primarily focused on heavy CPR investors;
3. there is a nontrivial amount of sanctioning that can be classified as error, lagged punishment, or "blind" revenge.

We observed 176 instances of sanctioning across the eight experiments. In no experiment did we observe fewer than 10 instances. The frequency of sanctions was inversely related to the cost of imposing the fine and dramatically increased with the stiffness of the fine. Further, our results, although reminiscent of strategy 2, did not strictly support the conclusion that subjects were playing an equilibrium of this form. Except for one experiment, where net yield was over 95%, yields were too low and sanctioning levels were too high to be consistent with imperfect equilibria.

The second and third results relate to the reasons for sanctioning. From post-experiment interviews and personal observations, we offer four explanations for the higher-than-predicted level of sanctioning: (1) one round punishment—the person fined was the highest or one of the highest investors in the previous round; (2) lagged punishment—the person fined was one of the highest investors in the CPR in a round prior to the previous one; (3) blind revenge—the person fined was a low CPR investor and was fined by a person fined in a previous round; (4) error—no obvious explanation can be given for the action (trembling hand).

In summary, 77% of all sanctioning was aimed at investors who in the previous round were above-average investors in the CPR. An additional 7% was aimed at subjects who had been heavy investors in the CPR in earlier (but not the most recent) rounds. We classify 5% as blind revenge and the remaining 11% as errors.[22]

The evidence from these experiments suggests why individuals in field settings might not want to rely on sanctioning alone. Individuals who have the capacity to sanction one another without the ability to communicate about joint strategies and the use of sanctions face an insuperable handicap to increasing efficiency. The final question to which we return is whether communication and sanctioning together foster sustainable high yields.

Covenants With a Sword—Communication and Sanctioning

Our last two decision environments investigate the consequences of combining a one-shot opportunity to communicate with either: (1) an experimenter-imposed sanctioning mechanism or (2) an opportunity to decide whether or not to adopt a sanctioning mechanism endogenously. These experiments began like those in the design with sanctioning alone. After round 10, subjects were given an announcement that they would have a single 10-minute discussion period. In experiments with an imposed-sanctioning mechanism, subjects were also given an announcement (prior to discussion) similar to that of the sanctioning alone environment. In experiments where subjects had an opportunity to choose a sanctioning mechanism, the announcement informed them that at the end of 10 minutes they would vote on: (1) whether to institute a sanctioning mechanism and (2) on the level of fines if they did institute one. The only restriction on the sanctioning mechanism was that the fee to fine ratio was 1/2. The voting rule was strict majority with the status quo being a repeated base-line experiment without a sanctioning mechanism.

Imposed Communication and Sanctioning

The structure of the three experiments in this design is:

$$X, X, \ldots, X, C, X\text{–}S, X\text{–}S, \ldots, X\text{–}S, X.$$

In the first experiment, the participants rapidly focused on the problem of deciding upon a joint investment strategy. They spent most of their ten minutes calculating various options to ensure that they had discovered an optimal strategy. They decided to invest 4 tokens each in Market 2 and the remaining 21 tokens in Market 1. Further, they agreed to fine one another if anyone put more than 4 tokens in Market 2. One subject characterized their strategy in the following way: "If everyone puts in 4 tokens, we are going to be making 42 cents more money in the individual accounts. This is the highest." A second subject characterized their unanimous agreement: "Does everyone agree to this? OK, now we have agreed that everyone will put 4 tokens in and if anyone puts any more in, we are all going to fine them. Is that all agreed, now?" With this specific agreement to which everyone nodded assent, the subjects returned to their terminals and made investments for 16 more rounds without a single defection nor any use of the sanctioning mechanism. They obtained 98% of maximum net yield from the CPR and did not waste resources on fees or fines.

In the second experiment, the subjects did not find the optimal strategy but devised a complex rotation system to ensure that they all received what they thought would be maximal returns. They decided that each subject would invest 6 tokens in Market 2 and the right to invest 2 more tokens each round would be rotated first to Subject 1, then to Subject 2, on through Subject 8. One subject suggested that they not fine at all, but another argued: "No, let's fine anyone who breaks our rules. If they break our rules, then we should fine 'em!" After further discussion, the subjects agreed that they would use the sanctioning mechanism to fine anyone who deviated from "their rules." For two rounds they kept their agreement. On round 13, one subject invested 7 rather than 6 and was immediately fined by one of the other subjects. On round 19, two subjects invested one more token than agreed upon and were immediately sanctioned by one subject each. No more defections were attempted and no more fees were paid to assess fines. In this experiment, the subjects achieved 86% of maximum net yield (since they had miscalculated the optimum). Their net return dropped to 79% when fees and fines were deducted from their earnings.

In the third experiment, the subjects never discussed the possibility of devising a joint strategy even though they mentioned how the overinvestment of some of the subjects during the first 10 rounds had made it difficult for the rest of them. The closest they got to an agreement was to discuss fining those who were obviously overinvesting—for example, "those who invested over 21 tokens in Market 2." A considerable amount of their discussion time was wasted in awkward silence. They finally asked whether they had to sit there the entire ten minutes. After verifying that no subject wanted to use the remaining two minutes of their time for further discussion, the experimenters let the subjects return to their terminals.

Following the communication period, the subjects achieved an average of 70% of net yield from the CPR, up from −14% in pre-discussion rounds. A total of twenty $.40 fees were paid to impose the same number of $.80 fines on other subjects. The fines were directed toward subjects who had invested heavily in Market 2 in the prior round. Net yield fell to 24% with fees and fines deducted from earnings.

Imposed Communication and Endogenous Sanctioning

In order to make the choice of a sanctioning mechanism meaningful, subjects in this decision environment were randomly drawn from the pool of subjects from our imposed sanctioning design. The structure of the four experiments in this design is:

$$X, X, \ldots, X, C, X, X, \ldots, X$$

or X, X, . . . , X, C, X–S, X–S, . . . , X–S, X.

Subjects decided upon a joint investment strategy and established a sanctioning mechanism in only 2 of the 4 experiments. In one they chose a fee to fine ratio of $.10/$.20 and in the other a ratio of $.20/$.40. Net yield averaged 91% of maximum following the communication round. The level of defection from their agreements was very low. Net yield fell slightly to 86% when fees and fines were deducted.

In one of the experiments where subjects rejected the adoption of a sanctioning mechanism, they did adopt an agreed-upon joint strategy to invest 4 tokens in the CPR (a joint strategy very close to optimal). In the first few rounds following discussion, they sustained their agreement, but by round 16, four subjects invested more than their agreement. From then on, the level of defections steadily rose. Overall they had an average net yield of 36% and a defection rate of 42%—the highest defection rate of any communication experiment where an agreement was reached. The other experiment in which a sanctioning mechanism was not chosen is an outlier. Across all of our CPR experiments with the baseline institution, this is the only experiment where yields in the first 10 rounds were essentially maximal. When given the opportunity to discuss the decision problem and choose a sanctioning mechanism, the group: (1) agreed that they did not need a mechanism and (2) agreed that no one should try to get "greedy"—i.e., invest too much in the CPR. The group held together for a few rounds, after which yields began a gradual decline. This decline was due primarily to a gradual increase in Market 2 investments by two subjects. By round 25, net yield had dropped to 56% of optimum. Net yield for all rounds following the discussion session averaged 76% compared to 90% prior to round 10.

We have traced back to the specific sanctioning/no communication experiment in which each of these subjects participated. Of the 32 subjects in these four experiments, 18 voted for and 14 voted against the implementation of a sanctioning mechanism. Of the 14 who voted no, 11 had previously participated in a sanctioning experiment with a fee to fine ratio of $.20/$.80. Of the 18 who voted yes, only 3 had been in a $.20/$.80 design. We infer from this result that the high level of sanctioning activity in the $.20/$.80 design, the lack of overall efficiency gains, and the presence of blind revenge combined to impede the willingness of participants to choose a sanctioning mechanism.

It is possible that the experience of the first ten rounds of the constituent game had an effect on mechanism choice. To examine this possible hysteresis effect, two additional experiments were conducted. In these two experiments, the opportunity to communicate and to adopt a sanctioning mechanism was available at the outset.

The structure of these two experiments is:

C, X, X, . . . , X   or   C, X–S, X–S, . . . , X–S, X.

In both of these experiments, the subjects quickly agreed to an investment strategy and a sanctioning mechanism to punish defectors. Across the two experiments net yields averaged 95%, and 94% with fees and fines included.

The payoff consequences of selecting or not selecting a sanctioning mechanism were very different across the experiments in this design. The groups choosing some form of sanctioning institution earned average yields of 93% in the post-discussion phase. Indeed, yields this high suggest that this set of institutions, endogenously chosen, approximate the conditions necessary for a cooperative game. The groups not choosing some form of sanctioning institution earned average yields of only 56%, with serious decay.

The results from this set of communication and sanctioning experiments suggest that some subjects can find yield-improving joint strategies, design a sanctioning mechanism, use the sanctioning mechanism, and achieve a high rate of conformance to their joint strategies. On the other hand, prior negative experience with institutions that individuals view as punitive and inefficient is not conducive to the design of better institutions nor to a willingness to use them.

Conclusions: Self-Governance Is Possible

The inconsistency between predicted results and observed behavior in prior research stimulated the research presented in this article. In one-shot and finitely repeated games, communication alone is not predicted to have an effect on behavior. Earlier experimental studies of social dilemmas have, however, shown that communication alone leads to more efficient outcomes. We confirm these results in complex CPR environments.

With regard to communication alone, we obtain the following results (summarized in Table 8.3):

1. In the low endowment CPR environment, average net yield increased from 35% when no communication was allowed to 99% when communication was allowed on a repeated basis.
2. In the high endowment CPR environment, average net yield increased from 21% when no communication was allowed to: (i) 55% when communication was allowed only once, and (ii) 73% when communication was allowed on a repeated basis.

These results raise several puzzles. Because the subgame consistent equilibrium prediction for games with communication (one-shot or repeated) is the same as that for games without communication, opportunities for "mere jawboning" should make no difference. But they do. Further, the equilibrium prediction is the same for both low and high endowment environments. The high endowment environment, however, exhibits lower net yield and fosters less effective communication.

Table 8.3
Aggregate Results For All Designs*

Experimental Design	Average % Net Yield CPR	Average % Net Yield CPR**	Defection Rate
Baseline 10TK***	34	—	—
Baseline 25TK	21	—	—
One-Shot Communication 25TK	55	—	25
Repeated Communication 10TK	99	—	5
Repeated Communication 25TK	73	—	13
Sanction 25TK	37	9	—
One-Shot Communication Sanction 25TK	85	67	1
One-Shot Communication 25TK No Sanction Chosen	56	—	42
One-Shot Communication 25TK Sanction Chosen	93	90	4

* All computations are for periods in which the treatment was in effect. Nash equilibrium for all designs is 39% net CPR yield. Not applicable is represented with a —.

** Minus fees and fines.

*** TK corresponds to tokens per subject.

The finding that CPR appropriators in the field invest substantial resources in sanctioning activities stimulated our exploration of sanctioning behavior in the laboratory. With imposed sanctioning and no communication we find:

3. Subjects are willing to pay a fee to place a fine on another subject far more than predicted.
4. In the high endowment environment, average net yield increases from 21% with no sanctioning to 37% with sanctioning. When the costs of fees and fines are subtracted from average net yield, however, net yield drops to 9%.

Thus, subjects overuse the sanctioning mechanism, and sanctioning without communication reduces net yield.

The finding that CPR appropriators in the field invest substantial resources in both communication and sanctioning activities stimulated our exploration of these joint behaviors in the laboratory. Examining only the high endowment environment, we find:

5. With an imposed sanctioning mechanism and a single opportunity to communicate, subjects achieve an average net yield of 85%. When the costs of fees and fines are subtracted, average net yield is still 67%. These represent substantial gains over baseline where net yield averaged 21%.
6. With the right to choose a sanctioning mechanism and a single opportunity to communicate, subjects who adopt a sanctioning mechanism achieve an average net yield of 93%. When the costs of fees and fines are subtracted, average net yield is still 90%. In addition, the defection rate from agreements is only 4%.
7. With the right to choose a sanctioning mechanism and a single opportunity to communicate, subjects who do not adopt a sanctioning mechanism achieve an average net yield of only 56%. In addition, the defection rate from agreements is 42%.

Thus, subjects who use the opportunity to communicate to agree to a joint investment strategy and choose their own sanctioning mechanism achieve close to optimal results. This is especially impressive in the high endowment environment, where defection by a few subjects is very disruptive.

For those who predict cooperation in repeated settings based on trigger strategies, our findings are not supportive. In no experiment where one or more subjects deviated from an agreed-upon joint strategy did the subjects then follow a trigger strategy of substantially increasing their investments in the CPR.[23] In fact, in some experiments where one or more subjects deviated from an agreed-upon joint strategy, some subjects subsequently *reduced* their investments in the CPR. When subjects discussed the problem of how to respond to one or more "free riders," they overtly rejected the idea of dumping all of their tokens into the CPR.[24]

To return to our starting point, Hobbes's assertion, these experiments suggest that covenants, even without a sword, have some force, while swords without a covenant may be worse than the state of nature. Best of all the conditions we examined are covenants with an *internal* sword, freely chosen or made available as an institutional option.[25]

What Are the Implications?

Two major implications follow from the results of this paper. The first relates to policy analysis. Policymakers responsible for the governance and management of small-scale, common-pool resources should *not* presume that the individuals involved are caught in an inexorable tragedy from which there is no escape. Individuals may be able to arrive at joint strategies to manage these resources more efficiently. To accomplish this task they must have sufficient information to pose and solve the allocation problems they face. They must also have an arena where they can discuss joint strategies and perhaps implement monitoring and sanctioning. In other words, when individuals are given an opportunity to restructure their own situation they frequently, but not always, use this opportunity to make credible commitments and achieve higher joint outcomes without an external enforcer. We cannot replace the determinate prediction of "no cooperation" with a determinate prediction of "always cooperate." Our findings challenge the Hobbesian conclusion that the constitution of order is only possible by creating sovereigns who then must govern by being above subjects, by monitoring them, and by imposing sanctions on all who would otherwise not comply.[26]

The second major implication relates to behavioral theory. In finitely repeated social dilemma experiments, a wide variety of treatments that do not change the theoretically predicted subgame consistent equilibrium outcomes do change subjects' behavior. This raises a *substantial* question whether our subjects conceptualize their decision task in the way theorists do. For instance, if subjects believe the game is being repeated according to some exogenous probabilistic mechanism, then there are equilibria supporting more cooperative behavior if the subjective continuation probability is not too low. Or, it may be that subjects are acting as boundedly rational players in the sense of Selten, Mitzkewitz and Uhlich (1988). In this case, the observed improvement in yield could be the result of boundedly rational equilibrium, as Selten et al. observe in a duopoly context. We intend to explore these intriguing possibilities in future research.

Notes

1. Harsanyi and Selten (1988, 3) add that in real life, "agreements may be enforced externally by courts of law, government agencies, or pressure from public opinion; they may be enforced internally by the fact that the players are simply unwilling to violate agreements on moral grounds and know that this is the case." To model self-commitment using noncooperative game theory, the ability to break the commitment is removed by trimming the branches that emanate from a self-commitment move to remove any alternative contrary to that which has been committed. In a lab setting, this would mean changing the structure of the alternatives made available to subjects after an agreement, which was not done.
2. See, for example, Taylor (1987), Hardin (1971, 1982), Campbell (1985), McLean (1981), Moore (1987). The term "social dilemma" is introduced by Dawes (1975, 1980).
3. See Bianco and Bates (1990) for a theoretical analysis of the capabilities and limits of assigning leaders strong sanctioning powers, and Samuelson et al. (1986)

for an experimental investigation of the choice of a Leviathan-like mechanism to solve social dilemmas.

4. See Gardner, Ostrom, and Walker (1990) and Ostrom, Gardner, and Walker (N. d.) for a detailed exposition of the terms we use and the models we have developed.

5. See Ostrom (1990), National Research Council (1986), Berkes (1989), Pinkerton (1989), Wade (1988) for a discussion of successful, failed, and fragile efforts to self-organize and govern, small-scale CPRs. Michael Hechter's recent synthesis of self-organizing capabilities within many social groups provides evidence across other domains (Hechter 1987; Williamson 1975, 1985). See, also, Kreps (1990) for a useful synthesis of literature relevant to endogenous commitments within firms.

6. The extensive literature on one-shot communication in dilemma games includes: Bornstein and Rapoport (1988); Bornstein et al. (1989); Caldwell (1976); Dawes, McTavish, and Shaklee (1977); Dawes, Orbell, and van de Kragt (1984); Dawes, van de Kragt, and Orbell (1988); Edney and Harper (1978); Jerdee and Rosen (1974); Kramer and Brewer (1986); Braver and Wilson (1984, 1986); Orbell, Dawes, and van de Kragt (1990); Orbell, van de Kragt, and Dawes (1988, 1991); and van de Kragt et al. (1983, 1986).

7. See Isaac and Walker (1988, 1991) and Ostrom and Walker (1991) for a discussion of relevant literature.

8. See works cited in Note 5.

9. Investment in the CPR beyond the maximum net level is termed "rent dissipation" in the literature of resource economics. One can interpret this environment as a limited access CPR (see, for example, Clark 1980; Cornes and Sandler 1986; and Negri 1989).

10. This specification actually has a number of other possible interpretations. For instance, if one defines $F(\Sigma x_i)/\Sigma x_i = y$, and defines y to be a public good, then one has the payoff functions for a voluntary contribution mechanism as in Isaac and Walker (1988). Alternatively, one can define y in the same expression to be an externality, in which case one has payoff functions for Plott's experiments on externalities in product markets (Plott 1983). For further details, see Ledyard (1991).

11. During recruitment, subjects are told they will participate in a 1–2 hour decision-making experiment. Although the exact endpoint is not revealed, it is explicitly bounded from above. Further, all subjects are experienced and have thus experienced the boundedness of an experiment that lasted between 10 and 30 rounds.

12. We use the word "fine" not in the context of redistribution. What is crucial here is that real resources are used up, and not merely redistributed, by efforts to sanction.

13. Besides the symmetric imperfect equilibria given above, there are many asymmetric equilibria. Take any permutation of the identity matrix—for instance,

1 sanctions 2, 2 sanctions 3, and so on. Then these permuted sanctions also support the same outcome as strategy 2 does. Notice that if mistakes are what cause deviations, then an equilibrium like strategy 2 will generate n fines every time a mistake takes place, which is considerably more than the 0 fines generated by the subgame consistent equilibrium strategy 1.

14. Net yield accrued as a percentage of maximum = (Return from Market 2 minus the opportunity costs of tokens invested in Market 2)/(Return from Market 2 at the optimum minus the opportunity costs of tokens invested in Market 2). Opportunity costs equal the potential return that could have been earned by investing the tokens in Market 1.

15. A complete set of instructions is available from the authors upon request. In high endowment experiments, subjects were informed that their cash payoff would be one-half of the "lab" dollars earned in the experiment. This was done so that total payments in high and low endowment treatments would be approximately equal.

16. At the end of all experiments, subjects were paid privately (in cash) their individual earnings. All subjects had participated previously in an experiment using the constituent game environment. The number of rounds in earlier experiments had varied from 10 to 20. Subjects were recruited randomly from this pool of experienced subjects to ensure that no prior experimental group was brought back intact. Walker, Gardner, and Ostrom (1990, 1991) provide a detailed account of behavior in the constituent game environment.

17. In the one-shot communication experiments subjects received information on individual decisions after each round to facilitate a comparison of results in designs in which we add sanctioning alone or in conjunction with one-shot communication. Information was given by subject number, thereby preserving anonymity. This added information had no significant impact on observed yields.

18. As in the one-shot communication setting, each person was identified with a badge that was unrelated to their player number. This facilitated player iden-tification in our transcripts. If unanimous, players could forego discussion.

19. We also conducted a series of costly communication experiments where subjects had first to pay for opportunity to communicate. See Ostrom and Walker (1991) for a detailed discussion. Also, see Isaac and Walker (1988, 1991).

20. Earlier experiments focusing on sanctioning mechanisms without com-munication include Yamagishi (1986, 1988).

21. A comparison of the initial 10 rounds to the initial 10 rounds of baseline, suggests that the addition of anonymous information about individual decisions had no impact on investments.

22. A second set of sanctioning experiments was conducted as a check on the robustness of our original design. Readers of our earlier results conjectured that the lack of a significant improvement in net yield with the introduction of a sanctioning mechanism in our initial design could be due to a hysteresis tied to the decisions in the first 10 periods, periods in which there was no sanctioning

mechanism. In our second design, three new experiments were conducted in which the sanctioning mechanism was introduced prior to the first decision period. The fee to fine ratio was $.40 to $.80. Subjects used fines repeatedly in all three experiments. The results from our second set of experiments are consistent with those from our first design. There was no persistent yield-improving behavior which can be tied to the introduction of the sanctioning mechanism. In fact, when costs of fees and fines are incorporated we found a negative impact on net benefits.

23. It is well-known that inducing trigger strategy behavior in subjects is extremely difficult. For a recent attempt, see Sell and Wilson (1991).

24. One player resisted the suggestion made by another player to dump all of the tokens into the CPR by stating that "we screw ourselves too."

25. We did not explore the effect of an external agent assigned responsibility to monitor and sanction behavior because in this research we were interested in the feasibility of internal enforcement.

26. See Ostrom (1987, 1989, 1991) for an elucidation of an alternative theory to that of Hobbes.

References

Berkes, Fikret, ed. 1989. *Common property resources, ecology and community-based sustainable development.* London: Belhaven Press.

Bianco, William T., and Robert H. Bates. 1990. Cooperation by design: Leadership, structure, and collective dilemmas. *American Political Science Review* 84 (March): 133–47.

Bornstein, Gary, and Amnon Rapoport. 1988. Intergroup competition for the provision of step-level public goods: Effects of preplay communication. *European Journal of Social Psychology* 18:125–42.

Bornstein, Gary, Amnon Rapoport, Lucia Kerpel, and Tani Katz. 1989. Within- and between-group communication in intergroup competition for public goods. *Journal of Experimental Social Psychology* 25:422–36.

Braver, Sanford L., and L. A. Wilson. 1984. A laboratory study of social contracts as a solution to public goods problems: Surviving on the lifeboat. Paper presented at Western Social Science Association, San Diego, April.

———. 1986. Choices in social dilemmas. Effects of communication within subgroups. *Journal of Conflict Resolution* 30(1): 51–62.

Caldwell, Michael D. 1976. Communication and sex effects in a five-person prisoners' dilemma game. *Journal of Personality and Social Psychology* 33(3): 273–80.

Campbell, R. 1985. Background for the uninitiated. In *Paradoxes of rationality and cooperation*, edited by R. Campbell and L. Sowden. Vancouver: University of British Columbia Press, 3–41.

Clark, Colin W. 1980. Restricted access to common-property fishery resources: Game-theoretic analysis. In *Dynamic optimization and mathematical economics*, edited by Pan-Tai Liu. New York: Plenum Press, 117–32.

Cornes, Richard, and Todd Sandler. 1986. *The theory of externalities, public goods, and club goods.* Cambridge: Cambridge University Press.

Dawes, Robyn M. 1975. Formal models of dilemmas in social decision making. In *Human judgement and decision processes: Formal and mathematical approaches*, edited by Martin F. Kaplan and Steven Schwartz. New York: Academic Press.

———. 1980. Social Dilemmas. *Annual Review of Psychology* 31:169–93.

Dawes, Robyn M., Jeanne McTavish, and Harriet Shaklee. 1977. Behavior, communication, and assumptions about other people's behavior in a commons dilemma situation. *Journal of Personality and Social Psychology* 35(1): 1–11.

Dawes, Robyn M., John M. Orbell, and Alphons J. C. van de Kragt. 1984. Normative constraint and incentive compatible design. Department of Psychology, University of Oregon, Eugene.

Dawes, Robyn M., Alphons J. C. van de Kragt, and John M. Orbell. 1988. Not me or thee but we: The importance of group identity in eliciting cooperation in dilemma situations: Experimental manipulations. *Acta Psychologica* 68:83–97.

Edney, Julian J., and Christopher S. Harper. 1978. The commons dilemma: A review of contributions from psychology. *Environmental Management* 2(6): 491–507.

Gardner, Roy, Elinor Ostrom, and James Walker. 1990. The nature of common-pool resource problems. *Rationality and Society* 2:335–58.

Hardin, Russell. 1971. Collective action as an agreeable N-prisoner's dilemma. *Behavioral Science* 16(5): 472–81.

———. 1982. *Collective action.* Baltimore: Johns Hopkins University Press.

Harsanyi, John C., and Reinhard Selten. 1988. *A general theory of equilibrium selection in games.* Cambridge: MIT Press.

Hechter, Michael. 1987. *Principles of group solidarity.* Berkeley: University of California Press.

Hobbes, Thomas. 1960. *Leviathan.* Oxford: Basil Blackwell. Originally published in 1651.

Isaac, R. Mark, and James M. Walker. 1988. Communication and free-riding behavior: The voluntary contribution mechanism. *Economic Inquiry* 24(4): 585–608.

Isaac, R. Mark, and James M. Walker. 1991. Costly communication: An experiment in a nested public goods problem. In *Laboratory research in political economy*, edited by Thomas R. Palfrey. Ann Arbor: University of Michigan Press, 269–86.

Jankowski, Richard. 1990. Punishment in iterated chicken and prisoner's dilemma games. *Rationality and society* 2(4): 449–70.

Jerdee, Thomas H., and Benson Rosen. 1974. Effects of opportunity to communicate and visibility of individual decisions on behavior in the common interest. *Journal of Applied Psychology* 59(6): 712–16.

Kramer, R. M., and Marilyn M. Brewer. 1986. Social group identity and the emergence of cooperation in resource conservation dilemmas. In *Experimental social dilemmas*, edited by Henk A. Wilke, David M. Messick, and Christel G. Rutte. Frankfurt: Verlag Peter Lang, 205–34.

Kreps, David M. 1990. Corporate culture and economic theory. In *Perspectives on positive political economy*, edited by James E. Alt and Kenneth A. Shepsle. New York: Cambridge University Press, 90–143.

Kreps, David M., Paul Milgrom, John Roberts, and Robert Wilson. 1982. Rational cooperation in the finitely repeated prisoners' dilemma. *Journal of Economic Theory* 27:245–52.

Ledyard, John O. 1991. Is there a problem with public good provision? California Institute of Technology, Pasadena. Mimeo.

McLean, Iain. 1981. The social contract in leviathan and the prisoner's dilemma supergame. *Political Studies* 29(3): 339–51.

Moore, Clement Henry. 1987. Prisoners' financial dilemmas: A consociational future for Lebanon? *American Political Science Review* 81(1): 201–18.

Nash, John F. 1950. The bargaining problem. *Econometrica* 18:155–62.

———. 1951. Non-cooperative games. *Annals of Mathematics* 54:286–95.

National Research Council. 1986. *Proceedings of the conference on common property resource management*. Washington, DC: National Academy Press.

Negri, D. H. 1989. The common property aquifer as a differential game. *Water Resources Research* 25:9–15.

Ophuls, W. 1973. Leviathan or oblivion. In *Toward a Steady State Economy*, edited by H. E. Daly. San Francisco: Freeman, 215–30.

Orbell, John M., Robyn M. Dawes, and Alphons J. C. van de Kragt. 1990. The limits of multilateral promising. *Ethics* 100(4): 616–27.

Orbell, John M., Alphons J. C. van de Kragt, and Robyn M. Dawes. 1988. Explaining discussion-induced cooperation. *Journal of Personality and Social Psychology* 54(5): 811–19.

———. 1991. Covenants without the sword: The role of promising in social dilemma circumstances. In *Social norms and economic institutions*, edited by Ken Koford. Ann Arbor: University of Michigan Press.

Ostrom, Elinor. 1990. *Governing the commons: The evolution of institutions for collective action*. New York: Cambridge University Press.

Ostrom, Elinor, and James Walker. 1991. Communication in a commons: Cooperation without external enforcement. In *Laboratory research in political economy*, edited by Thomas R. Palfrey. Ann Arbor: University of Michigan Press, 287–322.

Ostrom, Elinor, Roy Gardner, and James Walker. N.d. *Rules, games, and common-pool resources.* Ann Arbor: University of Michigan Press. Forthcoming.

Ostrom, Vincent. 1987. *The political theory of a compound republic: Designing the American experiment.* 2d rev. ed. Lincoln: University of Nebraska Press.

————. 1989. *The intellectual crisis in American public administration.* 2d ed. Tuscaloosa: University of Alabama Press.

————. 1991. *The meaning of American federalism: Constituting a self-governing society.* San Francisco: Institute for Contemporary Studies Press.

Pinkerton, Evelyn, ed. 1989. *Co-operative management of local fisheries. New directions for improved management and community development.* Vancouver: University of British Columbia Press.

Plott, Charles R. 1983. Externalities and corrective policies in experimental markets. *Economic Journal* 93:106–27.

Samuelson, Charles D., David M. Messick, Henk A. M. Wilke, and Christel G. Rutte. 1986. Individual restraint and structural change as solutions to social dilemmas. In *Experimental social dilemmas*, edited by Henk A. M. Wilke, David M. Messick, and Christel G. Rutte. Frankfurt: Verlag Peter Lang, 29–54.

Sell, Jane, and Rick Wilson. 1991. Levels of information and contributions to public goods. *Social Forces* 70(1): 107–24.

Selten, Reinhard. 1971. A simple model of imperfect competition where 4 are few and 6 are many. *International Journal of Game Theory* 2:141–201.

Selten, Reinhard, Michael Mitzkewitz, and Gerald R. Uhlich. 1988. Duopoly strategies programmed by experienced players. University of Bonn Special Research Project 303, discussion paper B–172.

Taylor, Michael. 1987. *The possibility of cooperation.* Cambridge: Cambridge University Press.

van de Kragt, Alphons J. C., John M. Orbell, and Robyn M. Dawes. 1983. The minimal contributing set as a solution to public goods problem. *American Political Science Review* 77 (March): 112–22.

van de Kragt, Alphons J. C., Robyn M. Dawes, John M. Orbell, S. R. Braver, and L. A. Wilson. 1986. Doing well and doing good as ways of resolving social dilemmas. In *Experimental social dilemmas*, edited by H. Wilke, D. Messick, and C. Rutte. Frankfurt am Main, FRG: Verlag Peter Lang, 177–204.

Wade, Robert. 1988. *Village republics. Economic conditions for collective action in South India.* Cambridge: Cambridge University Press.

Walker, James, Roy Gardner, and Elinor Ostrom. 1990. Rent dissipation in a limited-access common-pool resource: Experimental evidence. *Journal of Environmental Economics and Management* 19:203–11.

————. 1991. Rent dissipation and balanced deviation disequilibrium in common pool resources: Experimental evidence. In *Game equilibrium models II: Methods, morals, and markets*, edited by Reinhard Selten. Berlin: Springer-Verlag, 337–67.

Williamson, Oliver E. 1975. *Markets and hierarchies: Analysis and antitrust im-*

plications. New York: Free Press.

———. 1985. *The economic institutions of capitalism: Firms, markets, relational contracting*. New York: Free Press.

Yamagishi, Toshio. 1986. The provision of a sanctioning system as a public good. *Journal of Personality and Social Psychology* 51(1): 110–16.

———. 1988. Seriousness of social dilemmas and the provision of a sanctioning system. *Social Psychology Quarterly* 51(1): 32–42.

9

Humankind in Prehistory: Economy, Ecology, and Institutions

Vernon L. Smith*

This essay is about who we were in prehistory and how we were shaped by economic principles.[1] Of the many models that one encounters in the antiquities literature of humankind, unabashedly economic models are rare. Such models are easily dismissed as reductionist economic determinism because they appear not to account for the richness of culture. The tale of humankind I relate here is based on a relatively simple model of the influence of opportunity cost and human capital accumulation. It explains mankind's evolution from our genesis in bipedalism through tool manufacturing to anatomically modern *Homo sapiens*, hunting big game, planting seeds and harvesting crops, and developing art and language.

* A much shorter version of this paper was printed, as my presidential address to the Western Economic Association, in *Economic Inquiry* (January 1992), under the title of "Economic Principles in the Emergence of Humankind." I am indebted to Bob Heizer for first prevailing upon me to research and write on the economics of hunting and gathering; to Paul Martin for significant encouragement as well as detailed comments and corrections; to Richard Klein for helpful corrections; and to Adrienne Zihlman for references and comments leading to revisions in the second section. None of them can be held accountable for any misinterpretation of the history or science. Finally, I thank Robert Heilbroner and my friend Ed Ames for their comments.

Crucial to this development and consistent with the theme of this volume, prehistoric man developed institutions that conditioned his use of resources. Property rights evolved as an essential part of man's institutional environment as a result of the changing constraints of the natural and technological environment. These property rights could evolve in the absence of a centralized state because they depended on reciprocity, mutual dependence, and state-like forms of control achieved through broadened kinship ties, customs, and culture. While early property rights were not always private or transferable, they did constrain individual and group behavior by limiting access to scarce resources. In this sense, the successful evolution of humankind is closely related to the customs and culture that shaped prehistoric property rights.

Life Emerged Early, Bipedalism and *Homo* Very Late

The Earth and other planets, formed by the condensation of gas that produced our solar system, are about 4.5 billion years old. Elementary life forms, found in Australia and South Africa, appear 3.8–3.5 billion years before present (B.P.), which is about as early as life as we know it could have emerged. But multicellular animals are not found in the fossil record until much later, some 650 million years B.P., and those of modern form that are believed to be antecedents of humankind appear about 550 million years B.P.

In Africa, sometime between 10 and 5 million years ago, bipedal protohumans almost certainly split off from the forerunners of today's chimpanzee and gorilla. This is indicated directly by the fossil record and by genetic comparisons between living people and other primates. During this period a globally cooler and drier climate shrunk forests in favor of grasslands and savannas (Klein 1989, 29–35, 180–181; Laporte and Zihlman 1983). This was a conditioning factor. Grassland ungulates (hoofed mammals) increased in number and diversity as the cost of harvesting their food declined, and the resulting economic stress on forest dwellers brought the extinction of many ape species in Eurasia. But at least one ape species in Africa adapted by becoming more of a ground dweller (Klein 1989, 181). These environmental changes may have made bipedalism an economizing response in several ways: it was easier to carry food and young; heat stress would have been reduced by exposing less body surface to direct sunlight; the freeing of hands for using, carrying, and later fabricating, tools; the decreased energy requirements of locomotion; and, finally, improved ability to see over obstructions, grass and shrubs.

Although bipedalism predates the earliest recorded stone tools, early humankind may have used wood, bamboo, and other perishable material for simple fabricated tools, much as Chimpanzees (genetically the nearest relative of humans) will make, transport and use sticks to reach for food.[2] In fact it can be argued that an elementary reliance on implements may have predated bipedalism and helped to account for our protohuman ancestor's ability to flourish in Savanna environments (Laporte and Zihlman 1983, 105–7).

Although bipedalism was the important opportunistic response (for us), it was not a unique experimental adaptation by nature to the demands of a Savanna environment. Apparently the other response was to become a more effective quadrupedal knuckle-walker, to evolve into the modern chimpanzee, and to continue to exploit woodland as well as Savanna environments (Zihlman 1991). If our ancestral protohumans were adaptively attempting bipedalism as grasslands expanded, then mutations favoring bipedalism would have economic value.

At some point, perhaps 4–3 million years B.P. (proposed in Zihlman and Cohn 1988), early bipedal hominids developed reduced body hair and thermo-regulatory (body cooling) sweat glands. Hair reduction would have necessitated skin pigmentation to protect against ultraviolet radiation. These developments, especially in combination with bipedalism, would have greatly enhanced survival and foraging productivity in open grassland and savanna mosaic environments.

The cooler dryer trend in climate that is associated with the emergence of bipedalism accelerated from 2.5 to 2 million years B.P. This coincided with rapid evolutionary change in hominids and other African mammals leading to a more carnivorous, larger-brained, and more tool-dependent lineage of *Homo* whose expanding niche may explain the decline of other African carnivores (Vrba 1985; Walker 1984).

The earliest firmly documented stone tools (attributed to *H. habilis*) are found at the Hadar site in Northeast Ethiopia adjacent to the Red Sea; they are conservatively dated at 2.5–2.4 million years B.P., but could be as old as 3.1 million years (Harris 1983). These and other sites in Zaire, Olduvai and elsewhere show that stone tools were widely used in Southern and Eastern Africa by 2 million years B.P. These early tools, while crude by later standards, were diverse, but the diversity (based upon experimental replication) appears to have been controlled by the random shape of the original blank not by deliberate design (Toth 1985). The tool kit and their suggested uses included flakes (for cutting and splitting), scrapers (for butchery), and cobble missiles (for hunting or defense). The combination of such stone tools with fragmentary animal bones clearly demonstrate an increased interest in meat by *H. habilis* over earlier hominids; but it cannot be definitely said that they were great hunters. Most of the assemblages are found near ancient stream or lake beds where animals would have congregated. Although the bones often show evidence of scarring from stone tools this does not prove that meat was obtained by hunting instead of by scavenging the kills of other carnivores. Whether it was more cost efficient for these early humans to take meat from such formidable carnivores than to dispatch the prey themselves is an open research issue. A recent study of Hazda scavenging finds that "scavenging returns were highly variable, depending on carcass encounter rates, carcass size and completeness on encounter, and success at displacing the original predators" (O'Connell, Hawkes, and Jones 1988, 356). The authors conclude that even if early hominids had no difficulty displacing competing carnivores, scavenging could only have been intermittently successful in savanna environments comparable to those in the Hazda study.

At the beginning of the Pleistocene, approximately 1.8–1.7 million years ago, *H. habilis* was replaced by *H. erectus*, generally thought to be the direct ancestor of *H. sapiens* and of you and me. Today we are still in the Pleistocene epoch (or Quaternary) enjoying a warming interglacial period which began about 14,000 years B.P.[3]

The significance of the Pleistocene is that the evolutionary, cultural and economic development of humankind was accelerated during the ebb and flow of the earth's cycles in glaciation. There have been 17 major glaciations in the last 1.7 million years and eight during the last 730,000 years. At the peak glaciation nearly a third of the earth's surface was covered by ice sheets; and the sea level dropped by 400–500 feet. This caused the joining of land masses that were isolated in the warm stages: Siberia with Alaska, Australia with New Guinea and Southeast Asia with Java. Gulfs such as the Persian were river valleys above sea level. Within the past 1 million years interglaciations as warm as the one we are now experiencing have lasted only about 10,000 years whereas the periods of glaciation have lasted more like 100,000 years. (Perhaps this will comfort those concerned with global warming.) Consequently, our ancestral development occurred under mostly glacial conditions, to which we adapted well. These cycles of glaciation made possible a world-wide redistribution of plants, animals, and humankind (Klein 1989, 34–35).

Out of Africa: Exodus I

A prominent contemporary view of the emergence of modern humans is the "out-of-Africa model" in which humankind first evolved in Africa then spread throughout Eurasia (Gould 1988; Stringer 1990) in an initial wave beginning about 1 million years B.P. In Africa the displacement of *H. habilis* by *H. erectus* may be explained by the increased emphasis on tool use and by carnivory. *H. erectus* was much better endowed with a locomotor skeleton, had a larger brain plus the typically human external nose.[4] These endowments suggest improved exertion capacity and hunting, gathering, or scavenging skill.

The greater adaptability of *H. erectus* is demonstrated by this people's colonization of previously unoccupied dry regions of Africa about 1.5 million years B.P. and by their dispersal to Northern Africa and thence into colder regions such as Eurasia and China, and to Java after 1 million years B.P. Generally, in the African and eastward expansion paths of *H. erectus* one finds evidence of tool use which required more investment in human capital—planning, foresight, and preparation effort—than is associated with *H. habilis*. Thus the finding that most of our current growth is due to investment in human capital probably applies with even greater force to the last 2 million years of hominid development. The tool kit now includes hand axes, cleavers and other large bifacial tools used for butchery, bone breaking and perhaps wood working (wood spears appear toward the end of this period). Also it is likely that *H. erectus* could control the use of fire; the oldest evidence is 1.5 to 1.4 million years B.P., although more convincing evidence does not appear until 500,000 years ago[5].

A long standing puzzle is the geographical distribution of these tools in Southeast Asia; here the tools are less standardized and there is a paucity of hand axes but no shortage of chopper tools. At one time this led to the conclusion that *H. erectus* was culturally retarded, that they had minimal capacity for standardizing the manufacture of stone tools. Yet it is hard to believe that the same race of people who made hand axes in Africa and Northwest Asia, and who had trekked to Southeast Asia had unintentionally lost this sophisticated craft. A hypothesized solution has now been offered by the observation that the line across Southeast Asia below which one finds alleged "cultural retardation" corresponds to the distribution of naturally occurring bamboo. This is an area which today contains over 1000 species of bamboo, a raw material that can be fabricated into knives, spears, projectile points, and traps (Pope 1989). It would appear that *H. erectus*, far from having suffered cultural degeneration in bambooland, was simply responding to the locally high opportunity cost of making standardized tools, such as hand axes, from stone.

Out of Africa: Exodus II

Up to about 500–400,000 years B.P., most human fossils are those of *H. erectus* in Java, China and Africa. The exceptions are assigned to early *H. sapiens*. The European fossils suggest an anticipation of the later Neanderthals. The trend was different in Africa where *H. erectus* appears to have evolved in the direction of modern *H. sapiens*, while fossils in Southeast Asia maintained their similarity with *H. erectus*. Artifacts in the latter region continue to be dominated by flake and chopping tools with an absence of hand axes. Early *H. sapiens*' hand axes and other stone artifacts were better made, and they invented a technique for predetermining flake size so that tools could be more deliberately designed, but such artifacts were generally uniform in function and style over wide areas and a long period of time (Klein 1989).

Neanderthals—traditionally believed to be our immediate ancestors—are thought to be a Eurasian descendant of *H. erectus*. They appeared 130,000 years ago or earlier, had a brain case at least as large as living people, and, judging from the skeleton and muscle/ligament markings on the bones, had exceptional physical strength (Trinkaus 1986). They were adapted to cold climate, and made tools of wood (e.g. spears), but bone tools are rare. Judging from the animal bones at numerous sites, Neanderthals successfully hunted deer, bison, aurochs (wild cattle), sheep, goats and horses. They cared for family members who were handicapped or incapacitated, and were the first people who practiced intentional burial, perhaps with ceremony; they may have adorned their bodies with ocher. But their unusual adaptation was not viable, and they disappeared about 30,000 years ago (Klein 1989; Gould 1988).

Although modern *H. sapiens* or Cro-Magnons traditionally had been thought to originate 50–40,000 years B.P., and to have overlapped Neanderthals, recent claims find anatomically modern humans as early as 90,000 years B.P. (Valladas et al. 1988). Thus Neanderthals may have overlapped Cro-Magnons for over 50,000 years, and according to one view, are not central stock but a side branch. The contemporary view, supported by fossil and genetic evidence, is that modern humans evolved within the period 200,000–50,000 years B.P. in Africa.[6]

Prior to this, time body form and behavior (based on tool assemblages) evolved together (Klein 1989, 1992). Subsequently, behavioral evolution accelerated, within a constant bodily form. Thus, "The people of Cro-Magnon carved intricate figures of horses and deer and painted their caves with an esthetic power never exceeded in the history of human art" (Gould 1988, 16). After 40–35,000 years ago artifact assemblages varied tremendously across neighboring regions, and the pace of change accelerated dramatically (Klein 1989, 360–398). Cro-Magnons fashioned bone, ivory and antler into projectile points, awls, punches, needles and art objects. Compared to the Neanderthal, their stone crafts included more blades with longer cutting edges and numerous shouldered projectile points of the kind suitable for spears, arrows and darts. Also graves, houses and fireplaces were more elaborate. Ceramic fired clay appears about 28,000 years B.P.

Eurasian Cro-Magnons hunted in savannas and grasslands principally for mammoth, bison, reindeer, antelope and horse—all large gregarious herbivores—that provided meat, hide, and sinew, as well as bone, antler and ivory. Like the American Indian and the plains settlers, it is likely that they burned the dried droppings ("buffalo chips") of large animals where wood was unavailable (Klein 1989, 366). After 20,000 years B.P. the artifacts include the atlatl (spear thrower), arrows, stone inserts in antlers, harpoons, leisters (three pronged fish spear), eyed needles, and all manner of clothing—jackets, shirts, trousers, etc. Conclusive evidence for the bow and arrow appears 12–10,000 years ago (Tyldesley and Bahn 1983), but a much earlier origin is likely given the frequent occurrence of stone points similar to those used for arrow tips in historical times.

In Europe 34,000–11,000 years B.P., there is widespread evidence that humankind had the means of making large numbers of kills of a single species. They ate ungulates, fish, molluscs, birds and seals. The staples were reindeer, red deer, horse, ibex and bison. Evidence of the mass slaughter of horse and reindeer suggest they were driven into cliff enclosed canyons, or off "jumps." The Cro-Magnons were adept at the battue (beating underbrush to drive game), the drive line, the stampede, and the pit trap.

Humankind: Super Predation and World Expansion

Modern *H. sapiens* spread from Africa through Europe and Asia in the last 50,000 years, jumped to Australia by about 40,000 years B.P., entered Alaska perhaps 14–12,000 B.P., the lower 48 states of North American by 12,000 B.P., and within the next 1000 years reached the southern tip of South America. The last stages of this worldwide expansion were Madagascar, New Zealand, and Antarctica which were occupied by humankind only in the last 1000 years.

A plausible theoretical hypothesis is that North America was discovered by advanced Paleolithic people who crossed the exposed Bering land bridge, connecting Asia with Alaska, 14–12,000 years ago. The Bering terrain was unsuitable for gathering plants but the subarctic grasses supported the cold-adapted mammoth, bison, and caribou. Communal hunting parties, armed with stone weapons, and able to control fire, were big-game hunters par excellence. Their descendants found an exposed land corridor between the Western and Midcontinent ice sheets in Canada (Klein 1989, 390) and made their way ultimately into Montana, then South and East throughout the United States. As suggested by Martin (1990), they entered a continent that was an unprecedented "home-on-the-range" for now extinct mammoth, mastodon, ground sloth, two species of extinct bear, a cheetah, the giant beaver (*Castoroides*, the size of a black bear, and the largest North American rodent), horse, tapir, two species of peccary, camel, llama, two species of extinct deer, the stag moose, pronghorn, shrub ox, two species of musk ox, yak, two subspecies of bison (*B. occidentalis* and *B. antiquus*), both larger than the surviving *B. bison* known to the plains settlers, the dire wolf, a saber-toothed and a scimitar-toothed "tiger," and many other less familiar megafauna. Many of these animals, such as the ground sloth, were slow and would have been easily hunted, or like the mammoth, mastodon, and horse were large gregarious herding animals. The herding behavior of these great animals implied low search cost for hunting parties armed with stone projectile points and strategic knowledge of animal behavior; their great size meant high value per kill; while some prey such as the extinct plains bison may have been easier to hunt than their living relatives. Since there were no property rights in live animals, only in harvested animals, there was no incentive to stay the spear in anticipation of tomorrow's reproductive value as with modern domesticated cattle—descendants of the Old World auroch. The resulting mass harvesting pressure on animals may have caused or contributed to the extensive megafauna loss on the North American continent by 11,000 years B.P. Their hunting parties left behind Clovis fluted points—a work of craftsmanship in stone—found from Florida to Nova Scotia, in the high plains, the Southwest, across the Midwest, and in the South. These points are 7–15 centimeters long, 3–4 centimeters wide with concave bases, and a fluting extending from the base to one-half the length of the point. They were flaked by percussion and the base edges ground down to prevent cutting of the thongs securing them to a throwing or thrusting spear—a design that would allow the weapon to sustain lateral stress if it remained in the hand of the hunter after penetrating the prey.

That Clovis hunters killed mammoth is well documented; also that these animals had become extinct by 11,000 years B.P. (Haynes 1964, 1988), although they " . . . had been in North America for over one million years" (Martin 1990, 111). Numerous mammoth kill sites in the western United States show direct evidence that the mammoth was harvested by hunters. Some sites also contain the bones of camel and horse,[7] but no incontrovertible evidence exists that these animals were hunted in North America, although the horse was one of the most widely hunted animals in the Paleolithic Old World. The horse became extinct in North America (where it originated) only about 10–9000 years B.P. (Mead and Meltzer 1984, 446). It was reintroduced by the Spanish in the sixteenth century and has thrived in the wild down to the present under the arid conditions of Arizona, Nevada and Utah. The Clovis point was replaced by the Folsom point between 11,000 and 10,000 years B.P.; it is less widely dispersed than the Clovis and is associated with the extinct *Bison antiquus*, which is much larger than surviving American Bison. The Scottsbluff and similar projectile points date from about 9000 years ago and are associated with the slightly smaller extinct *Bison occidentalis*. It appears likely that Paleo-Indian procurement of Bison occurred in mass kills, sometimes of several hundred animals at a time. This is illustrated at the Olsen-Chubbuck site in Colorado (Wheat 1967) where, 8500 years B.P., 200 *B. occidentalis* were stampeded into an arroyo 5–7 feet deep, and dispatched with Scottsbluff projectile points. At least 50 of the animals apparently represented a wastage kill since they showed no evidence of butchery for consumption. Dozens of such kill-butchery sites are found in Colorado, Wyoming, Montana and Nebraska (Frison 1986; Todd 1986). Many sites are stampede jumps or traps, with several thousand years of use. Perhaps the species survived in the form of the plains bison by dwarfing (Edwards 1967); indeed this could have been an adaptive response to the greater vulnerability of the larger subspecies to predation.[8] In any case despite the enormous carrying capacity of the land from Alberta to Texas, which in historical times supported perhaps 60 million bison, we were left with far fewer large species than the fossil record of the Pleistocene would lead one to expect.

Martin (1968, 1984, 1990) has summarized the evidence for the world-wide extinction of late Pleistocene megafauna. In Africa and Asia 15–20 percent of the genera disappeared 80–60,000 years B.P.; in Australia 94 percent were lost from 40–15,000 years B.P.; North and South America experienced a 70–80 percent loss in the last 15,000 years, with an abrupt North American loss of mammoth, mastodon, ground sloth, and such dependent predators and scavengers as the saber toothed cat and (in much of its range) the condor 11,000 years ago. The horse and two subspecies of bison were gone by 9–8,000 years ago. This worldwide pattern correlates suspiciously with the chronology of human colonization leading to Paul Martin's hypothesis that extinction was directly or indirectly due to "overkill" by exceptionally competent hunter cultures. This model explains the light extinctions in Africa and Asia where modern humankind "grew up," allowing gradual adaptation to humankind's accumulating proficiency as a superpredator; it explains the abrupt massive losses in Australia and the Americas—the only habitable continents that were colonized suddenly by advanced stone-aged humans. But the control cases for Martin's "experiment" are the large oceanic islands such as Madagascar and New Zealand; both were colonized within the last 1000 years, and both suffered a wave of extinctions at this time (Dewar 1984; Trotter and McCulloch 1984; Anderson 1989).[9] One wonders, if extinction was due to climatic change, why Madagascar extinctions were not coincident with those of Africa 220 miles off its coast, and those of Australia were not coincident with New Zealand extinctions; and why European and Ukrainian mammoths became extinct 13,000 years B.P. while in North America they survived another 2000 years. Previous great extinction waves had affected plants and small animals as well as large animals, but the late Pleistocene extinctions are concentrated on the large gregarious herding, or slow moving, animals—the ideal prey of human hunters. Such large genera are also the animals that are slower growing, have longer gestation periods, require longer periods of maternal care, and live longer. Consequently they were more vulnerable to hunting pressure because reductions in biomass require more time to recover. The theory is bold—some say fanciful. A counter argument is that there is little direct evidence of hunting; that Paleolithic peoples "probably" relied on plants. But if the fossil record of hunting is "small," the fossil evidence of gathering is virtually non-existent (Klein 1989, 219, 364–5).

A second counter argument is that there would not have been an incentive to overproduce in excess of immediate needs; that this occurs only in modern exchange economies (Frison 1986, 213). But this argument fails to recognize that in the absence of private property rights, there is no intertemporal incentive to avoid the kind of waste associated with large kills. What controls the slaughter of domestic cattle is the comparative value of dressed versus live beef (Smith 1975, 745). Since no one owned the mammoth, their harvest value (net of hunting cost) contrasted sharply with their zero live procreation value to the individual hunter. A third argument finds it incomprehensible that mere bands of men could have wiped out the great mammoth and two subspecies of bison.[10] It takes a particularly skilled modern rifleman to stop a charging African elephant in time to prevent injury, and extant bison react quickly and violently when they sense danger (Frison 1986, 188–192).

Such observations may simply tell us that these particular subspecies have survived because they were selected for their successful defensive characteristics. We know nothing of the behavioral properties of extinct species which may have been far more approachable than their surviving relatives. While the African and Indian elephants are both members of the same genus, their fossil similarities fail to inform us that the Indian elephant is docile and easily trained for circus display, while the African elephant is not. No one has successfully domesticated the African zebra; in contrast, the Tarpan horse has been domesticated since ancient times (5000–2500 B.P.). *Equus* includes horses, asses and zebras—all behaviorally distinct animals.

Interpretations and Hypotheses From the Prehistoric Record

Several principles and hypotheses stem from an economic interpretation of this brief survey of the prehistorical record.

1. *Hunting and gathering provided the technology and institutions for the first affluent society.*

One of the great myths of modern humankind is the belief that life in the Paleolithic was intolerably harsh, or as presumed (without evidence) by Hobbes, "solitary, poor, nasty, brutish and short." It may have been none of these. What is just as likely is that hunting and gathering provided the first affluent society (Sahlins 1972); it sustained and promoted humankind for almost all of their 2.5 million years of existence. The Hobbesian belief obscures the striking continuity in the ability of prehistoric humans to adapt to changes in their environment by substituting new inputs of capital, labor and knowledge for old, and to fabricate new products when effort prices were altered by the environment, or by new learning. Late Pleistocene human skeletons show a mortality pattern like that of historic hunter-gatherers, and "rarely show evidence of serious accidents or disease . . ." (Klein 1989, 385). Their teeth were healthy probably because their diets contained little sugar. Historically, among the hunting and fishing peoples of Africa, Australia, the Pacific Northwest, Alaska, Malaya, and Canada, malnutrition, starvation, and chronic diseases were rare or infrequent. Studies of the African Kung Bushman (Lee 1968) show that these people worked only 12–19 hours per week; their hunting and gathering activities scored well on several measures of nutritional adequacy; and their labor bought much leisure in the form of resting, visiting, entertaining and trance dancing.[11] Similarly, African Hazda hunters worked no more than two hours per day, with time for gambling, other social activities, or investment. Much of the diversity in our ancestral development must have been due to the extent to which different peoples employed released time from subsistence for different forms of investment in human capital.

Although studies of the prehistoric record place great emphasis on the intellectual development of humans—brain size, tool use, the control of fire—their prowess as hunter-gatherers was likely also due to their physical superiority over other animals. After all, tool development was slow and limited until the explosive development of the late prehistoric period. But human physical superiority is striking. As J. B. S. Haldane once noted, only man can swim a mile, walk twenty and then climb a tree.

2. *Opportunity cost has conditioned the cultural and economic development of humankind.*

This principle was articulated succinctly by the Kung bushman who was asked by an anthropologist why he had not turned to agriculture (as his neighbors had done). His reply: "Why should we plant when there are so many mongongo nuts in the world?" (Lee 1968, 33). Why indeed, unless tastes and opportunity cost combine to demand it? Bipedalism itself occurred at a time when the cost of an arboreal existence was stressing primate populations. An economical adaptation was to subsist in the spreading savannas and grasslands that were replacing the forest. The great migrations out of Africa, the invention of weapons for big game hunting, Eskimo adaptation to hunting sea mammals, humankind's eventual turn to agriculture; these can all be interpreted as responses to changes in opportunity cost whether driven by environmental change, by human learning, or their conjunction. A telling example of the influence of effort prices on prehistoric human choice is found in Lee's (1968) study of 58 extant hunter-gatherer societies the world over. There is a strong correlation between a society's distance from the equator and the relative importance of hunting over gathering in its diet. In the Arctic the hunting of land and sea-mammals predominated, while in the temperate latitudes up to 39 degrees from the equator, gathering was much the more important economic activity.

Economic models of human development and change are often held suspect because they appear not to account for the richness of culture. But culture and institutions can be interpreted as providing the information system for transmitting the learning embodied in the unconscious response to opportunity cost and as providing the rules of the game that prevent the "tragedy of the commons." Thus hunter cultures use ceremony and ritual to enhance recognition of the value and significance of the chase and its technology of execution. Culture is the means of transmitting human capital from generation to generation; of forming in the young an indelible impression of the hunt. The magnificent Cro-Magnon art preserved on the walls deep in the narrow crawl spaces of French and Spanish caves have been given this interpretation: "Imprinting enormous amounts of information in memory called for . . . the use of confined spaces, obstacles and difficult routes, and hidden images to heighten the natural strangeness of underground settings . . . piling special effect on special effect in an effort to ensure the preservation and transmission of the tribal encyclopedia" (Pfeiffer 1982, 132).

Another example of the hidden economic function of culture is the magical practice of the Naskapi Indians of Labrador, who, when the caribou were scarce and the tribe hungry, resorted to scapulimacy, a divination in which the shoulder blade bone of a caribou was heated by fire until it cracked. As cracks appeared, they were interpreted by a diviner in terms of the local geography and caribou haunts, as trails, one of which the hunter should follow if he was to be successful. Speck (1935) reports having observed 12 successful hunts out of 19 divinations, noting that the unsuccessful cases were always attributed to the failure of the diviner to correctly read the scapula map. All this is interpreted by Speck as showing the capacity of the Naskapi for belief in magic. But is scapulimacy functional? One function of course is to sharpen the hunter's concentration, and to impress upon all the need for great dedication. Moore's (1957) study of magical practices led him to the conclusion that they served immediately practical economic ends. The effect of Naskapi magic was to cause the hunter to choose a random route, steering him away from previously successful hunting routes, and preventing the caribou from being sensitized to regularities in hunter behavior.[12] What the Naskapi in effect seem to have discovered was that reading shoulder blades had survival value. "People are capable of formulating any number of strange ideas, not necessarily directed towards any particular end, but if they do have a practical application and are successful, they may persist. And if they persist long enough people will begin to believe in them" (Reader 1988, 139). If they are believed, I might add, they will be incorporated into educational rituals so that the tribal learning is not lost to each new generation.

3. *Prehistoric H. sapiens accumulated human capital.*

Economic success as a hunter-gatherer required an endowment of human capital normally associated only with the agricultural and industrial revolutions: learning, knowledge transfer, tool fabrication skill and design, and social organization. The aboriginal use of fire for game and plant management demonstrates that prehistoric humans possessed knowledge of the phenology of trees, shrubs, and herbs, used fire to enhance the growth and flowering of certain food plants (huckleberry and hazel bushes, bear lilies, wild rice, etc.), and to suppress the growth of competitors.[13] Effective game and wild plant management required people to know where, when, how and with what frequency to burn. Aboriginals knew that the growing season for wild plants can be advanced by spring burns designed to warm the earth, that in dry weather fires should be ignited at the top of hills to prevent wild fires,[14] but in damp conditions they should be set in depressions to avoid being extinguished, that the burning of underbrush aided the production of acorns by the oak trees, and attracted moose, deer and other animals who feed on the tender new shoots that follow a burn.[15]

Humankind was a fire creature beginning with *H. erectus*, and fire "revolutionized human society and its relationship to the natural world" (Pyne 1991). Anthropogenic fire redefined or reformed food, dentition, facial muscles, tools (wood spears could be fire-hardened, trunks fire-carved into dugout canoes) and the ecology of humankind's environments. The Australian aborigines were the "black lightening" that ignited Australia with their arrival some 40,000 years ago where they lived abundantly by fire stick farming: burning to increase access to roots and tubers, to recycle nutrients more quickly in dry regions, and to increase grass and plant yield; to flush or kill game; to increase plant food for a new cycle of game production.

The life of a hunter-gatherer is one of commitment to an intellectually and physically demanding activity requiring skill, technology, social organization, division of labor, knowledge of plant and animal behavior, of climate, seasons, and winds, the habit of close observation, inventiveness, problem solving, risk bearing and high motivation. These demands would have been selective in humankind's cultural and biological evolution, and helped to develop the human capital and genetic equipment needed to create modern civilization. The aboriginal practice of awarding more wives to the most successful hunters would have favored the genetic selection of these traits.[16]

It was as a hunter-gatherer that humankind learned to learn: young hunters needed to be imbued with knowledge of animal behavior and anatomy, with the habit of goal-oriented observation, to learn that ungulates often travel in an arc so that success could be increased by traversing the chord, and so on. Knowledge of animal behavior could substitute for weapon development. From knowledge of animal anatomy it was but a short step to curiosity about human anatomy, the discovery that we are one with the animals, and to the first practice of medicine.

4. *Property rights are likely of ancient origin.*

Although humankind have made stone tools for at least 2.5 million years, the archeological record of property rights is more obscure. Nonetheless, the similarities between the cultural materials of late-Pleistocene and aboriginal peoples suggest that such social traditions originated at least as early as the period 40,000–20,000 years B.P. Cultural materials (amber, sea shells, stone tools) often occur hundreds of kilometers from their points of origin indicating intergroup contacts over wide areas (Klein 1989, 376–8). No such evidence of social contact occurs before the late-Pleistocene, when the archeological record shows a vast increase in property: bows and arrows, atlatls, seed grinding stones, boiling and storage vessels, kilns for firing clay, boats, houses, villages, animal drawn sledges, the domesticated wolf. New tools and techniques allowed new products of gathering and hunting to substitute for the loss of big game. Previously, gathering emphasized the seeds and plants that could be eaten while on the move. Now the seeds gathered were inedible without soaking, grinding and boiling. This upsurge in personal paraphernalia implies more sedentary, less nomadic, hunting and gathering. Knowledge of the seasonal cycles of plants and animals, of the use of fire in resource management, of techniques of storing, drying and preserving foods, all combine to make life more sedentary. But with the accumulation of personal property and real estate would come more complex property right and contracting arrangements.[17] Dalton (1977) has summarized the economic, but also the important political function, of the ceremonial exchanges of Northwest

America and Melanesia, such as the potlatch, kula, moka and abutu, which in substance are elaborate multilateral contracting mechanisms. The valuables exchanged (bracelets, pearl shells, cowries, young women) bought not only other commodities in ordinary exchange; they bought kinship ties with the exchange of daughters, military assistance if attacked, the right of refuge if homes and property had to be abandoned, and emergency assistance in the event of poor harvest, hunting or fishing. They bought political stability in stateless societies, and a property right environment that facilitated specialization and ordinary exchange. Property rights thus precede the state and property included private goods such as land, fishing sites, livestock, and cemetery plots, but also public goods such as crests, names, dances, rituals and trade routes that could be assigned to more than one individual or group.

How is it possible that property rights and exchange could exist prior to the advent of the state and of central enforcement? The answer is to be found in reciprocity, mutual dependence, and state-like forms of control achieved through broadened kinship ties and the outright purchase of political stability. If I grow beans and you grow corn, and we exchange our surpluses, we each have a stake in protecting our respective property rights. If either of us plays the game of 'steal' rather than the game of 'trade' this will end our prospect of maintaining a trading relationship tomorrow. Once humankind opted for less nomadic forms of hunting and gathering, such reciprocal relationships would have been vastly more important. Transients always, and even today, pose a more demanding problem of property right enforcement, than those who are in more permanent contact with each other.[18] The conditions of reciprocity would have been powerfully present once the agricultural revolution came, but I suggest that they already existed in hunter-gatherer communities that were managing and harvesting from relatively fixed resource bases. Moreover, stateless societies did not have to rely entirely on voluntary forbearance based on the incentive support from reciprocal relationships. They also purchased political stability by paying tribute and by kinship exchange and "gift-exchange."[19]

Evidence for the existence of property rights and social contracting in stateless societies is incontrovertible. Heizer (1955) notes that in North America the private ownership of fishing and hunting grounds, nut trees, and seed gathering areas was common. Among the Karok (Kroeber and Barrett 1960), owning the right to fish a particular eddy or channel of a river was independent of who owned the land along the river, and the right was transferable by bequest or sale. Similarly, an individual would own sealing rights to a particular coastal rock. Peter Freuchen (1961), who lived with the Greenland Eskimos at the turn of the last century, describes the social organization and trading behavior of these prehistoric hunting-fishing people. Among their social contracts was a simple incentive compatible rule for allocating the skin among hunting team members when the prey was the dangerous polar bear: "The hunter who fixed his spear first in the bear gets the upper part. That is the finest part, for it includes the forelegs with the long mane hairs that are so much desired to border women's kamiks (boots) with" (Freuchen 1961, 53).

5. *Humankind was an intense user of the environment for self-interested ends.*

Although today we associate environmental damage, including extinction, with the advent of industrial society and human population growth, it is likely that prehistoric humans had a comparable, or perhaps more severe impact, on their environment. This is because the species that have survived to the present represent the less vulnerable plants and animals. If Paul Martin is correct, that the wave of animal extinctions beginning with the "invasion" of Australia 40,000 years B.P. and ending with the occupation of Madagascar and New Zealand, were of anthropogenic origin, then the losses were of species that had inadequate defensive capabilities. The winnowing left the more stubbornly resistant species, able to survive all but major destructions of habitat. Major losses of hunted game animals in the prehistoric period can also help to account for the enculturation of self-serving conservationist principles in the myths, rituals and beliefs of aboriginal societies. Thus the Choctaw had rules regulating the game that could be killed by one family. The Kaska trapped marten in a game area only every two or three years. The Iroquois and many other tribes spared the females of hunted species during the breeding season. The Yurok had "game laws" the violation of which would cause loss of "hunting luck." Many tribes believed that game is watched over by supernatural deities who are angered if too many animals are killed or if they are merely wounded.[20] Thus tribal property rights, though not always private and transferable, encouraged resource stewardship.

A second source of ecological change induced by prehistorical peoples was their transportation of seeds in hunter-gatherer migrations throughout the world. The introduction of botanical exotics into new regions has often been noted by archaeologists who have observed the association of various plants with campsites and dwellings; the wide distribution of wild squash appears to be associated with humankind. Other plants whose patterns of incidence suggest that they were spread by early humans include mulberry, black walnut and buckeye trees, elderberry, nettle, scurvy grass, sweet flag, crabapple, cactus, and lotus (Heizer 1955, 12–13).

Finally, the human use of fire is thought to have had a profound effect on the ecology of the environment. Many authors who have studied patterns of land burning by primitive peoples have concluded that many of the world's great grasslands were produced by periodic burning (Heizer 1955, 9–12; Lewis 1980). Where tree growth is favored by weather conditions, periodic burning will select for particular species such as the pine forests in southern New York, and to the West, which have been attributed to Indian burning. Similarly, the disappearing grassland areas in northern Alberta are attributed to Canadian restrictions on traditional Indian burning (Lewis 1980, 76–77).[21]

6. *Long plateaus without change are punctuated with revolutionary leaps in biological and economic development.*

There were essentially three prehistoric revolutions in the development of mankind, prior to the agricultural revolution: bipedalism, the invention and development of tools, including fire, and the explosive accumulation of human capital by Cro-Magnon peoples. As I have already argued, bipedalism, which became adaptive somewhere in the period 10 to 5 million years ago, was probably a bioeconomic response to the cooler, dryer climate that reduced the proportion of forested lands in Africa. Then sometime between 5 and 3 million years ago our protohuman ancestors discovered the value of stone tools so that by 2.5 million years B.P. they are being fabricated by *H. habilis*. From the stone tool breakthrough down to about 40–30,000 years B.P., the record shows discrete improvement in tool use and fabrication (including fire) as *H. erectus* displaces *H. habilis*, followed by early *H. sapien*; then the Neanderthals arrive, make their indelible mark, but disappear some 30,000 years ago. The Cro-Magnon people produced an astonishing creative outburst—in tools, art and hunting-gathering techniques—beginning sometime after 40,000 years B.P. (Pfeiffer 1982). This great acceleration in human capital formation, and Cro-Magnon's rapid spread throughout all the major continents, set the stage for the agricultural revolution. It did this partly by giving our immediate ancestors the knowledge of animals and seeds required by the agricultural way of life, but probably also by hastening the demise of the megafauna that were the favored game of the chase, and thus tipping the opportunity cost balance in favor of tilling the soil.

What accounts for the sudden acceleration of human economic and cultural development after 40,000 years B.P? Cro-Magnon people had already been firmly established in Africa for perhaps 60,000 years, and had already begun their spread throughout the world. I believe the most likely cause is the emergence of language.[22] The ability to communicate effectively by the spoken word would make possible the accumulation and diffusion of knowledge on an unprecedented scale. The experience and knowledge of the elderly—at the time men and women only 40 years of age—would be a valued source of information. Since this human capital needed to be preserved and drawn upon, it explains why older and incapacitated people were cared for, and their value recognized by proper burial and enshrined in art. In aboriginal societies the medicine man or woman was often a person handicapped from birth or crippled by injury. Thus, "Kokopelli," widely revered in the rock art of the southwestern Four Corners area and Mexico is depicted as a hunchbacked arthritic figure who is associated with paintings of corn, deer, goats, atlatls, and bison, and often carries or plays a flute. With the advent of spoken language the value of information relative to physical strength would have changed dramatically and human society would have been highly motivated to preserve and transmit it to new generations. Based upon a reconstruction of the fossil evidence it is thought by many that the Neanderthals had a vocal tract more like an ape than the Cro-Magnon. If so, this might explain the extinction of Neanderthals, and their failure to develop the tool, art and hunting-gathering proficiency of competing Cro-Magnon peoples.

The affluence made possible by improvements in food acquisition methods would have provided the released time necessary to give attention to language development and to the rituals, ceremony and socializing that demand communication capacity. Big game hunting placed new demands on planning, organization, coordination and cooperation that depended on communication. It was the spoken word that allowed ideas and complex thought to be externalized. Memory, operated on by ritual, allowed knowledge to be preserved and, most important, accumulated. Writing, invented by 5000 years B.P. (and thereafter in many dispersed cultures), vastly accelerated the human capacity to preserve and accumulate thought.[23] But by this time humankind's vast knowledge of seeds, eggs and animals had already fomented the agricultural revolution made all the more necessary by the disappearance of so many of the great game animals.

The Agricultural Revolution; Reversion in America

In the Near East, beginning about 10,000 years ago, our ancestors abandoned the hunter-gatherer way of life that had served humankind so well over the vast stretch of at least 3 million years. The evidence appears in the form of several early Neolithic farming villages dated from 9500 to 9000 years B.P. (Zohery and Hopf 1988). Plant cultivation in this area appears to coincide closely with the domestication of animals. Sheep and goats were domesticated first, but cattle and pigs followed closely thereafter.[24] Domesticated plants consisted of only 8 or 9 species of local grains such as wheat, barley and the legumes—lentils, peas and chickpeas. Sometime later bitter vetch and flax are added to the crops. About 3000 years after grain agriculture, various fruits—olive, grape and fig—are cultivated. All these plants were domesticated forms of the wild varieties that were indigenous to the area.[25] Subsequently plant cultivation appears in Egypt, the Balkans, and the West Mediterranean 7000 years B.P., Central Europe and the Ukraine 6500 years B.P., and Scandinavia about 5000 years B.P. Evidence for agriculture in New Guinea, where there were virtually no animals suitable for hunting, is dated 9000 years ago (Reader 1988).

In North America although the earliest evidence of agriculture is in Mexico, 10–9,000 years B.P., products were added slowly, one by one, over thousands of years as if cultivation were a hobby used to supplement hunting and gathering. When the first Europeans arrived in the sixteenth century there was great variability among the North American tribes in their dependence on agriculture versus hunting and gathering. In California acorns and hunting were important means of subsistence. In the Pacific Northwest salmon fishing supplemented by gathering was paramount. On the Great Plains many tribes, such as the Pawnee,

Cheyenne and Arapaho, had well-developed horticulture and pottery arts. The peaceful Pueblos of the Southwest grew cotton, corn, beans, tobacco and squash.

The influence of opportunity cost on tribal choice of culture is well illustrated by the effect of the reintroduction of the horse to North America by the Spanish. The Spanish mustang—a docile and easily domesticated member of the *Equus* family—was a revolutionary innovation to the Plains indian causing many tribes to revert to the bison hunt as a permanent way of life. Wedel (1936) reports that the introduction of the horse caused the Pawnee to change from a sedentary tribe devoted to agriculture to one in which the chase and maize culture were equally important sources of sustenance. More dramatically the Cheyenne and Arapaho abandoned their villages, agriculture and pottery arts to become bison hunters (Wedel 1940; Strong 1940). Consequently the fierce "fighting Cheyennes" known to the plains settlers were almost entirely a recent creature of the horse. Tribes such as the Apache, who were already subsisting on bison when the Spanish arrived, simply adapted the horse to their hunting culture.

Although Cornado and other conquistadors lost or abandoned horses in the sixteenth century, it was not until the permanent colonization of New Mexico in the first half of the seventeenth century that peaceful Indians, forced to tend their horses, learned horsemanship from the Spanish. During this period, horses and knowledge of them were acquired by the Apaches and other tribes, and by the 1650s the colonial settlements faced the formidable Apaches, on horseback, whose raids became legend. All the power of Spain in America failed to subdue them. Then out of the Rocky Mountain headwaters of the Arkansas River appeared a little known tribe of hunter-gatherers who abandoned their homelands and took to the Plains on horseback. They became great bison hunters and by 1725 invaded the Apache lands of Colorado, Kansas, Oklahoma and West Texas. Entire tribes of Apache who had been the scourge of the Spanish disappeared. The invading Comanches exterminated the Eastern tribes and drove the Western tribes into Arizona and New Mexico. The Comanches were the greatest warriors ever to ride the high plains and plateaus of Texas. They were without peer on horseback, with men, women and children skilled in the saddle. Their raiding parties ranged up to 1000 miles, and across the Rio Grande deep into Northern Mexico; their loot sometimes consisted of hundreds of horses in a single moonlight raid. They were known for their " . . . boast that the warrior tribes permitted Spanish settlements to exist on the fringes of Comanche territory only to raise horses for them" (Fehrenbach 1983, 36). The Spanish were never again to muster any semblance of control of West Texas; nor were the white Americans able finally to control bison country until 1875 when the remnants of the fierce Comanche tribes finally surrendered at Fort Sill, and the bison were all but exterminated and replaced by the long horn steer. For a century and a half the history of the American West was a history of fear and terror of the Comanches who, prior to the arrival of the mustang, had picked berries and dug roots while hunting miscellaneous game in the Eastern Rockies, and were a threat to no one.

Genesis: A Folk Memory of Conflict Between Two Cultures?

The remnants of our prehistoric past that reside in our cultural traditions today is well illustrated by a fascinating interpretation of Genesis as a myth of conflict between the agricultural and hunter-gatherer way of life, written from the perspective of the latter (Hamblin 1987). According to this reconstruction the Garden of Eden represents the economic affluence achieved by humans as hunter-gatherers who lived abundantly on the plants, animals and fishes placed on Earth by God for the benefit of humankind. Then Eve broke the cultural command not to eat the fruit of the tree of knowledge. But what "knowledge" was contained in this fruit? It was knowledge of the reproductive cycles of seeds, eggs and animals, which was the human capital foundation of agriculture.[26] Some were already practicing agriculture and departing from their ancestral imperative, causing a bifurcation of the cultural message. The warning against this dangerous new direction is expressed in the punishment of Adam and Eve: " . . . cursed is the ground for thy sake; in sorrow shalt thou eat of it. . . . Thorns and thistles shall it bring forth to thee; and thou shalt eat the herb of the field" (Genesis 3: 17–18).

Eve bore two sons who were split on the ancestral imperative: Cain became a tiller, while Abel was a herder of sheep.[27] Cain made offerings of the fruit of the ground to the Lord, while Abel offered the first of his flock. Abel's offering was respected by God, but Cain's was not. So Cain killed Abel, implying that the culture was in danger of losing the skills of the hunter-gatherer in which case there could be no turning back from the world of thistles and thorns. Then came the flood, all the game animals are in danger of extinction, and so on.[28]

This allegorical interpretation is plausible in many ways. First, the timing is right; second the location is right; and third, the events described correlate with what is known about this period and place. The first evidence of agriculture appears about 9500 years B.P. in the fertile crescent of the Tigris and Euphrates rivers. Surely this was not an unclimatic event after more than 5 million years of bipedalism, 2.5 million years of tool use, and a very successful adaptation to hunting and gathering. Moreover, the Sumerians invented and were using the first written cuneiform language 6–5000 years B.P., a language which produced many epic poems that obviously influenced the Hebrew story of Genesis. The Sumerians had a cuneiform word for "Adam" which meant "settlement on the plain." They also had a word for "Eden" which meant a "fertile plain." Interestingly there was no word for "Eve," but their word "ti" had two meanings: "rib" and "to make live." The Hebrew scholars, not appreciating this dual meaning, concocted their story that God gave life to Adam's rib creating the first woman. The Sumerian tablets, besides telling us of "Adam," "Eden," and the "lady of the rib," also tells us of a Great Flood and of their King Gilgamesh who went down to the Gulf in search of the Tree of eternal life.[29]

Moreover, it is known that there was a sudden warming trend 7–6000 years B.P. shrinking the ice caps and raising the sea level. The Persian Gulf would have filled with water during this period reaching its current level about 6000 years B.P. These considerations have suggested to Juris Zarins (Hamblin 1987) the hypothesis that the Garden of Eden was located at the upper end of the Persian Gulf, for it is written: "and a river went out of Eden to water the garden; and from thence it was parted, and became of four heads . . . the . . . Pison . . . Gihon, Tigris . . . and . . . Euphrates" (Genesis 2: 10–14). Of course the Tigris and Euphrates still flow, while the Pison and Gihon probably refer respectively to the Wadi Batin, a fossil river in Iraq, and the intermittently flowing Karun River in Iran.

Finis

The significance of prehistory to humankind, circa 2000, is that all we are today—our great cultural attainments, and ever growing potential, our biological and human capital achievements—are a product of that prehistory. If there is much that is new in historical time it is because we have continued what began in prehistory, but have had so many millennia to accumulate the human capital made possible once our hunter-gatherer ancestors learned to learn. If we are a "kinder and gentler" species today than were our ancestors who slaughtered the great mammoth and bison on two continents; if we can care enough to launch a massive effort to save three great whales trapped in a hole in the Arctic ice; if we can debate reintroducing the timber wolf into Yellowstone Park; it is because we can now afford to do all these things and have learned to treasure the value of individual responsibility for preserving and managing natural resources.

But change has been episodic, not linear, as we have leaped from one long confining plateau to another less than a half-dozen times since we escaped—so improbably—our primate origins which took three billion years of sporadic change to create. Through all these sweeping changes is discernable the blurred outline of continuity in humankind's development of the capacity to respond to effort prices, to create cheaper techniques and products to substitute for dearer ones, to develop property rights, and to accumulate and preserve knowledge, our most precious capital asset.

Notes

1. It is, and must be, a speculative extension of what we know from the paleoanthropological and biological records. This is because what we know about prehistorical humankind is interpreted from the artifacts and remains that our remote ancestors left behind and that have survived biodegradation, from backward extrapolation of what we know from the study of extant prehistorical societies during the last 96 years (Boas 1897), and from genetic differences

between humans and other primates today. One of our most important characteristics as humans is to pattern-search our data, and try to make dumb facts speak with understanding. I make the case that economic principles help us to achieve this understanding. The theme is one of 'natural,' as distinct from 'political,' economy (Hirshleifer 1978), but, as will be seen below, I think the outlines of 'political' economy emerged in antiquity.

2. Nonhuman primates, such as baboons and chimpanzees, are known to prey on small vertebrates. There is also evidence of elementary forms of planning and cooperation among chimpanzees in their predatory activities; they also transport materials to use as tools. " . . . some level of predation as well as tool use is not unique to the Hominidae. Much, if not all, of the evolution of these activities in the hominid lineage was therefore primarily a shift in emphasis rather than the introduction of completely novel behavioral patterns (Trinkaus 1986, 110–111)."

3. Glaciation of the earth actually begins before the Pleistocene about 14 million years B.P. in the middle Miocene. See Klein (1989, 29–35) for a summary of late Cenozoic ice age climate and its significance for humankind.

4. "Such a structure (the external nose) would have enabled members of *H. erectus* to retrieve moisture from exhaled air . . . (which could be) used for humidifying the next breath without using additional body moisture . . . Such a system would have been more efficient at conserving body fluids . . . (which) would have been important for a diurnal primate exploiting resources in open country, especially in relatively arid regions" (Trinkaus 1986, 120). In fact it is possible that these people were capable of running prey to exhaustion (Trinkaus 1986, 128). (American aboriginals had the capacity literally to run down a horse or deer by pacing the animal.)

5. See Klein (1989, 171, 218) for references.

6. For a controversial study placing our common mitochondrial DNA ancestor at 200,000 B.P., and two rebuttle notes, see Vigilant et al. (1991); Templeton (1992); and Hedges et al. (1992).

7. In North America, horse bones are among the most common Pleistocene fossils (Martin and Guilday 1967, 41–42).

8. Dwarfing may have provided a higher biomass growth rate enabling the bison to overcome a high rate of Paleolithic harvesting of megafauna. "Human technology, including use of missile weapons, greatly reduced the counterattacking defensive advantages of larger size and emphasizes concealment and speed of flight. At this point of increased pressure of human predation, the genetically selected optimum body size of many forms declines sharply" (Edwards 1967, 149). Hammond (1961, 321) has noted that a considerable reduction in size has occurred since the beginning of the century in the major beef breeds of cattle. This is due to deliberate selection for early maturation in body proportions. Under appropriation, investment favors the smaller animals with a higher biomass growth rate. But under common property conditions, Paleolithic hunters (also the Hazada and Ache: Hawkes, O'Connell, and Jones 1991) selectively harvested the larger,

slower growing animals.

9. Caughley (1988) offers a population diffusion and growth model to account for the geographical and temporal distribution of radiocarbon dates at prehistoric sites (many of them moa bird kill sites) in New Zealand. According to this model colonization began on the northeast coast of the South Island 1050–900 B.P. and diffused at an accelerating rate throughout New Zealand. Accordingly, the population increased about 3 percent per year (doubling every 20 years), and sea elephants, sea lions and about 25 species of birds became extinct. Earlier, similar models were used (see Caughley 1988) to structure hypotheses concerning the colonization of Australia more than 30,000 B.P. and the colonization of North and South America about 11,000 B.P.

10. Yet it has been estimated that a population of only 15,000 people in northern Eurasia would need to consume up to 60,000 horses or 10,000 bison per year (Vereshchagin and Baryshnikov 1984, 508).

11. Some African hunter-gatherer tribes, such as the pygmies, have fared well because they depended on trade with their agricultural neighbors (Reader 1988, 155). But for the Kung, it is the opposite; their neighbors have survived draughts and poor crops by joining the Kung in gathering mongongo nuts and other wild plants. During the third year of a draught phase the Kung consumed an average of 8.3 percent more calories and 55 percent more protein than the estimated daily recommended allowance for people of their stature and activity (Lee 1968; Lee and Devore 1976). But see Hawkes and O'Connell (1981) for a critique of Lee's interpretation of the Kung data: Lee's foraging calculations do not include the time spent in processing food. The mongongo nut requires considerable cracking/roasting time, which correspondingly reduces the net caloric yield per hour of labor.

12. This is of course precisely the normative argument for using Nash mixed strategies in certain games of conflict.

13. As stated by a Karok woman "They . . . burn the brush . . . so that good things will grow up. . . . Some kinds of trees are better when . . . burned off. . . . But some . . . disappear . . . the Manzanita . . . does not come up when it is burned off. . . . They are careful lest the(se) trees burn" (Lewis 1973, 50–51).

14. As explained by a Cree Indian: "See, you start a fire at the top of a meadow in the afternoon, when you feel the wind change, the way the cool air does at that time. This way the fire burns toward the low part of the meadow. . . . Its safe. You have to know the wind" (Lewis 1980, 82).

15. Modern experiments have tested the Amerindian policy of burning to improve game productivity. Thus deer in recently burned over chaparral cover show marked increases in numbers, size and improvement in health (Biswell 1967, 81).

16. Among the Ache hunter-gatherers of Eastern Paraguay the most successful hunters devote more, not less, time to hunting than less successful hunters. They also share disproportionately their surplus with people outside their family group. In return they gain increased access to extramarital mates producing illegitimate

children, and a higher survivorship of their offspring (Kaplan and Hill 1985; Hawkes 1990).

17. Of course we have no idea as to whether the early property rights systems were based on regimes of private property. By property rights, I mean rules governing the actions of individuals. Aboriginals had concepts of both private and tribal property, and both probably originated in this early period with the great increase in individual (or group) possessions.

18. This is illustrated in John Hughes's (1982) account of the seasonal closing of the Alaska cannery where he worked in the summer of 1951. A half-Eskimo winter watchman was removing the locks and chains from various items of property. When asked why, he stated that locks were not needed now that the Christians were gone. For a discussion of the role of "repeat business" in inducing cooperation in the absence of enforcement see Hirshleifer (1978). Also see Hawkes (1991) for a discussion of reciprocal altruism or "delayed reciprocity" wherein those in close relationship share resources in return for future shares, and for a generally incisive analysis of "sharing" in the context of individual incentives and game theoretic interactions.

19. For an economic analysis of the Kula Ring, see Landa (1983).

20. See Heizer (1955, 4–7) for these and many more examples.

21. Lewis quotes the reminisces of a Beaver Indian woman: "Why the bush is so thick is because they (Indians) stop burning . . . From about five miles from here you could see straight prairie right to Childs Lake and that timber. Did you ever see them prairies? . . . It was really prairie, just prairie, you know; here and there you see little specks of woods, and if there were trees there, they were quite high" (Lewis 1980, 76). The imposition of fire prevention policies for many prior decades led to the great Yellowstone Park holocaust of 1988. Similar policies imposed on the Australian Aborigines " . . . resulted in the sporadic eruption of gigantic wild fires feeding on several years' accumulation of litter, causing leaf scorch heights of up to 20m, with the death of mature woodlands of . . . (Cypress pine) which the policy was intended to protect . . . " (Jones 1980, 125).

22. Linguists are split on the antiquity of language: radicals suggest that the roots of spoken language could go back 100,000 years, while traditionalists accept an origin of at most 15,000 years B.P. (Ross 1991). Of course the date for the common ancestor of modern humankind may be closer to 50,000 B.P. Klein (1992) notes that this is suggested by the archeological evidence for a radical biologically based change in human behavior 50–40,000 B.P. Under Klein's hypothesis the development of language would have been a later consequence of the biological change. I assume that the dates based on DNA studies are roughly correct, and that we have to account for a much later occurrence of the cultural revolution. There are still other perspectives, e.g. Sofeer (1990) argues that the biological and archaeological records are consistent with a socio-cultural innovation that introduced bi-parental provisioning of the young, division of labor and food sharing. But I would argue that these and all manner of other cultural

innovations could have been made possible by the development of language.

23. An interesting hypothesis, supported by the archaeological evidence, argues that the precursor of Sumerian writing was a clay token accounting system, appearing 11,000 B.P., used to preserve records and to facilitate the exchange of property (Schmandt-Besserat 1978). Thus the first forms of written language may have been invented as an aid to memory and security in contracting for property (Sumerian exchange included land, animals, vessels, bread, beer, clothing, furniture, etc.). Early symbols then evolved into Sumerian pictographic writing and ultimately ideographic and phonetic writing.

24. It would appear that sheep domestication predates agriculture in this region: " . . . most authorities now agree that the first species to be domesticated in the Near East was the sheep, 10,500 years ago or so" (Fagan 1989, 265).

25. In virtually all aboriginal societies studied in the last century, hunting was a preoccupation of men and gathering was the province of women. It therefore would appear likely that the agricultural revolution was due to women's knowledge of seeds, herbs and edible plants.

26. As noted in endnote 24, it was the woman, in this case Eve, who transmitted the agricultural human capital.

27. Not quite a hunter-gatherer so the allegory here is weak, but Abel was a nomad nonetheless. Sheep herding does appear to be an intermediate step in the turn from hunting.

28. As Ed Ames has pointed out to me a sharper contrast between hunting and tilling is found in Genesis, 25–27, where Esau was a hunter, whose birthright was bought by Jacob, the farmer-herder.

29. Incidentally, he found it, but it was stolen from him by a serpent!

References

Anderson, Atholl. 1989. *Prodigious birds*. Cambridge: Cambridge University Press.

Biswell, Harold H. 1967. The use of fire in wildland management in California. In *Natural resources quality and quantity*, edited by S. V. Ciriacy-Wanthrup and J. J. Parsons. Berkeley: University of California Press, 71–86.

Boas, Franz. 1897. The social organization and the secret societies of the Kwakiutl Indians. In *Report of the U.S. National Museum for 1895*. Washington.

Caughley, Graeme. 1988. The colonization of New Zealand by the Polynesians. *Journal of the Royal Society of New Zealand* 18:245–70.

Dalton, George. 1977. Aboriginal economies in stateless societies: Interaction spheres. In *Exchange systems in pre-history*, edited by J. Erickson and T. Earle. New York: Academic Press.

Dewar, Robert E. 1984. Extinctions in Madagascar. In *Quaternary extinctions*, edited by Paul S. Martin and Richard G. Klein. Tucson: University of Arizona Press, 574–593.

Edwards, William Ellis. 1967. The late-Pleistocene extinction and diminution in size of many mammalian species. In *Pleistocene extinctions*, edited by Paul S. Martin and Herbert E. Wright, Jr. New Haven: Yale University Press.

Fagan, Brian M. 1989. *People of the Earth*. Boston: Scott, Foresman and Co.

Fehrenbach, T. R. 1983. *Lone Star*. New York: American Legacy Press.

Frison, George C. 1986. Prehistoric, plains-mountain, large-mammal communal hunting strategies. In *The evolution of human hunting*, edited by M. H. Nitecki and D. V. Nitecki. New York: Plenum Press, 177–223.

Freuchen, Peter. 1961. *Book of the Eskimos*. Cleveland: World Publishing.

Gould, Stephen J. 1988. A novel notion of Neanderthal. *Natural History* 97 (June): 16–21.

Hamblin, Dora J. 1987. Has the Garden of Eden been located at last? *Smithsonian* 18 (May): 127–135.

Hammond, J. 1961. Growth in size and body proportions in farm animals. In *Growth in living systems*, edited by M. X. Zarrow. New York: Basic Books.

Harris, J. W. K. 1983. Cultural beginnings: Plio-Pleistocene archaeological occurrences from the afar, Ethiopia. *The African Archaeological Review* 1:3–31.

Hawkes, Kristen. 1990. Showing off: Tests on an hypothesis about men's foraging goals. *Ethology and Sociobiology* 12:29–54.

———. 1991. Sharing and collective action. Department of Anthropology, University of Utah.

Hawkes, Kristen, and James F. O'Connell. 1981. Affluent hunters? Some comments in light of the Alyawara case. *American Anthropologist* 83:622–26.

Hawkes, Kristen, James F. O'Connell, and Nicholas B. Jones. 1991. Hazda hunting and human evolution. Department of Anthropology, University of Utah.

Haynes, Caleb Vance. 1964. Fluted projectile points: Their age and dispersion. *Science* 19 (June): 1408–13.

———. 1988. The first Americans: Geofacts and fancy. *Natural History* 97:4–10.

Hedges, S. Blair, Sudhir Kumar, Koichiro Tamura, and Mark Stoneking. 1992. Technical comments. *Science* 255 (February 7): 737–38.

Heizer, Robert F. 1955. Primitive man as an ecologic factor. *Kroeber Anthropologic Society Paper No. 13*. Berkeley: University of California Press.

Hirshleifer, Jack. 1978. Natural economy versus political economy. *Journal of Social Biological Structures* 1:319–337.

Hughes, Jonathan R. T. 1982. The great strike at Nushagack Station, 1951: Institutional gridlock. *Journal of Economic History* 42 (March): 1–20.

Jones, Rhys. 1980. Hunters in the Australian coastal savanna. In *Ecology in savanna environments*, edited by D. R. Harris. New York: Academic Press.

Kaplan, Hilliard, and Kim Hill. 1985. Hunting ability and reproductive success among male ache foragers: Preliminary results. *Current Anthropology* 26 (February): 131–33.

Klein, Richard G. 1989. *The human career*. Chicago: University of Chicago Press.

———. 1992. The archeology of modern human origins. *Evolutionary Anthropology* 1(1).

Kroeber, Alfred L., and Samuel A. Barrett. 1960. Fishing among the Indians of Northwestern California. *Anthropological Records* 21(1).

Landa, Janet. 1983. The enigma of the Kula Ring: Gift-exchanges and primitive law and order. *International Review of Law and Economics* 3:137–60.

Laporte, Leo F., and Adrienne L. Zihlman. 1983. Plates, climate and hominoid evolution. *South African Journal of Science* 79 (March): 96–110.

Lee, Richard B. 1968. What hunters do for a living, or how to make out on scarce resources. In *Man the hunter*, edited by Richard B. Lee and I. DeVore. Chicago: Aldine Publishing Co., 30–48.

Lee, Richard B., and I. DeVore. 1976. *Kalahari hunter gatherers: Studies of the Kung Son and their neighbors*. Cambridge, MA: Harvard University Press.

Lewis, Henry T. 1973. Patterns of Indian burning in California: Ecology and ethnohistory. *Anthropology Papers*, no. 1, Ballna Press.

———. 1980. Indian fires of spring. *Natural History* 83 (January): 76–83.

Martin, Paul S. 1968. Prehistoric overkill. In *Pleistocene extinctions: The search for a cause*, edited by Paul S. Martin and Herbert E. Wright, Jr. New Haven: Yale University Press, 75–120.

———. 1984. Prehistoric overkill: The global model. In *Quaternary extinctions*, edited by Paul S. Martin and Richard G. Klein. Tucson: University of Arizona Press, 354–403.

———. 1990. Who or what destroyed our mammoths? In *Megafauna and man: Discovery of America's heartland*, edited by L. D. Agenbroad, J. I. Mead, and L. W. Nelson. Flagstaff, AZ: Northern Arizona University.

Martin, Paul S., and John E. Guilday. 1967. A bestiary for Pleistocene biologists. In *Pleistocene extinctions*, edited by Paul S. Martin and Herbert E. Wright, Jr. New Haven: Yale University Press.

Mead, Jim I., and D. J. Meltzer. 1984. North American late Quaternary extinctions and the radio carbon record. In *Quaternary extinctions*, edited by Paul S. Martin and Richard G. Klein. Tucson: University of Arizona Press, 440–450.

Moore, O. K. 1957. Divination—A new perspective. *American Anthropology* 59:69–74.

O'Connell, James F., Kristen Hawkes, and Nicholas B. Jones. 1988. Hazda scavenging: Implications for Plio/Pleistocene hominid subsistence. *Current Anthropology* 29 (April): 356–63.

Pfeiffer, John E. 1982. *The creative explosion*. Ithaca: Cornell University Press.

Pope, Geoffrey G. 1989. Bamboo and human evolution. *Natural History* 98

(October): 49–56.

Pyne, Stephen J. 1991. *Burning bush: A fire history of Australia.* New York: Henry Holt and Company.

Reader, John. 1988. *Man on Earth.* New York: Harper and Row Publishers.

Ross, Philip E. 1991. Hard word. *Scientific American* 264 (April): 138–47.

Sahlins, Marshall. 1972. *Stone age economics.* London: Tavistock.

Schmandt-Besserat, Denise. 1978. The earliest precursor of writing. *Scientific American* 238 (June): 50–59.

Smith, Vernon L. 1975. The primitive hunter culture, Pleistocene extinction and the rise of agriculture. *Journal of Political Economy* 83 (August): 727–55.

Sofeer, Olga. 1990. Before Beringia: Late Pleistocene bio-social transformations and the colonization of Northern Eurasia. Symposium on Chronostratigraphy in North Central East Asia and America. Novosibirsk.

Speck, Frank G. 1935. *Naskapi, the savage hunters of the Labrador Peninsula.* Norman: University of Oklahoma Press.

Stringer, Christopher B. 1990. The emergence of modern humans. *Scientific American* 263 (December): 98–104.

Strong, William D. 1940. From history to prehistory in the Northern Great Plains. In *Essays in historical anthropology of North America.* Washington: Smithsonian Institute.

Templeton, Alan R. 1992. Technical comments. *Science* 255 (February 7): 737.

Todd, Lawrence C. 1986. Analysis of kill-butchery bonebeds and interpretation of Paleoindian hunting. In *The evolution of human hunting,* edited by M. H. Nitecki and D. V. Nitecki. New York: Plenum Press, 177–223.

Toth, N. 1985. The Oldowan reassessed: A close look at early stone artifacts. *Journal of Archaeological Science* 12:101–20.

Trinkaus, Erik. 1986. The Neanderthals and modern human origins. *Annual Review of Anthropology* 15:193–218.

Trotter, Michael M., and Beverly McCulloch. 1984. Moas, men and middens. In *Quaternary extinctions,* edited by Paul S. Martin and Richard G. Klein. Tucson: University of Arizona Press, 708–27.

Tyldesley, J. A., and P. Bahn. 1983. Use of plants in the European Paleolithic: A review of the evidence. *Quaternary Science Reviews* 2:53–81.

Valladas, H., J. L. Reyss, J. L. Joron, G. Valladas, O. Bar-Yosef, and B. Vandermeersch. 1988. Thermoluminescence dating of Mousterian 'Proto-Magnon' remains from Israel and the origin of modern man. *Nature* 331: 614–16.

Vereshchagin, Nikolai K., and G. F. Baryshnikov. 1984. Quaternary mammals in extinctions in Northern Eurasia. In *Quaternary extinctions,* edited by Paul S. Martin and Richard G. Klein. Tucson: University of Arizona Press, 483–516.

Vigilant, Linda, Mark Stoneking, Henry Harpending, Kristen Hawkes, and Allen Wilson. 1991. African populations and the evolution of human mitochondrial DNA. *Science* 253 (September 27): 1503–07.

Vrba, E. S. 1985. Ecological and adaptive changes associated with early hominid evolution. In *Ancestors: The hard evidence*, edited by E. Delson. New York: Alan R. Liss, 63–71.

Walker, A. C. 1984. Extinction in hominid evolution. In *Extinctions*, edited by M. H. Nitecki. Chicago: University of Chicago Press, 119–52.

Wedel, Waldo R. 1936. *An introduction to Pawnee archeology*. Washington: Smithsonian Institute.

————. 1940. *Culture sequences in the Central Great Plains*. Washington: Smithsonian Institute.

Wheat, Joe B. 1967. A Paleo-Indian bison kill. *Scientific American* 216 (January): 44–51.

Zihlman, Adrienne L. 1991. The emergence of human locomotion: The evolutionary background and environmental context. University of California, Santa Cruz, January. In *Human Origins*, edited by T. Nishida. 13th Congress, International Primatology Society 1 (forthcoming).

Zihlman, Adrienne L., and B. A. Cohn. 1988. The adaptive response of human skin to the savanna. *Human Evolution* 3(5): 397–409.

Zohary, David, and Maria Hopf. 1988. *Domestication of plants in the Old World*. Oxford: Oxford University Press.

About the Political Economy Forum and Authors

The Political Economy Research Center (PERC) is a nonprofit think tank located in Bozeman, Montana. For over ten years, PERC has been a pioneer in recognizing the value of the market, individual initiative, the importance of property rights, and voluntary activity. This approach is known as the New Resource Economics or free market environmentalism. PERC associates have applied this approach to a variety of issues, including resource development, water marketing, chemical risk, private provision of environmental amenities, global warming, ozone depletion, and endangered species protection.

In 1989, PERC first organized a forum aimed at applying the principles of political economy to important policy issues. The purpose of this forum was to bring together scholars in economics, political science, law, history, anthropology, and other related disciplines to discuss and refine academic papers which explore new applications of political economy to policy analysis.

The papers in this volume are the second in an annual series emanating from the Political Economy Forum. The topic in this case is informal solutions to the commons problem. Too often we assume that only strict private property rights can prevent the "tragedy of the commons," but in reality, elements of customs and culture play a big role in resource allocation.

We at PERC believe that forums of this type can integrate "cutting-edge" academic work with crucial policy issues of the day. It is becoming increasingly evident that the interface between government and the individuals in society is vital in determining the rate and direction of economic progress. We anticipate that future forums will provide equally stimulating ideas for other important policy issues.

James M. Acheson is professor of anthropology and marine studies at the University of Maine. He received his B.A. from Colby College and his Ph.D. in social anthropology from the University of Rochester. He has done fieldwork in the Purepecha speaking area of Mexico and in fishing communities of Maine. In 1974 to 1976, he served as social anthropologist with the National Marine Fisheries Service in Washington. His primary interests include: economic anthropology, maritime communities, Mesoamerica, and resource management. He is author of a number of books and articles, including *The Lobster Gangs of Maine*, published by the University Press of New England in 1988.

Terry L. Anderson is professor of economics at Montana State University and senior associate at the Political Economy Research Center in Bozeman, Montana. He received a Ph.D. in economics from the University of Washington. He has been a visiting professor at Stanford University, Oxford University, the University of Basel (Switzerland), Clemson University, and Canterbury University (New Zealand). Anderson's numerous books include *Free Market Environmentalism* (with Donald Leal); *Water Crisis: Ending the Policy Drought*; and *The Birth of a Transfer Society* (with P.J. Hill). He was a contributing editor of the first volume in the Political Economy Forum series, *Property Rights and Indian Economies*.

Thráinn Eggertsson is a native of Iceland. He was educated in England at the University of Manchester and in the United States at Ohio State University. Dr. Eggertsson is a professor of economics at the University of Iceland and has been a visiting professor at the University of North Carolina at Chapel Hill, Washington University in St. Louis, and at the University of Hong Kong. He has also worked for the Central Bank of Iceland and the O.E.C.D. in Paris. Professor Eggertsson's recent research has involved the economics of institutions. His book, *Economic Behavior and Institutions*, was published by Cambridge University Press in 1990.

Jean Ensminger teaches in the Department of Anthropology at Washington University, where she is a member of the Center in Political Economy. She is interested in the relation between economic change and social, political, and economic institutions. She has published articles on the process of state incorporation, changes in property rights, the role of women and the family in economic development and income and wealth among African pastoralists. Ensminger's latest book, *Making A Market* (Cambridge University Press), analyzes the transformation of institutions among the Orma of Kenya over the past century.

Roy Gardner is a research associate of the Workshop in Political Theory and Policy Analysis and professor of economics at Indiana University. He specializes in the theory of games and economic behavior, and has studied evolutionary stability of game equilibria in both biological and economic settings. Gardner has applied game theory to topics as diverse as class struggle in the USSR, the processes of veto and purge, spoils systems, elections, draft resistance, and alliance formation. His research has been funded by the German Science Foundation, the National Science Foundation, the U. S. Department of Agriculture, and the Alexander von Humboldt Foundation.

Dean Lueck is assistant professor of economics at Louisiana State University and has also taught at the University of Washington, Montana State University, and Brigham Young University. He received his Ph.D. in economics from the University of Washington. Lueck has conducted research in law and economics and natural resource economics. His articles have appeared in *Economic Inquiry*, the *Journal of Law and Economics*, and the *Journal of Legal Studies*. Lueck co-authored a chapter with Terry Anderson that appeared in the first volume of the Political Economy Forum series, *Property Rights and Indian Economies*.

Elinor Ostrom is co-director of the Workshop in Political Theory and Policy Analysis and Arthur F. Bentley Professor of Political Science at Indiana University. Her major academic interest is in the field of institutional analysis and design—the study of how rules-in-use affect the incentives facing individuals in particular settings, their behavior, and consequent outcomes. She has studied institutional arrangements related to metropolitan governance and natural resources both in the United States and the Third World. She is a fellow of the American Academy of Arts and Sciences. Her books include *Governing the Commons: The Evolution of Institutions for Collective Action*; *Crafting Institutions for Self-Governing Irrigation Systems*; *Local Government in the United States* (with Vincent Ostrom and Robert Bish); *Strategies of Political Inquiry*; and *Patterns of Metropolitan Policing* (with Roger B. Parks and Gordon P. Whitaker).

Russell D. Roberts was named the first director of the Management Center at the Olin School of Business at Washington University in St. Louis in 1991. The Management Center links the classroom with the real world through hands-on learning opportunities. Roberts has also taught at the University of Rochester, Stanford University, and UCLA. He was a national fellow and visiting scholar at the Hoover Institution from 1985 to 1987. He did his graduate work at the University of Chicago and undergraduate work at the University of North Carolina. Professor Roberts's main research interests are altruism, common property, and the interaction of public and private activity. In addition to his academic publications, he has written for *The New York Times* and *The Wall Street Journal*, and is currently writing a novel on international trade.

Andrew Rutten teaches in the Government Department at Cornell University. He is interested in the role of institutions, especially legal and political institutions, in economic development. He has published articles on American political economic history and demography. Rutten is currently working on a political economic history of the constitution of the United States.

Edella Schlager received a Ph.D. in political science from Indiana University. She is an assistant professor in the School of Public Administration and Policy at the University of Arizona. Her research interests involve refining, developing, and testing theories of collective action and institutional choice. This includes analyses of informal voluntary organizations as well as formally organized interests that attempt to control public authority. Her empirical focus is upon common property resources, in particular, coastal fisheries and ground water aquifers.

Peregrine Schwartz-Shea is associate professor of political science at the University of Utah. She received a Ph.D. in political science from the University of Oregon. Her research examines the application of rational choice theory to organizations, individual-group relations, and feminism. Recent papers have been published in the *Journal of Public Administration Research and Theory* and *Small Group Research* (with John Orbell).

Randy T. Simmons is professor of political science and head of the Department of Political Science at Utah State University where he was recognized as Researcher of the Year by the College of Humanities, Arts, and Social Sciences in 1986 and 1991. After receiving his Ph.D. from the University of Oregon in 1980, he spent two years in Washington, D.C., as a policy analyst in the Office of Policy Analysis of the Department of the Interior. He specializes in applying the methods and assumptions of economics to policy questions, especially to environmental and natural resource policy. His current policy interest is in the design of policy to allow indigenous people to benefit from wildlife. His book, *Politics, Markets, and Welfare*, with William Mitchell, will be published in 1993.

Vernon L. Smith is Regents' Professor of Economics and research director of the Economic Science Laboratory at the University of Arizona. He has authored or co-authored over 150 articles and books on capital theory, finance, natural resource economics and experimental economics. He has served on the board of editors of the *American Economic Review, The Cato Journal, Journal of Economic Behavior and Organization*, the *Journal of Risk and Uncertainty*, and *Science*. He is past president of the Public Choice Society, the Economic Science Association, and the Western Economic Association. He previously taught at Purdue, Brown University, and the University of Massachusetts. He has been a fellow of the Ford Foundation and the Center for Advanced Study in the Behavioral Sciences, and was a Sherman Fairchild Distinguished Scholar at the California Institute of Technology. He received an honorary Doctor of Management degree from Purdue University and is a fellow of the Econometric Society, the American Association for the Advancement of Science, and the American Academy of Arts and

Sciences. Professor Smith's *Papers in Experimental Economics* was published by the Cambridge University Press.

James Walker is a research associate of the Workshop in Political Theory and Policy Analysis and professor of economics at Indiana University. His major academic interest is the use of experimental methods in the investigation of individual and group behavior related to the voluntary provision of public goods and the use of common-pool resources. His articles have been published in the *Quarterly Journal of Economics* (with R. Mark Isaac), the *Journal of Environmental Economics and Management* (with Elinor Ostrom and Roy Gardner), and the *Economic Journal* (with Roy Gardner).